Ten Ways to Destroy the Imagination of Your Child

Ten Ways to Destroy the Imagination of Your Child

ANTHONY ESOLEN

WILMINGTON, DELAWARE

ISBN: 9781610170796
Library of Congress Cataloguing-in-Publication data is on record and available upon request.

ISI Books
Intercollegiate Studies Institute
3901 Centerville Road
Wilmington, DE 19807-1938
www.isibooks.org

Manufactured in the United States of America

For my mother, Jane Esolen,
who let me have a boy's life

Contents

Introduction

A Bad Day for Grendel

A few years ago, a vandal seized some forty or fifty thousand books from my college's library. He didn't want to read them, or even to sell them. He wanted simply to get rid of them, on the grounds that nobody would read them anyway. Some of the volumes he had branded for destruction were irreplaceable. I know, because I went into the back room where they were being held temporarily before the trucks came to haul them away. From that room I saved several dozen, including a definitive dictionary of medieval Latin, and the first great grammar book for Anglo-Saxon—you know, the language that Beowulf spoke on the night when he was tearing Grendel's arm off, and the monster knew that his end was near. "That was not a good day for Grendel," says the poet, deadpan. It was not a good day for the books, either.

There wasn't much we could do about it, because the vandal in question made more money than we did and had a nicer office. He was our librarian. It's ironic, but true, that one of the qualifications of the modern librarian is a distaste for books. They take up space, and space, the librarians complain, is limited. The books grow old, too. Their covers fray, the spines crack, the pages go dog-eared. Inattentive student workers stick them on the wrong shelves, where they can practically "disappear" for years. People borrow them and don't return them. Some people—I'm guilty of this—underline favorite passages, or write wry comments in the margins, so that the book eventually becomes a kind of successive crime scene. Here a priest wrote, "This is the modernist heresy all over again," but over there an infidel wrote, "Church, enemy of thought." That is not to mention fingerprints and inkblots and even bloodstains—from crushed mosquitoes, I guess.

Books are bulky and inconvenient—like rocks, and trees, and rivers, and life. It occurs to me that everything that can be said against the inconvenience of books can be said about the inconvenience of children. They too take up space, are of no immediate practical use, are of interest to only a few people, and present all kinds of problems. They too must be warehoused efficiently, and brought with as little resistance as possible into the Digital Age.

And there is the trouble. A good book is a dangerous thing. In the wrong hands, it is like a bomb housed within a couple of red pasteboard covers. It can blow the world wide open; it can, if it's Dante's *Divine Comedy*, blow the reader as high as heaven. It carries within it the possibility—and it is always *only* a possibility—of cracking open the shell of routine that prevents us from seeing the world. Our days pass by with the regularity of a conveyor belt at an airport, which we duly get on, and make our way with bland uniformity. A book is like a mischievous boy sticking out his foot at the end of the belt, or like some fantastic intellectual machine that jolts us awake, and we find that the belt is gone. Instead, we're riding in a stagecoach on a trail of dry ruts, and half-naked Indians are surrounding us from the hills, bows stretched and arrows picked to fly.

That's bad enough already. But children are worse than books. A book can make you see the world again, and so ruin your calm and efficient day. But a child does not need to see the world again. He is seeing it for the first time. The Gospel of John reports that when Jesus cured that blind man at the pool of Bethsaida, the people around him asked him what he saw. "I see trees walking," he said, looking at the men and women. The child is like that, except that in his imagination the trees really do walk, and people really may grow branches. Tolkien's Ents, the tree-herders, are like slow, stately moss-grown ancient oaks and maples and birches, if oaks and maples and birches could talk; it takes them nearly a full day to say hello at their parliament. The old Greco-Roman myth had Apollo chasing the virgin nymph Diana, and just when he was about to catch her in his arms, her wish to escape him forever was granted, and she was transformed into a laurel tree. In the child's world, because it is a fresh and new world, anything may happen. The fat frog on the lily pad is a Buddha. The one-legged man stumping down the road to the nearest bar was once a pirate, and killed three people in a quarrel over a game of rummy. The house next door has eyes and a nose and a smokestack at the top. The girl who lives in it, the one with the yellow blouse, is an angel.

Obviously this won't do. If we believe what we say, that "children are our greatest resource," then we need to do something about it. Resources are valuable because they are good, solid, dependable, and inert. Aluminum is a resource. Titanium is a resource. If a block of titanium were suddenly to say, "No, I think I should not like to form an alloy with my friend aluminum to build the side of that airplane," and walked off the assembly line or the conveyor belt and bought a ticket on a ship to Athens, then it would no longer be a resource. In fact, it would be a positive danger. It would be worse than useless. It would be an Enemy of the People. Granite is a resource. If a block of granite at the top of an arch were to wriggle loose whenever people weren't around to notice, to drop on the head of the governor, we might swear off building with granite for a while. Or we might use it all the more—but that is another matter.

In order for children to be transmuted into resources, then, a tremendous alchemical change must be wrought in them. The old alchemists of the early Renaissance sought the secret philosopher's stone, which would, in the right recipe, transform lead into gold. We smile at their folly. We know full well that you can't transform lead into gold. You can only transform gold into lead. This book is written to show you how to do that. The gold is nothing other than the child's imagination, which if it is not gold itself, can still work the miracle of old King Midas. "Nature only provides us with a leaden world," wrote the poet Philip Sidney, "but it is the poet that makes for us a golden one." If we can but deaden the imagination, then, we can settle the child down, and make of him that solid, dependable, and inert space-filler in school and, later, a block of the great state pyramid.

"But we don't want that!" my reader objects. Yes, dear reader, you do. Children make liars of us all. Almost everything we say about them is a lie. We believe exactly the opposite, and act accordingly.

Suppose you are a lover of books. You will not say, "Ah, books, yes, books are wonderful. Such treasures, books are! Myself, I don't have any, and I don't want any, or maybe just one, but I so love books!" Why, you would have books strewn about your flat. You would delight in their very bindings and the smell of their pages. You would not know what to do without them. You would not say, "Yes, I love books. That is why I have warehoused them in this special room, far away from company, and far from where I do anything of importance. I keep them locked up behind this glass case, and only take them out on special occasions." You would not say, "Books indeed, our greatest resource. They kindle readily, and make excellent bonfires."

If we loved children, we would have a few. If we had them, we would want them as children, and would love the wonder with which they behold the world, and would hope that some of it might open our own eyes a little. We would love their games, and would want to play them once in a while, stirring in ourselves those memories of play that no one regrets, and that are almost the only things an old man can look back on with complete satisfaction. We would want children tagging along after us, or if not, then only because we would understand that they had better things to do.

Now that simply is intolerable. For the first time in human history, most people are doing things that could never interest a child enough to make him want to tag along. That says less about the child than about us. If someone should say to us, "How would you like to spend most of your waking hours, five days a week, for the next four years, shut within four walls," we should go mad, that is if we had an imagination left. It is only by repressing that imagination that many of us can stand our work. Some years ago, American feminists, in their own right no inconsiderable amazons against both childhood and the imagination, invented something called Take Your Daughter to Work Day. "See, Jill, this is the office where Mommy works. Here is where I sit for nine hours and talk to people I don't love, about things that don't genuinely interest me, so that I can make enough money to put you in day care."

Consider, too, the problems of the poor fellow who has to manage the Human Warehouse, the faraway, sprawling school, stocked with hundreds or thousands of pupils. In the old days, let's say in a one-room schoolhouse, you could easily pick out which young lad or lass was blessed with a mischievous eye and a lively mind. They were the ones hanging upside down from a couple of planks nailed up to a tree in the schoolyard, or sticking bubble gum on the radiator, or reading *Ivanhoe*. So you got them a few more planks and a bucket of nails, or a paddle to the rear end, or *Waverley*. They could be dealt with. But the bigger the school, the more dangerous and upsetting a single act of imagination can be. The necessity to impose something like order rules it out. A vast enterprise like McDonald's can only function by ensuring that no employee, anywhere, will do anything sprightly and childlike in the way of cooking. I sometimes think that if a single boy at the grill tossed paprika into the french fries, the whole colossal pasteboard empire would come crashing down. Barbarians everywhere would be grilling the onions, or leaving the ketchup out, or commandeering the Swiss to take the place of the American The great virtue of McDonald's, that of the solid, dependable, inert routine, would vanish. As in what was once called "life," you'd never know what you were getting.

We must, then, kill the imagination. The ideal, of course, would be to cease having children, but that might have some adverse effect upon long-range economic prosperity, besides threatening certain industries with extinction—the manufacturers of tasteless clothing, for instance, and importers of refined sugar. Since we must have children, we should be sure to subject them to all the most efficient and humane techniques to fit them for the world in which they will live, a world of shopping malls all the same everywhere, packaged food all the same, paper-pushing all the same, mass entertainment all the same, politics all the same. We owe it to them, and, what is more important, they owe it to us. Now we have been doing a fine job of this for many decades. I will not, in this book, fail to give credit where credit is due. Far be it from me to claim, for instance, that I have invented day care. I confess that, when I was a little boy, I'd have found the idea perfectly revolting. Nor can I claim to have come up with the soul-leveling notion that boys and girls are just the same. I confess that, when I was growing up, I was fascinated, frustrated, appalled, and thunderstruck to find them different. But some people are born with genius, and others are but blessed with the knack for setting their superiors' inventions in some order. I am, I'm afraid, of that latter sort.

Here now, for the first time, are ten sure ways to Destroy the Imagination of Your Child. I do not claim that it is an exhaustive list. No doubt, many of my readers, blessed with a keener attention to the needs of the child, will have come up with others. But I am sure that a judicious application of even three or four of these methods will suffice to kill the imagination of an Einstein, a Beethoven, a Dante, or a Michelangelo.

Good luck!

Why Truth Is Your Enemy,
and the Benefits of the Vague

or

Gradgrind, without the Facts

> "Now what I want is Facts. Teach these boys and girls nothing but
> Facts. Facts alone are wanted in life. Plant nothing else, and root out
> everything else. You can only form the minds of reasoning animals
> upon Facts: nothing else will ever be of any service to them. This is
> the principle on which I bring up my own children, and this is the
> principle on which I bring up these children. Stick to Facts, sir!"
> —The opening of *Hard Times*, Charles Dickens

Those are the words of the schoolmaster Thomas Gradgrind, whose
philosophy of education is meant to reflect the smog-ridden
industrial desert of Coketown, where his enlightened school is
located. If what you want is industrial production, cheap and plentiful, and
if human beings are to be cogs and gears in the industrial machine, then of
course you will want to stick to flat unimaginative Facts. A cog should not
go soft, musing about the clouds in the sky. A gear should never wonder
what it would feel like to turn backwards.

It's easy for us to laugh at the naiveté of Mr. Gradgrind, we ingrates who
have inherited all the benefits of the revolutionary system that he represents. We forget that what was called "empiricism" in education—sticking
to facts, sir, and avoiding the training of the moral imagination in virtues
that can't be isolated in a glass dish or oxidized in a Bunsen burner—was
locked in a mighty struggle with the older tradition of the liberal arts—

1

introducing students to the best that has been thought, done, and written in the world, and, sometimes quite by accident, indulging dangerous flights of fancy, with every book like Aladdin's carpet, ready to whisk us away. The popular form of such an education was what young David Copperfield had, locked up in his room by his cold-hearted stepfather:

> My father had left a small collection of books in a little room up-stairs, to which I had access (for it adjoined my own) and which nobody else in our house ever troubled. From that blessed little room, Roderick Random, Peregrine Pickle, Humphrey Clinker, Tom Jones, the Vicar of Wakefield, Don Quixote, Gil Blas, and Robinson Crusoe, came out, a glorious host, to keep me company. They kept alive my fancy, and my hope of something beyond that place and time.

I pick up McGuffey's *Fourth Eclectic Reader* (1837) and find, to our shame, that along with precise rules of grammar and elocution, students are expected to expand what was once quaintly called their "souls," contemplating, for example, the meaning of those places where their forefathers fought to secure their liberty. "No American," writes Daniel Webster, "can pass by the fields of Bunker Hill, Monmouth, or Camden, as if they were ordinary spots on the earth's surface. Whoever visits them feels the sentiment of love of country kindling anew, as if the spirit that belonged to the transactions which have rendered these places distinguished, still hovered around, with power to move and excite all who in future time may approach them." The same short selection ushers on stage, in a single sentence, the beauties of Homer, Milton, Cicero, Raphael, and Michelangelo. It is, alas, no isolated lapse into imagination. Students elsewhere in the book will be transported to the Himalayas, the ruins of Babylon, Westminster Abbey, the volcano of Etna, the gates of Hell, and, more dreadful even than those, the whirlwind out of which God spoke to Job, commanding him to consider the glory of the creation about him:

> Hast thou given the horse strength?
> Hast thou clothed his neck with thunder?

That one image would be sufficient to quicken a dying imagination, undoing months of hard and programmatic labor.

So we ought to be grateful to the old Gradgrinds, without whom the first stage of modern education, with its demotion of a sense of beauty to an irrational and private feeling, would have been impossible.

In C. S. Lewis's *Voyage of the Dawn Treader*, a boy named Eustace Clarence Scrubb, brought up in a modern Gradgrindian school, bumbles into a cave with treasure in it, and makes the terrible mistake of putting a golden bracelet on his arm. He did this, says Lewis, because in his school all the boys and girls ever read about were factories and electrical output and population density and such like. Eustace didn't read the right sort of books, says Lewis, so he never did know what to do in case of dragons, and other sorts of eminently practical things like that. This of course is the same C. S. Lewis who, in *The Lion, the Witch, and the Wardrobe*, has four children enter into another universe by stepping into a clothes dresser, when, as everybody should know, a wardrobe is for hanging clothes in, and that is that.

So, if we want to kill the imagination—and we do want to do that—the Gradgrind method of sticking to the Facts is not a bad way to begin. Consider what it would be like to have row upon row of students seated at their geography lesson, while the rain drips down the gutter from outside the windows. I hear their voices in unison, droning on without inspiration or joy: "The Arkansas River is 1,469 miles long. It is the sixth longest river in the United States. Its source is in Colorado. It empties into the Mississippi River. It flows through Colorado, Kansas, Oklahoma, and Arkansas. It is irrigated for farms. The Rio Grande River is 1,885 miles long. It is the third longest river," and so on, until death, or the bell, whichever comes first.

But there are problems with the Gradgrind method. Let's see what they are.

A Horse Is a Horse, of Course, of Course

Early in the novel *Hard Times*, Mr. Gradgrind in his arrogance makes the mistake of taking in to his school a girl named Cissy (Gradgrind insists upon calling her "Cecilia"), whose father wants her to get a better education than he can give her himself. The father works as a horse breaker for a traveling circus, and so Cissy has lived all her life among tightrope walkers, magicians, fire-eaters, lady acrobats, elephants, midgets, and suchlike. Hardly a promising upbringing. For the trouble with Cissy, other than that she has a keenly developed sense of good and evil, and a lively imagination, is that she actually does know some Facts. And that proves to be a dangerous thing.

"Give me," says Gradgrind, for the benefit of Cissy and the whole class, "your definition of a horse."

Cissy, alarmed, can say nothing:

"Girl number twenty unable to define a horse!" said Mr. Gradgrind, for the general behoof of all the little pitchers. "Girl number twenty possessed of no facts, in relation to one of the commonest of animals! Some boy's definition of a horse. Bitzer, yours."

Whereupon Bitzer, a pale and gloomy boy with the habit of knuckling his forehead when he is not speaking, the pride of the Gradgrind system, replies:

Quadruped. Graminivorous. Forty teeth, namely twenty-four grinders, four eye-teeth, and twelve incisors. Sheds coat in the spring; in marshy countries, sheds hoofs, too. Hoofs hard, but requiring to be shod with iron. Age known by marks in mouth.

Thus (and much more), Bitzer.

"Now, girl number twenty," said Mr. Gradgrind. "You know what a horse is."

The irony is that Cissy knows more about horses than anybody in the classroom, certainly more than Bitzer, who is merely repeating phrases poured into him, like concrete into a form. She has ridden upon horses, seen them give birth, combed them and curried them, and watched as her father salved their sores or rubbed them with liniment. She knows them in a way that only life with them reveals. At the end of the novel, indeed, Mr. Gradgrind's spoiled son, Tom, will be spirited away from the clutches of the law, riding a horse provided for him by the circus people, and disguised as a clown. *Then* there will be no patter about the horse being graminivorous and shedding its coat in the spring.

And yet Bitzer is in possession of some facts about horses. He knows that they have twelve incisors. What's an incisor? Why should a horse have those, if he eats only grass? Will he eat anything besides grass, anything that an incisor might help him bite and crush? For instance, how does a horse eat a carrot? Or an apple?

Bitzer knows that horses shed their winter coats. How do they do that? Do the coats come off in patches? Do the horses rub up against rough trees or rocks to peel them away? What does the new coat look like?

Bitzer knows that you can tell how old a horse is by looking in its mouth. What would you be looking for there? Do the teeth grow long? Do they change color? Do the gums turn dark? Can you learn the age of other animals in the same way?

The judicious reader will see the problem. A Fact, by itself, does not seem to rouse the imagination. It merely is. It sits there like a rock. Yet its apparent impenetrability is a challenge to the mind. The Arkansas River is 1,469 miles long. How wide is it when it reaches the Mississippi? Can you sail a boat upriver? How far can you go? Is it a clear and fast river, or sluggish and muddy? If water from the river is used for farming, does that mean that it has been dammed up here and there? If it has been, are there big man-made lakes along its course? Can you swim in those lakes?

Now of course it is better that the students learn facts about the Arkansas River, than wander about the streams of Mount Helicon, where the Muses of Greek mythology danced and sang. It is better that they should learn that Mount McKinley is the highest peak in North America, than that they should trudge along with Frodo to Mount Doom in the heart of Mordor. It is better that they should learn that there are twelve tones in the Western musical scale, than that they should listen to a wood thrush singing from the thickets, trilling out his ethereal notes that have no name. But it would be better still if they had never heard of the Arkansas River, or Mount McKinley, or the twelve tone scale.

Such heights of ignorance could never be attained in Mr. Gradgrind's time, for the simple reason that in the middle of an industrial revolution you actually have to know some things to get some jobs done, and those jobs were often complicated, requiring a great deal of ingenuity. Suppose, for you, a tree is nothing but a source for lumber. That's fine. You're well on your way. But in Grandgrind's day you would then have to know about sawmills, and that would require, in turn, a pretty precise knowledge of waterpower, and how to use wheels, belts, and gears to turn the rotary motion of a wheel into just the right back-and-forth motion of the saw, complete with couplers to disengage the mechanism from the source of power. In other words, a sawmill, while not the Forest of Arden, is in its own right a fascinating place.

A great deal of that fascination can be found in William Stout's *The Boy's Book of Mechanical Models* (1917), now available in reprint, and doubly dangerous to the young mind, in that it encourages both the direct experience of mechanical forces and the spirit of irresponsible play. Thus Stout describes seeing a "wonderful electric writing telegraph" at the Saint Louis World's Fair: "Here a man sat at a desk with a pencil and wrote and drew pictures, while above him, on another piece of paper in a separate machine, a pencil guided itself in the same manner and drew the same lines. It was very interesting, especially when one thought of writing from one city to another, as can be done with this machine."

So Stout, while yet a boy—such was the state of unsupervised youth in his day—went home to devise a way to copy the machine in miniature. His scheme takes into account all kinds of facts. First, there is what I'd call the "grammar" of the telautograph, the structure that directs its motions to the desired goal. Then there are the parts themselves, and knowing by experience what sorts of work they can do. Then there's the material for the parts: wood, rubber, and metal.

Of course, Stout's machine is far too complicated an apparatus for our current schools, I am proud to say, let alone for a boy rummaging about his basement with spare wood and a toolbox. But Stout assumes that his readers will grasp the principles involved without much trouble: "You can see from this how," he says, "if you swing the pencil sideways so as to move this lever about its pivot *S*, that the pencil at the other end will slide sideways back and forth in exactly the same way as you move the first pencil." That's just one motion; a linked mechanism transmits the up-and-down motion, and the whole machine therefore will transmit any kind of motion of the pencil at all.

"Well," says my reader, nervously looking over his shoulder as his son transforms a ruler, a spool, and an ice cube into Lord Winter's catapult, "that may be the case for mechanical or physical facts, but surely it is safe to drum young heads with historical trivia, as dry as dust. If their minds are going to be as flat as Oklahoma, they should be as dry and dusty as Oklahoma, too." True enough, and many an imagination has been flattened by such an approach. Yet beware: historical facts can be dangerous, too. Webster could not have touched the imaginations of his audience, after all, if they had not known what Bunker Hill and Camden were.

Let's take a few examples. What could be duller, you say, than to memorize the dates of the various presidents of the United States? Not much. So the student properly instructed may learn that Franklin Pierce was president from 1853 to 1857. If the facts stopped there, that would be fine. But they might not stop there. He might learn that Pierce was an unpopular president, another fact, and this one more mysterious. He might read somewhere that Pierce's son died just before his father took office. He might hear that a great author named Nathaniel Hawthorne was a close friend of Pierce. And all at once a picture of a tragic man emerges in the mist, one who might have done well, had times been better. If the student then remembers that the Civil War began in 1861, and that Pierce was a Democrat while Lincoln was a Whig, and then a Republican, the mystery deepens, and questions begin to stir in the sleepy mind. What was it like to have been that man, watching the war that he did not prevent, with the Union armies commanded by his political enemy?

Or consider this piece of apparently harmless trivia: "The Normans conquered Sicily in the eleventh century." Ah, who cares about that? Nobody, so long as you have not made the mistake of introducing your student to geographical facts to boot. For if he knows where Normandy and Sicily are on the globe, he may ask the obvious question, "How did the Normans get down there? Did they go overland, or did they sail?" And that might lead him to investigate the construction of their boats, or who was in control of Sicily before they arrived. He might eventually find out that Viking raiders and traders had long been in contact with Constantinople, and that the Byzantine rulers there requested the help of the now Christian Normans in ousting their enemies, the Muslim Arabs, from Sicily. How did Vikings end up in Byzantium? It appears they trekked overland to the River Don in Russia, and then sailed down it to the Black Sea and Constantinople. It would be better if the student could not tell Sicily from Saskatchewan, and knew only that Vikings were Very Bad People with funny hats who sailed a lot.

Old history textbooks used to be full of battle plans; people had the quaint notion that the outcome of battles like Salamis, Lepanto, and Waterloo changed the course of history. One argument for getting rid of those plans was that they were dull. Actually, they were dull to the teachers, many of whom didn't care a rap about the structure of battles, but they could be dynamite for the young. Once when my family and I were

.ting Gettysburg, I got into a conversation with a teenager at the top of n observation tower. He was a tourist too, but he told me he came back to Gettysburg quite a lot, and showed me Little Round Top and described for me what happened there.

He reminded me of a couple of homeschooled boys I knew, who also got their hands on battle plans, pored over them, committed them to memory, and turned the basement into a battlefield. They drew out the woods and hills and rivers in chalk, marked the battalions with counters, and then played a game of strategy with declared decisions and dice, reenacting the battle not as it actually happened but as it might have happened. When they'd made a move or two on the sprawling "board" of the basement floor, they would then go outside to play it out with their arms and legs and voices. And all this was going on while the mother of one of the boys looked the other way.

I relay this all to you in order to ask: of what use to us now are Facts? Surely, in the case of the homeschooled boys, we have seen Facts run amok. The Gradgrinds in the days of Dickens saw the black smoke belching out of the stacks in Leeds and Manchester, and it gladdened their hearts. The thought of molten pig iron fairly made them giddy. Had Father Christmas dumped their stockings full of coal, they would have treasured the lumps like diamonds. But we now have a Service Economy, which mainly entails the transfer of money from one person to another for nothing of any inherent use. We also have a Welfare State, which is a perpetual motion machine, producing the dependency which it purports to alleviate. Now a man with a wrench who knows Facts about pipes and fittings simply won't do. We need a few such men, no doubt, but we don't want to encourage it. We want instead helplessness, narcissism, shallowness, and ignorance, and we want them in the guise of education. Drudgery will do; but drudgery to no practical end. We want Gradgrind, without the Facts.

Memory? What Memory?

How, then, to do away with the Facts? The first thing is to keep the memory weak and empty.

That may sound counterintuitive. "We don't teach by rote memorization," say our educators today, raising their chins in pride. "We prefer to teach critical thinking. We prefer to tap into the imagination."

So long as teachers keep harping on that one string, we won't have to fear that our schools will turn out the next Dante or Mozart. That is because a developed memory is a wondrous and terrible storehouse of things seen and heard and done. It can do what no mere search engine on the internet can do. It can call up apparently unrelated things at once, molding them into a whole impression, or a new thought. The poet T. S. Eliot understood this creative, associative, dynamic function of a strong memory. The developed imagination remembers a strain from Bach, and smells spinach cooking in the kitchen, and these impressions are not separate but part of a unified whole, and are the essence of creative play. Without the library of the memory—which the Renaissance poet Edmund Spenser compared to a dusty room full of wonders in the attic of the mind, where a wise old man pores over his books, and a little boy called Anamnesis, "Reminder," sometimes has to climb a ladder to go fetch them—the imagination simply does not have much to think about, or to play with.

We sniff at memorization, as hardly worth the name of study. That is wise of us. For the most imaginative people in the history of the world thought otherwise. "Zeus became enamoured with fair-haired Memory," sings the ancient Greek poet Hesiod, "and she produced the nine Muses with their golden diadems, who enjoy festivities and the delights of song." The great epic poets invoked the Muses not to stir in them something supposedly "original," which usually is merely self-centered and peculiar, but to give them the twin gifts of memory and prophecy. "They breathed into me their divine voice," says Hesiod, "that I might tell of things to come and of things past, and ordered me to sing of the race of the blessed gods who live forever, and always to place the Muses themselves both at the beginning and at the end of my song."

It is not surprising that, for the Greek mind, the Muses—of epic, history, astronomy, music, dance, tragedy, comedy, lyric poetry, and sacred poetry—should be daughters of Memory. The Greek lad knew his poetry, which was for him also history and moral training, *only* by memory. Imagine the evening sun setting over the mountains of Greece, while boys and girls, men and women, young and old, gather round the traveling *rhapsode*, who strums his lyre as he was taught by his master, and sings them the songs of Achilles who grew enraged at his general Agamemnon, or of Odysseus home at last, disguised as a beggar, looking at an old dog dying on a dungheap, a dog he has not seen in twenty years. You have learned all the great stories by hearing them, and you can sing plenty of passages in your own right: of Orestes confronting his mother Clytemnestra after she murdered his father; of Medea, harboring vengeance against the husband, Jason, for whom she had killed her own brother; of wise Athena and sly Aphrodite and proud Hera, striving for the golden apple. And see now what those great memorizers the Greeks did: they invented historiography, political science, democratic systems of government, philosophy, geometric proof, comedy and tragedy, and a tradition of sculpture of the human form unsurpassed until the Renaissance. So crucial was memory to the training of the Greek mind that Plato worried whether writing would actually compromise matters. In *Phaedrus*, Plato's Socrates relates a legend of the wise Egyptian king Theuth, who one day was approached by an advisor recommending the invention of writing, to enhance the memory and wisdom of his people. But Theuth replied:

> "O man full of arts, to one it is given to create the things of art, and to another to judge what measure of harm and of profit they have for those that shall employ them. And so it is that you, by reason of your tender regard for the writing that is your offspring, have declared the very opposite of its true effect. If men learn this, it will implant forgetfulness in their souls; they will cease to exercise memory because they rely on that which is written. . . . And it is no true wisdom that you offer your disciples, but only its semblance; for by telling them of many things without teaching them you will make them seem to know much, while for the most part they know nothing; and as men filled, not with wisdom, but with the conceit of wisdom, they will be a burden to their fellows."

Plato never conceived of the flattening distractions of the internet.

When Mozart was a little boy, the story goes that his father took him to Rome, to show him the music of the place, and to introduce the child wonder to important people. He wangled a way into the Sistine Chapel for the evening service of Tuesday of Holy Week. On that night, year after year for well over a century, the choir sang the *Miserere Mei* by Giorgio Allegri, a pupil and friend of the great composer Palestrina. No one had ever seen a score of that unusual and haunting piece—composed for a double choir with four voices (the boy sopranos, the countertenors, the tenors, and the basses), with each part carrying a melody of its own, as was the rule in Renaissance polyphony. No one had seen the score, because the Church considered the piece so precious that it might only be passed down by ear, by memory, from one choirmaster to the next, over the generations.

"Son," said Leopold Mozart, as they knelt in the chapel, "do you think you can remember this piece?"

"Yes, father," said Wolfgang. And he did. When word got around Rome that a boy had committed the *Miserere* to memory, flawlessly, the Pope, not angry but curious, called the Mozarts in for an audience, and gave him more music to remember. This same boy had written his first composition, the surprisingly complex little Andante in C, at age five, and would write his first opera, successfully staged, at age fourteen.

True, Mozart was a prodigy. But we should not let down our guard, merely because a Mozart comes along only once or twice in a century, at best. We want to ensure that none come along at all, *and* we want to ensure that one of the keys without which Mozart could not have blossomed—the training of the memory—will not be available for the many thousands of people who fall short of Mozart, but who might otherwise revive a dying culture. Why, the very music that Mozart heard on that night is music of the memory. The choirboys singing it—not professionals, note well—were not looking at anything on a page. They never had been given any page to study at all. Multiply that choir by the many thousands of churches across Europe, and multiply that year by the centuries since the choirmasters of the high Middle Ages began to transform chant into polyphonic melodies, and you will see how terrible can be the power of memory.

"But that's only a danger in high society," says the unwary reader. "We're uncultured hicks from the backwoods. We watch car racing and national politics."

It is true that watching politicians is well worth a trauma to the head. But be advised. It is precisely among the peasants and nomadic shepherds, among the common people of any age and clime, that memory has worked its dangerous wonders.

Here I might mention the shape-note singers of Appalachia, who preserved in rough-hewn popular form, whether they were aware of it or not, that same sort of choral polyphony that rang in the churches of Europe. Our children can barely hum a flattened tune or two, and the "music" they listen to on the radio is impossible to remember, as it has neither melody nor intelligible structure. But not so long ago you could gather a few dozen ordinary people at a chapel on a mountain in Kentucky, and someone might call out, "Wondrous Love," and without need of a musical score, the voices would rise in complex harmonies—with the *middle*, or tenor, part carrying the melody, the boys and the women above, and the deeper male voices below.

But an even more fearsome story of the power of memory comes from Anglo-Saxon England, a generation or so after the people had begun to turn to the gospel of Christ. Caedmon, a cattle herd for the local monastery, is sitting at the table with his friends one evening. They are having a feast. Now if you are a German, in those days, you need three things for a feast. You need food, you need beer, and you need *poetry*. Nothing written down; all these cattle herders and blacksmiths and shepherds and stable boys were illiterate. The poems were stories passed down from of old, in complicated yet memorable rhythm, about ancient heroes and gods, like Sigemund who slew the dragon in his lair. They could go on for many hundreds of lines, these songs. And you had to sing them, too, to the strains of a harp, making its way down the table from one man to the next.

Caedmon, feeling awkward, left the feast—"beership" is approximately the word for it in Anglo-Saxon—and went to tend the cattle before going to bed. In his sleep an angel of the Lord appeared to him, saying, "Caedmon, sing me something."

"But I don't know anything to sing," said Caedmon, "and that's why I left the beer-feast."

"Nevertheless," said the angel, "you *can* sing."

"What shall I sing?"

"Sing me the First Making."

At which point Caedmon, in the rhythms of the old heroic pagan poetry he had heard all his life, broke into this little hymn:

> Now let us laud the Lord of Heaven's realm,
> the Measurer's might and his mind-plan,
> work of the Glory-Father, as every wondrous thing,
> Chieftain eternal, he established from of old.
> He first shaped for the sons of earth,
> the high roof of heaven, holy Creator;
> the middle-yard mankind's Lord,

Chieftain eternal, adorned after that,
made the earth for men, the Master almighty.

When he awoke the next morning, he told his superior about it, and he, the bailiff for the monastery, took Caedmon to the abbess, who then instructed some of the literate monks to tell Caedmon a story out of Scripture, to see if he could transform it into poetry. They did, and Caedmon returned the next day with a polished poem, composed out of the treasures of his memory, though he could neither read nor write. It was a gift from God, they concluded, and took Caedmon in as a monk, where he proceeded to hear more and more of the stories from the Old Testament, the gospels, the Acts of the Apostles, the lives of the saints, and to transmute them into the music of poetry.

Caedmon thus began a tradition in English that would reach its pinnacle a thousand years later, in Milton's *Paradise Lost.* Appropriately so, since Milton—who could read a passel of languages, including of course ancient Greek and Latin and Hebrew—never read *Paradise Lost*, though it was his own poem. He never read it, because he was blind when he wrote it; it dwelled, with all its thousands and thousands of lines and interwoven images, in his imagination, and his memory. But that was no new thing in the world, either. Tradition has it that Homer was blind. Not only did he never read his *Iliad* and *Odyssey*. It may well be that he never *wrote* them down, either. For hundreds of years they too were passed down, by memory, before a few editors *after* the Golden Age of Athens decided to produce a definitive text.

The memory, then, is not to be taken lightly. In children, it is surprisingly strong. Adults scoff at remembering things, because they have—so they say—the higher tools of reason at their disposal. I suspect that they also scoff at memory because theirs is no longer very good, as their heads are cluttered with the important business of life, such as where they should stop for lunch and who is going to buy the dog license. But educators of old, those whom we now recognize rightly as mere drillmasters, exposed children to a shocking wealth of poetry and music, and indeed would often set their lessons to easily remembered jingles, as did Saint John Bosco, working with the street boys of late nineteenth century Turin, and as Marva Collins in Chicago did more recently, with unnerving success. The memorization and recitation of poetry was one of the hallmarks of the so-called

Integrated Humanities Program at the University of Kansas, in the late 1960s, under the direction of the Renaissance scholar John Senior. The intensely personal encounter with poetry, which memorization requires, began to change so many lives that the trustees of the university, appropriately alarmed, shut the program down. It lives on, however, in many a new Catholic school inspired by Professor Senior's method.

No, if we want to stifle the imagination, we should hold that memory in check. We can do this in two ways. We can encourage laziness, by never insisting that young people actually master, for example, the rules of multiplication, or the location of cities and rivers and lakes on the globe. Then we can allow what is left of the memory to be filled with trash. One of my old professors, the medievalist George Kane, used to tell me that the farmer down the road from him when he was a boy in Saskatchewan recited *Paradise Lost* by memory as he plowed his fields. Imagine the threat of such a man. A government official walks up to him, some bureaucrat from Ottawa intending to regulate him out of business, perhaps. The official smiles. And, just like that, there floats into the farmer's mind the words of another bureaucrat just as he was about to enter Eden:

> So farewell hope, and with hope, farewell fear;
> Farewell remorse; all good to me is lost;
> Evil be thou my good, by thee at least
> Divided empire with Heav'n's King I hold
> By thee, and more than half perhaps shall reign,
> As man ere long, and this new world shall know.

To have a wealth of such poetry in your mind—a wealth of knowledge about man, set to music—is to be armed against the salesmen and the social controllers. It allows you the chance of independent thought, and independence is by nature unpredictable. We prefer the predictable. Therefore, for children, books with silly, flat, banal language are best, so as to prepare them for the manageable and socially productive "songs" they will remember when they are adults:

> Rice-a-Roni, the flavor can't be beat!
> Rice-a-Roni, the San Francisco treat.

A Lump without a Skeleton

Unfortunately, not even the dullest life—not the most garish and gabbling schoolbooks, not the plasticene sterility of a day-care center, not even the wasted seasons spent gaping at a computer screen—will prevent the child from hearing about something that is real and good and ennobling. Even Facts will poke their noses under the tent. At this point the wise social planner must be shrewd. He must rob those Facts of their power by keeping them random and unorganized. As it turns out, he may now do this quite well, *by appealing to the very imagination which his policies must damage or destroy.*

Let me explain. We have accepted what I should call the Jellyfish Theory of the Imagination. According to this theory, the imagination abhors all structure, all rules. It likes to float along in a sea of impressions—usually provided for it not by real life but by the easy substitutes for life on television and in video games—sometimes allowing an "image" to pass through one end that had recently come into the other. It may be that, in the Land of the Jellyfish, the citizens can tell one jellyfish from another, but to us they look exactly alike. Every jellyfish looks like a lump without a skeleton. So, too, the free verse that students are encouraged to write, to express their feelings—again, to emit from one end the flotsam that has found its way into the other. That, too, reads like a lump without a skeleton. So, too, the music that washes up on the popular airwaves, without melody, without control, without meter, without even the precision of identifiable notes.

I could multiply examples. Do not teach history or geography, because these things demand some kind of overarching structure to make sense of it all. Do "unit studies" instead, spending a month on Egypt, another month on Japan, at whim; like the wave-borne drifting of a jellyfish. Do not teach English grammar. Rather, let the students learn to write by repeating the sniggers and grunts of popular chat. Do not teach the multiplication tables. Do not teach physics at all. Turn science into biology, biology into ecology, and ecology into shapeless cuddles. And while you are doing these things, proudly announce it to the world: "The teachers at Classical High hamstring their students with Rules, with Grammar, with Timelines, with Maps, with Blueprints, with Compositions. But *we* are too creative for that.

We foster the imagination." You see how it goes. If the mind has legs, we can at least keep those legs from developing any muscle and bone.

About a hundred years ago, a cartoonist named Rube Goldberg became famous for his sprawling single-panel cartoons of complicated machines, with crazy concatenations of levers and pulleys and chickens and lawn mowers and scotch tape and baseballs and whatnot, all put together to achieve a trivial result. In one such cartoon, a man drinking soup pulls a string with his arm that flips a spoon attached to a pulley, catapulting a cracker in the direction of a bird on a perch, that leaves his perch to catch the cracker, dumping a cup full of salt into a small bucket, that pulls a string on two pulleys, that flips the lid of a cigarette lighter, that lights a rocket attached to a sickle, that cuts the string attached to a clock's pendulum, that swings back with a handkerchief attached to it, to wipe the man's mouth.

If that seems merely absurd, you have never beheld the serpentine belt on a recently manufactured car—a belt that turns the fan, the alternator, the power steering, the water pump, and so forth. Goldberg's machines were wildly imaginative, really a gleeful celebration of the spirit of invention. In more recent times, Nick Park of *Wallace and Gromit* fame has revived that spirit, with Wallace sliding off his tilting bed into his trousers and through a trap door in the bedroom, down to the kitchen table below, where robot arms slap a shirt over his head and half a sweater on each arm. The Coyote in the old Road Runner cartoons was a failed Wallace, always purchasing some absurd heap of junk from the ever-present Acme Company—magnetized iron bird seed pellets, jet propelled roller skates—only to find the physics of the machine turn against him, causing the projecting ledge of a cliff to fall on his head, or something similarly disconcerting.

None of this playfulness is possible without a deep sense of structure—without a skeleton upon which to hang one's welter of experience. Some people probably still recall the story of Archimedes in the bathtub, rushing out into the streets without his clothes, crying out, "Eureka," meaning, "I have found it!" But they probably don't know what Archimedes found, and why it was important. The story goes that he had discovered the physical law of the displacement of water. That is, an object will displace an amount of water equal to its own weight. What this means is that you can pretty well predict whether an object will float. Does gold float? Well, that depends. A lump of gold will sink. But if you hammer gold thin enough and spread it out in the shape of a boat, then the amount of water it would have to push out of the way to bring water up over the hull will be heavier than the weight of the gold. So the golden boat would float.

Archimedes' mind had structure to it, and that allowed him to devise the most wonderful inventions, real masterpieces of the imagination. One of the simplest but most elegant was the Archimedean screw or drill, still used, apparently, in the Low Countries. It was a way of getting water to climb a staircase, so to speak. You turn the screw in the water, and the combined action of your rotary motion and the spiral incline of the screw draws the water up. It was no surprise that Archimedes was in great demand. During the siege of his city of Syracuse, he invented catapults and other ballistic devices (literally, machines that throw things around); he once boasted that if he had a lever long enough, he could move the world. But he died during that siege, when a soldier—who had been under orders to take the valuable man alive—mistook him for a fool and killed him. What was Archimedes doing when he died? He was doing what we must ensure that no boy will do again. He was tracing blueprints in the sand.

Structure—a "grammar" that orders every part in its appropriate place—is important not only for the physical sciences, but for every kind of intellectual endeavor. It allows us to do more than weave a fancy from the bits and pieces of our private experience. We can, by the power of structure, weave a whole artistic universe.

Let's take the hardest cases of all, the structures that our wise teachers are most unwilling to hand over to their students. I am speaking of grammar and arithmetic. Surely, you say, if we want to destroy the imagination we ought to be doing nothing *but* teaching grammar and arithmetic, until the students' minds are fairly choked to death with them.

Not so fast. Consider a man who was perhaps the most imaginative writer in English in the last century, J. R. R. Tolkien. In one of his essays he tells an amusing anecdote of something he overheard while he and other young recruits for the British army were listening to a lecture on "map-reading, or camp-hygiene, or the art of sticking a fellow through without (in defiance of Kipling) bothering who God sent the bill to." Suddenly a little man at a nearby table nearby said, dreamily, "I think I shall express the accusative case by a prefix!" Tolkien beamed within. So, he thought, I'm not the only one! I'm not the only half-mad inventor of an imaginary language! "What a pondering of alternatives within one's choice," noted Tolkien many years later, "before the final decision in favour of the daring and unusual prefix, so personal, so attractive; the final solution of some element in a design that had hitherto proved refractory."*

Tolkien, you see, was a linguist, fascinated by the power and beauty and structure of language, especially as he saw it at work in medieval epic. He was saturated with the strange beauty of Welsh (just *looking* at a sentence like "Y mae llygaid gwyrddion ganddi hi," "She has green eyes," will make you think you have opened a door onto a lovely and dangerous planet), the lilting of Finnish (wherein it is absolutely against the phonetic *rules* to put two consonants together at the beginning of a syllable), and the rugged muscles of Old Icelandic. Tolkien could not simply write *The Lord of the Rings*. That man of irrepressible imagination, who has been solely responsible for ruining countless ordinary minds and lending them the light fantastic, had to create an entire world, with geography (maps are a beloved aid for finding your way through Mirkwood or Rohan), history (what happened to the Silmarillion—the Elvish plural for Silmaril, similar to many Welsh plurals—helps to explain events many centuries later, when the hobbit Frodo seeks to cast the last Silmaril, the last Ring of Power, into the crater of Mount Doom), language (you are a Tolkien piker if you can read only Elvish but not Old Elvish), and unchangeable moral laws (most dangerous of all for a young mind to encounter). Without the habit of seeking out structure in language, he never would have had the skill to endow his fiction with it. Had he never known what it might be like to mark the accusative with a prefix, we never would have had Gollum and Frodo struggling for the ring at the top of that hellish mountain, in a moment that both decides the fate of Middle Earth, and that brings to a terrific climax a hundred events that have come before.

The best thing to do to strangle the next Tolkien in his educational crib would be to *pretend* to teach grammar, like so. "Now, class," says the Teacher, "we are going to do a little grammar. Frankly, the whole subject is pointless. It's all a set of picky little rules that apply here and there, at random. Try to remember the picky rules, but if you don't, nobody is going to care much, because nobody knows them anyway." To be candid, the only dangling participles most teachers can identify are those in the diagrams of health books for sixth graders—but more on *that* later.

---

* Christopher Tolkien, ed., *The Monsters and the Critics and Other Essays* (Boston: Houghton-Mifflin, 1984).

This approach to grammar has two considerable advantages. First, it is an absolutely futile way to teach anything at all. The students will learn no grammar. They won't know the difference between causative *lay* and stative *lie*. They won't be able to identify the subject of a sentence. Indeed, they won't be able to identify a sentence. They will never have the linguistic wrenches, pliers, hammers, and chisels to fashion a grammatical spree like the following, from the comic novel *Joseph Andrews*, by Henry Fielding. The good parson Abraham Adams hears a scream in the night and comes upon a man overpowering a woman. He knows what to do:

> He did not, therefore, want the entreaties of the poor wretch to assist her; but lifting up his crabstick, he immediately leveled a blow at that part of the ravisher's head where, according to the opinion of the ancients, the brains of some persons are deposited, and which he had undoubtedly let forth, had not Nature (who, as wise men have observed, equips all creatures with what is most expedient for them) taken a provident care (as she always doth with those she intends for encounters) to make this part of the head three times as thick as those of ordinary men, who are designed to exercise talents which are vulgarly called rational, and for whom, as brains are necessary, she is obliged to leave some room for them in the skull; whereas, those ingredients being entirely useless to persons of the heroic calling, she hath an opportunity of thickening the bone, so as to make it less subject to any impression, or liable to be cracked or broken; and, indeed, in some who are predestined to the command of armies and empires, she is supposed sometimes to make that part perfectly solid.

What a magnificent satire that is, against the "heroes" whose bravery consists in oppressing the weak, and against mighty generals and emperors, for whose brains Nature need leave no room in the skull at all, so little are they needed for the government of armies and states! But teachers will undoubtedly call that carefully structured sentence, building to its absurd climax, a run-on, because it happens to be long. They might as well call Michelangelo's paintings on the Sistine ceiling run-ons, because they happen to be big.

But the second advantage is more powerful than the first. Imagine a serpent whispering into the ear, "Young lady," or "Young lad," as the case may be, "do not fear those rigid threats of Death. Bad grammar will not kill you. How should it? It is itself weak and foolish. All structure is foolish. Be *creative*. Do what you please. So what if some old fashioned Tyrant up above calls it gibberish? It will be *your* gibberish. There are no rules. Isn't this apple shiny, though?" And so what we kill is not only the possibility that the students will learn English grammar, but that they will learn the grammar of anything at all—law, moral philosophy, mathematics, history, you name it.

What about arithmetic? There can't possibly be any imagination in manipulating numbers, right? Here again our schools have achieved a great victory *over* the imagination, by pretending to *support* it. And again they have done so by denigrating the memory, depriving children of the skeletal structure of arithmetic: the dreadful "rules."

When I was a boy, we had to memorize the multiplication tables in the second grade, up to 12 x 12 = 144. Let's set aside the fact that it takes a deal of intelligence and some ingenuity to accomplish that task. Forget that you would have to learn that anything multiplied by 5 ends in 5 or 0, alternately. Forget that if you were sharp you'd see that odd times odd is odd, and everything else is even. Forget the patterns showing up among the 2s, 4s, and 8s. Forget the nice progression in the 9s, with the tens digit gaining one and the ones digit dropping it: 09, 18, 27, and so forth. What that memorization did was to free you up to become comfortable with numbers themselves, and with the structure of arithmetic. Once you had done that, you could play with numbers creatively, long before you'd ever suspected the existence of algebra or calculus, with their toboggan curves and their infinite series and their radio waves, their transcendental numbers and the mysterious i, the square root of -1, whose existence we must leave to philosophers to determine.

Let's take an example from *Ray's New Higher Arithmetic* (1880), the pinnacle of a series of books that sold over 120,000 copies in America in the nineteenth century. Now, higher arithmetic is a subject no longer taught at all, because, it is said, calculators make it unnecessary for us actually to *understand* the numbers that appear on the screen. But the author of the series, Joseph Ray, MD, had the odd notion that a high school student could perform what look like extraordinarily difficult operations for all kinds of practical purposes: figuring interest, stock dividends, areas of land, and volumes. Because he could depend on the student's knowing the basic operations cold, he could lead them to understand how numbers could be used to solve some tricky problems. He shows, for instance, that there's a perfectly logical way to imagine what it is to take a square root of a number, by laying that number out as an area, like a square field, and then using squares and rectangles inside the field to fill it up, determining what the length of the field must be. That takes considerable imagination: the number can't be a funny looking sign on a page, but must take shape, assume a kind of concrete existence. The number 576 isn't just a number, but a nice square field, 24 feet on a side.

Deriving square roots (and cube roots!) just by adding and multiplying squares and rectangles or cubes and prisms is probably too hard for most teachers now, let alone students. Here is an easier problem, from early in the book:

Multiply 387295 by 216324.

Simple drudgery, you say. Ah, but here's the trick of it. Do the operation by performing *only three* sets of multiplication. That is, 216324 has six digits in it, and you'd think, if you were not imaginative with numbers, that you would therefore have to perform six sets of multiplication, first by 4, then by 2, and so on. It isn't so.

The trick is to see—and imagination is a power that allows us to combine things and recombine them, seeing them anew every time—that 216324 has a pretty set of digits. It has a 3, and a 24, and a 216. But 3 x 8 = 24, and 24 x 9 = 216. These things you just *know;* they are tools for your cleverness to fool about with, as a machinist learns the feel of a wrench or a drill press. This means that if you multiply by the 3 first, putting the product in the correct position, directly under the 3, and then multiply *that* product by 8, putting the new product directly under the 4 of 24, and then multiply *that* product in turn by 9, putting the new new product directly under the 6 of 216, you will have done all the multiplication you need to do. Then you add up the three products, instead of the six that you otherwise would have made; and you are done.

Students who never master the foundations of arithmetic will never learn such play. Suppose, in baseball, a player has 257 official at-bats and makes 73 hits. What is his batting average? Here are the possible responses a student may give, from most desirable to least:

"I am sorry, Mr. James, but I am being trained for absolute dependence upon a technocratic state. I have no idea what your question means."

"I don't know. I think you would have to divide one number into the other, but I'm not sure which should go into which."

"You have to divide 73 by 257. I'd need a calculator to do that. I have no idea what it would be."

"You have to divide 73 by 257. I think it's less than .300, but I'd need a calculator to find out."

"It's less than .300. Give me a pen and paper and I'll do the division."

And then, the answer that is only possible from a strong memory and a developed imagination that such a memory can foster:

"If it were 70 for 250, he'd be batting 70 x .4 = .280. So it's more than .280, because the extra 3 for 7 is much more than that. Add a hit to one side and take it away from the other: if it were 71 for 250, he'd be batting .284. Then the extra 2 for 7 wouldn't change the average much at all, because 2 for 7 is .286 (as everybody knows). So the average is .284."

The fact is, playing with numbers can be great fun. You're playing backgammon and desperately need a 5 and a 3 on the dice. What are your chances of getting it? The best hand in cribbage is a jack and four fives. What are the chances of that? When you look at the decimal expansions of fractions with the denominator 7, 11, and 13, they do something really peculiar:

$$1/7 = .142857 \quad 1/11 = .090909 \quad 1/13 = .076923$$

You'll notice that if you take the first three digits of each expansion, and add them to the last three digits, you'll get the same number, 999:

$$142 + 857 = 999 \quad 090 + 909 = 999 \quad 076 + 923 = 999$$

The rule continues for 2/7, 2/11, 2/13, and so on. Why is that? Hint: Multiply 7 x 11 x 13, and think about the result very hard, and use your imagination.

When I was a boy, we used to take baseball cards and flip them against the side of the schoolhouse outside at recess. It was a sort of contest. If your card came closer to the wall, or "topped" the other fellow's card, you got to keep them both. In general we liked to play with two kinds of cards: new ones with nice sharp sides for easy flipping, and cards for "bums" like

Dave Ricketts or Dooley Womack or somebody else that nobody wanted. And how could you tell that nobody wanted them? That's simple. From the *numbers* on the back. It was like playing with dynamite. Educators could blast a solid numerical imagination to rubble by detonating it with the highly abstract and highly verbal "new math," and could leave the memory dormant by not pestering it with such things as tables and rules of operation. But plenty of those gains were lost by the baseball cards, as boys who could not define "the distributive property of multiplication over addition" yet could pore over the spilling statistics on the backs of card after card, committing them lovingly to memory, as if they were the holy words of a strange and powerful language. Which, of course, they were.

There's Dullness, and There's Dullness

Imagine row after row of students slumped over their books, scratching their heads, gaping in incomprehension at their lesson, while the teacher in the front of the room drones over the minutiae of the grammar of what they are reading. Now imagine, in the next room, a popular professor of physics giving a lesson on air pressure and propulsion by attempting to set off a rocket by steam. The boys flock around him; he's young and chatty and easy to like, while the grammarian is old, crotchety, and distant.

That's the contrast set up in the film *The Browning Version* (1951), and as soon as we see the two classrooms we know which one we'd prefer to be in. That is exactly what the screenwriter expects. As it turns out, the physicist is more showman than scientist, and not a great showman at that. His first attempts at propulsion fail, until he takes a suggestion from a student named Taplow who is not even in his class, but rather in the deadly Greek class next door. Now *that* is the place where imaginations wither and die; except that *they* are the ones playing with nitro glycerine, although most of the students do not know it. They are reading, or desperately struggling to read, Aeschylus' *Agamemnon*, the first play in his trilogy that ponders the meaning of good and evil, vengeance and law, nature and the city. Clytemnestra has waited ten years for the return of her husband Agamemnon, who sacrificed their daughter to the goddess Artemis in return for favorable winds as his ships sailed off to Troy. Ten years she has waited, having taken a lover in the meantime, brooding, fearing that the man will not return,

then at last exulting when her sentries send the fire-signal from mountaintop to mountaintop, to alert her that Agamemnon is coming home. She
tells him, with devastating irony, that she has been longing to see him. In
the end she tangles him in a net and butchers him in his own house. When
the people of Argos come running, she stands above the body with bloody
knife in hand, boldly, with no apology.

"How fine that is, sir!" exclaims the same Taplow. "That she could
stand over the corpse of her own husband!" And the schoolmaster nods in
appreciation.

That is the picture of an imagination come alive, never to die again.
The students in the other class may have been entertained for a spell, but
Taplow's mind, under the influence of the potent Greek of Aeschylus, is on
its way to being rendered perfectly useless for hack work, for mass market-
ing, and for sloganeering politics.

So we want to make sure we overwhelm the students with the right
kind of dullness. In *The Weight of Glory*, C. S. Lewis wrote that a schoolboy learning Greek might eventually come to understand that he can have
again and again, but only after the hard work of study, the joy he feels when
a passage of stupendous poetry suddenly makes sense. Maybe he reads of
Odysseus's dog Argos, "Flash," lying flea-ridden and half dead on a dungheap, trying bravely to wag his tail as he sees his master home after twenty
years, recognizing the man when the human beings around him fail to do
so. Or he might fight through Latin inflectional endings to read the words
of Aeneas from Virgil's *Aeneid*, the saddest hero of ancient epic, as before
his final battle with his enemy Turnus he advises his son about what to
expect and not expect from his life:

Disce, puer, virtutem ex me verumque laborem,
Fortunam ex aliis.

Hard work and manhood learn from me, my boy;
Good fortune you can learn from someone else.

And the moment of understanding, the vision of a truth that is precious precisely because it turns us away from easy and comfortable con-
solations, a truth made the more splendid by poetry that burns itself into

the memory, will have made the laborious study worthwhile. We want to avoid, then, the sometimes necessary dullness of the beginnings of a great task. Yet we do want dullness. What should we do?

I think that the answer has already been suggested in this chapter. Demand drudgery, but not drudgery that has as its end the mastery of facts, or of an intellectual structure within which to retain and interpret the facts, or of a great work of imagination for which the facts of grammar or arithmetic or whatever are the doorkeepers. Keep the students busy *and* idle at the same time. Put them in groups, to pull down the intelligent. Have them make posters full of unrelated bits of data. Encourage the easy and slipshod. Have them study Germany by cooking a bowl of bean soup, or frying some wienerschnitzel (rather like studying baseball by grilling a hot dog). Make them write what they have cribbed from a "source," normally the gabbling internet, and then don't bother to check for grammar or style, or even to see whether the student actually wrote the work himself. At all costs have the assignments devour *time*. Call them "creative" if you like. Appeal to the student's vanity—never a difficult maneuver—and enlist his good will as you rob his days. Time was the eater of things, said the old poets, but now we are saddled with young people whom we don't know what to do with, and who have no idea what to do with their time. *Schola edax temporis sit*—let school be the eater of time.

Let me finish this chapter with an anecdote. I once met a bird-watching couple in Nova Scotia, who had taken hundreds of photographs of the birds they had seen (sometimes while lying in the snow or standing in icy water to wait for their approach). This couple, not college-educated, could speak about each species with wry anecdotes, genuine affection, and detailed information. They said that the arctic terns see more daylight in a year than any other creature on earth, migrating 22,000 miles in a great circle from pole to pole, spending their days in the northern summer and then in the southern summer, and back again. They said they had managed to feed through the winter an oriole that had strayed too far north. They sewed grapes on a string and dangled the makeshift feeder from a tree. They said that the spruce grouse was so stupid a bird that you could "freeze" one of them in a tree and snatch it by hand. They were a treasure-house of things to know about birds, because they loved them; and the more they learned about birds, the warmer their love grew.

A fact may not be much, by itself, but it points toward what is true, and even the humblest truth may in time lead a mind to contemplate the beautiful and the good. A blue jay will give a certain kind of warning shriek to alert his fellows that a hawk is nearby. Ponder that fact awhile, and perhaps the common pest of the backyard feeder, so familiar to us that we miss his bold brave beauty, will resume his proper mystery.

Method 1

Keep Your Children Indoors
as Much as Possible

or

They Used to Call It "Air"

One of the disadvantages of our civilization is that too often stress of circumstances places square pegs in round holes in the artificial economy of our lives. A man of splendid frame, who should be exploring the wilds, must sit at a desk; a brain teeming with fine imagination is deadened by routine work in a factory. Nature never practices such misfit politics.

—From *The Book of Knowledge* (1923)

I grew up in a small town in northeastern Pennsylvania, in a region where coal mining was just about to gasp out its last blue breath. That meant that what we called the "woods" were crisscrossed with old mining trails, and pocked with what we boys called "canyons," but were really stripping holes twenty to forty feet deep, sometimes cluttered with junk that people had driven up to the hole to abandon: cars, refrigerators, tubs, bowling balls. One time there was a refrigerator poised nicely at the edge of a canyon, and my cousins and I dutifully pushed it over to see it crash.

There was also a stone foundation for something; to this day I have no idea what. Perhaps a housing for a generator? Whatever it was, it promptly became our "hut." We took some scrap wood up there, cut down a couple of birches, nailed them together for what might have been the most inept roof imaginable, and cut a hole in it for a coffee can smokestack. I don't know if my cousins ever slept in it; I was a few years younger, and never did. Some other boys in the neighborhood caught wind of it and, as was the warlike custom in our town, found it and smashed it. For years I'd go up there on an idle afternoon and check it out, musing about how it could have been built differently, and kicking a piece of what used to be our roof. For all I know, there is still a stick or two of it there.

Mining leaves waste, and that too roused the imagination. On the far side of town, huge mounds of fine coal flakes, called "culm," towered over the neighborhoods. You didn't really get dirty from anthracite culm, just as you don't get dirty from glass. You might get the flakes caught in your shoe, or your hair, if you fell in it, but that's about it. So, many boys rode what we called "dirt bikes," those irresponsible and unhygienic things, up the sides of the mounds, trying to zigzag to the top before stalling in a smooth rut. I never had such a bike—that door of the imagination had been shut to me by an unreasonable fear of falling. But I did climb goat-like along the sides of a fifty-foot high scree of loose coal on our side of town. You couldn't fall from that, though you might slide a long way and rip your ankle. There on that mountain of debris I made a terrific discovery. The slabs of coal were often stamped with pictures: fossils of ferns and grass.

I'd stuff my pockets with them, or tuck the bigger rocks under my arm, and lug them home. The deadening of the imagination was already well advanced in my town, and that meant that, although I had collected one hundred and fifty of these things, nobody could tell me what they were, nor did anybody care to find out. I did learn that I was most likely to find a fossil in slab-shaped, glossy black rocks, and that if I split them along a horizontal seam, I'd often find excellent ones inside, just at the weak points of the rock. I suppose that wasn't a coincidence, but I'm not a geologist and can't be sure about it. Often the fossils were colored in strange oranges and pinks and greens, like the eerie rainbows you find in spilled oil on the pavement. I suppose that there's some connection there, too.

I never found a fossil of an animal, but grasses there were, usually streaked with a rusty red, and a lot of ferns. Those were the best; you could usually see the tiniest veins in the tiny leaves, perfectly preserved. I kept these fossils in a big sack under the porch. Then we moved to another house, and time and chance and spring cleaning, which happen to all things, happened to them.

There was another place I used to haunt, a heap of rocks left on a ridge by a retreating glacier. The heap had gotten covered with thin topsoil, making it impossible for anything to grow there except for a few stunted birches, a lot of moss and lichen, and blueberries. From that high place, with no trees in the way, I could see fifteen miles northeast and southwest, while to the southeast a mountain, actually a big ripple in the rug of the land, loomed up against me a mile away, with my town's streets struggling up it, and houses with strange people in them. In the summer I'd go there with my dog, just to look around, or think, or pick blueberries—because in July the place would be carpeted with them. I'd stay for a few hours and pick enough to fill a three-quart pitcher, with the dog happily panting under a birch tree, and sometimes nibbling the berries off the bush. There were a lot of edible things up there in those woods: mushrooms and wintergreen, for instance. A few old-timers picked mushrooms. My family picked blueberries. The rest, ignored. Wild roses grew there; I didn't know what they were. Waxwings, grosbeaks, all kinds of warblers, falcons, yellowhammers—I know them only now, after many years. For all that we knew of any of these things, they might have been occupying a parallel planet.

In winter I'd go there too, often trudging through snow. When it got really cold, sometimes the snow would form a hard crust on top, and you could walk on it without crashing through. The crystals, miniature prisms, would glint all the colors of the rainbow, though often the shadows on the snow were a cold light blue. In one of the "canyons," the water froze green, and again I do not know why, nor was there anybody around to tell me.

Standing on that glacial knob, or walking with the collie down the abandoned trails, I thought about things. I thought about death. It's said that young men make the best soldiers in part because they can't imagine themselves dying. I could imagine it; but mostly I was aware of the mysterious passage of time, and the changeableness of things. The plants that printed their forms on the coal had died thousands and thousands of years ago. The men who cleared the trails had died. There might well have been underground shafts nearby, abandoned and forgotten. The chassis of an abandoned bus once carried children to school; those children had grown old by now, and possibly the driver had died. I was surrounded by a world of change, scarred and pitted, and I loved it, and wanted it never to change.

I proved the existence of God up there, many times. I thought about people, mainly enemies at school and how I would get even with them; then later I thought about girls. I wasn't always alone, though. There was a nice cliff up there, which we called "the cliff," although its real name was

Corey Cliff, a name almost certainly forgotten by now. On the bald rocks adjoining that cliff, my cousins, in the immemorial tradition of boys everywhere, painted their initials and the date. For many years that witness of their existence and their conquest still shone out in the sun.

Please don't get the idea that my cousins and I were outdoorsmen. Fortunately, we were not. The world in which we had to make our way had already committed itself to being walled up. Our town had, accordingly, joined with two nearby towns to build a vast, hulking "school" in what used to be a part of those woods, complete with up-to-date swimming pools, tennis courts, and gymnasia. The classrooms *within* this school—which, as schools have done, began to devour more and more of the pupil's day, that he might be managed more efficiently—were originally built *without walls*, following the citified fad of the time, exactly as a high-toned lady from Tennessee would buy her perfume from Paris and nowhere else. They called these rooms "pods," borrowing a term from the same natural world that such schools ensure that their pupils will never explore. For a few years the school indulged that pretense of expansiveness and free investigation, but when the students refused to be controlled, they went back to walls, walls within walls.

And outside the walls? Fewer and fewer people; children still, and oldtimers, and the occasional drunk.

Contemporary life happens within walls; for the first time in the history of the human race, most people will spend most of their lives indoors. Therefore we must prepare the young for such a life. But as Robert Frost writes in "Mending Wall,"

Something there is in us that doesn't love a wall,
That wants it down.

So we must replace the great world about us with an artificial world, where not the imagination but the stray nervous tics of the brain may roam for a while and then rest. We must give the walled up child the illusion of the hills and plains. We must replace air with virtual space. More about that soon.

The Threat Outside the Door

Few parents grasp the danger of children playing outside. The most enlightened educators do grasp it, and have taken steps to ensure that children will be left to their own devices, outdoors, as little as possible. They have shortened the summer vacation, parceling out free days here and there through the school year. The effect is to keep children from developing the habit of learning things outside of school—things such as I will describe elsewhere in this book. After all, it takes children a week or so just to get used to the summer, and a week or two at the end of August to prepare for the new school year. Then, too, schools have heaped books upon the children to tote around during the summer, much as you would heave sacks of grain and skins of wine atop a camel before crossing a desert. The idea is not to instill a love of reading excellent literature. Recall that so-called great works of art are dangerous, as they rouse the imagination. No, summer reading ensures that no mental break occurs between June and September, no respite from the sedative.

As for the school day itself, both parents and educators want it to be as long as possible. Children, like fleas and lice, burrow into their parents' hair. Since parents wish to have children, yet to be unencumbered by them, they happily agree to have the effective school day take up all the daylight hours and then some: from the early march to the bus stop, to the long ride to the faraway asylum, through the school day (which is interrupted only briefly for that oiling of the human machine, which is called "lunch"), to the long ride back home, to the piles of homework that amount to little more than drudgery, graded by machine, or merely logged by the teacher as having been gotten through, but never really pored over, nor regarded as the work of a struggling human mind.

All of this the parents will accept, as canceling out years of their children's lives, which otherwise would have to be genuinely lived, with all the risks that genuine life must run. It also frees the parents. They may, with a clear conscience, go forth bravely to be what is called "themselves," along with millions of others who are being themselves, working at jobs that don't need to be done among people they don't really like. That is the Real World, and the routine of the school day and the night of homework prepare us for it.

But every so often a parent will look at the thin arms of his son or daughter and the weird pallor of a face exposed to hours of fluorescent light, and think that perhaps the child had better "play outside." This sentimentalism must be resisted.

Why? We may believe, naively, that to play outside is just to shift the arena, to play outside rather than to play inside. No doubt it is always better to have children play inside rather than outside. But the greatest danger of playing outside is the outside itself. *That* is the source of fascination. That can ruin everything.

First, there is what was once called *the sky*, what looks on earth like a vast dome above us, usually a deep blue, but purple and crimson and burning orange and pale yellow at sunrise and sunset, with even a wash of hardly visible green at times between the yellow and the blue. The sky, as you may know, is full of interesting and harmful things, clouds heaping up in towers, fleecy streaks of mist, birds in flight, and, when the sun has set, those odd points of light called *stars*. Some of these are suns whose light has gone out, millions of light-years away, or are red giants, about to explode or to collapse in upon themselves and die. Antares, the red heart of the Scorpion low in the southern summer sky, is perhaps one of these. Other stars are not stars at all but planets, not twinkling, but shining steadily, and moving across the apparent patterns of the stars night by night, red Mars and yellowish Saturn and bright white Jupiter, usually exceeded in brightness only by Venus and the moon.

In *The Divine Comedy*, after Dante has agreed to allow the shade of the ancient poet Virgil to lead him on a pilgrimage through the underworld, he and his guide approach the shores of a dismal river, where "naked and exhausted souls" await, with apprehension, what is to become of them. Suddenly a boat comes into sight, with an old man poling it across the swamp. Charon, the ferryman of the dead, greets them in this pleasant fashion:

> Woe to you, crooked souls!
> Give up all hope to look upon the sky!
> I come to lead you to the other shore,
> into eternal darkness, fire and ice.

What he says, in Italian, is *"non isperate mai veder lo cielo,"* meaning, theologically, that they must not hope to see heaven. But the Italian *cielo* means both "heaven" and "sky." Both meanings are in play here. Charon brings the souls news that there will forever be a lid on their world. They will not see heaven; and that means that they will not see the sky. Now Dante and his medieval contemporaries did not assume that heaven was up in the stratosphere, or even on some star or other. It is a place beyond place, and more real than any created place, whose location, as his heavenly guide Beatrice will say in the *Paradiso*, is in the mind of God. But the vastness of the sky will naturally lead the mind to contemplate infinities; it is wholly apt to associate the sky with expansiveness of the spirit, with joy and freedom and holiness. In the same way, the mind is apt to associate that lid of the earth with fixity, frustration, and the small cramped knot of evil that the damned soul becomes.

Imagine, then, never being able to look upon the sky. That would drive us mad; and madness, unless it is of the sort that is predictable and spends money, would damage our economy. In *Lady Windemere's Fan* by Oscar Wilde, Lord Darlington says, "We are all in the gutter, but some of us are looking at the stars." That is bad. We want our children to look at the gutter, or, at the very least, the movie theater or arcade across the street. What we want is to raise human beings that are not burdened with the yearning to look upward—unless they are seeing in the sky some career opportunity as a commercial pilot or a server of diet cola on airplane flights. We want to remove the organ of longing for the sky; call the procedure an *ouranotomy* or something of the sort. The sky suggests the vastness of creation and the smallness of man's ambition. It startles us out of our dreams of vanity, it silences our pride, it stills the lust to get and spend. It is more dangerous for a human soul to fall *into* than for a human body to fall *out of.*

But the sky is there, and the best we can do is to prevent the child from stopping to notice it. At this task we have been remarkably successful. It has been many years since I have seen a child, of any age, lying on a grassy field and staring up at the sky. The most likely reason I'll give in another chapter: they do not have *time* to do it. Yet there is another reason, which I'll illustrate by that efficient advancement in mental management called the *billboard*.

Consider the billboard as any spritz of noise that obtrudes between the mind and the sky: "cheap rates," "you can be sexy too," "billions and billions served." The itch to be what is called "important" functions as a billboard, as does the itch to be "doing something productive" or to be playing a video game or to be sitting in front of a television. Fill the visual field with neon lights. Smog is useful, too: I mean both the fumes that come from millions of automobiles, and the smoky darkness of lust. A child that has been blared at and distracted all his life will never be able to do the brave nothing of beholding the sky. He will not be able to ask, with the Psalmist,

> When I consider the heavens, the work of thy fingers, the moon and the stars, which thou hast ordained;
> What is man, that thou art mindful of him? and the son of man, that thou visitest him?

He will find the psalm itself too dull. He will want to change the channel. And since the sky is only itself, he will turn to other things—things that we will choose for him, while encouraging him to believe that he has chosen them himself. For that too is a great threat the sky poses to us: there is nothing you can do with it. It challenges the spirit to open itself unto it, and once that happens, there is no telling where the spirit will lead. It bloweth where it listeth.

The Greeks, whose gods lived atop Mount Olympus, built their temples as close to the sky as they could, and worshiped their deities of light and intelligence in the open air, with the priest performing the ritual sacrifice in the temple portico. We in more northern climes have had to put roofs over our heads as we worship, but the brilliant inventors of the Gothic style sought to make their churches soar higher and higher, with ever thinner walls, perforated with stained glass windows and the light of day pouring through. Saint Francis of Assisi, the little poor man of God who preached to the birds, sang his canticle to Brother Sun and Sister Moon, noblest of all the creatures above. In the beginning, we learn in Genesis, God created light—to fill the heavens, and the mind of man. The priest-poet Gerard Manley Hopkins in "Harrahing in Harvest" could look up at the autumn sky and exclaim,

> What wind walks! what lovely behaviour
> Of silk-sack clouds! has wilder, wilful-wavier
> Meal-drift moulded ever and melted across skies?

From that glory he gleans the love of his Savior. Christian or no, the reader still afflicted with imagination will be stirred into a flight of the heart when Hopkins calls us all to open our eyes, to see, and to wonder:

> These things, these things were here and but the beholder
> Wanting; which two when they once meet,
> The heart rears wings bold and bolder
> And hurls for him, O half hurls earth for him off under his feet.

The object of our schooling, note well, is not to ensure that such poetry as this will never be written again. Of course it can hardly be written, when it can hardly be *read*. Our aim is more complete. It is to ensure that the feelings that inspired Hopkins' work will never be understood again. To this end, we wish to make the sky at once banally familiar and utterly ignored. We should say that it does not really exist, that its blue is an optical illusion, and suchlike. A touch of science here, but only a touch, can go a long way. Here let us note with satisfaction a curious success of our educational program.

A century ago, there were no classes in astronomy in any of our grade schools or high schools. Yet anyone could tell you why you might build your house with the windows facing south, and why the planets seemed to move, and why, above the Tropic of Cancer, we never will see our shadows directly under our feet, and what the latitudes on a map have to do with where the North Star is in the middle of September. Now we have plenty of units and classes on astronomy, and our students are as familiar with the sky as Iowa farmers are with oarlocks and topmasts. Some of my own students are hard put to point toward the west—despite the fact that that is where we are all going.

In C. S. Lewis's *The Voyage of the Dawn Treader*, Eustace Clarence Scrubb (the boy, as I've noted, who was ignorant of dragons), subjected to the imagination-killing regime of a school called Experiment House, is swept off into the land of Narnia where for the first time he must actually encounter the elemental realities of wind, and sea, and sky. Meeting Ramandu, a kindly old man who says he is a "retired star," Eustace remarks that in his world a star is only a huge ball of gas. Ramandu replies, "Even in your world, that is only what a star is made of, and not what it is." But Eustace is not stolid enough for us. We must raise students who do not care what a star is, nor what it is made of, because the only stars they trouble to gaze at are the kind that flame out after a moment or two: the stars of mass entertainment. Click, goes the remote control.

Second, outside is dangerous because it contains a world that has not yet been managed into submission. As I write, I am watching a pair of cedar waxwings fluttering about the lower branches of a black spruce tree. Waxwings eat almost nothing but berries. They are gregarious and carefree, wandering about in large flocks in search of blueberries, barberries, blackberries, cranberries, whatever happens to be ripe. I have seen two dozen of them at once cull all the berries from a small holly tree. The waxwings I am watching are engaging in some pretty courtship. Mr. Waxwing, the suitor, has been combing the branches of the spruce, picking up a berry in his bill, and passing it over to Miss Waxwing, who says thank you very nicely and eats it up. Evidently the Waxwings have not been instructed in political correctness.

Not that nature is always so domestic. In his novel *Jayber Crow*, Wendell Berry describes the roaring of the Kentucky River in full flood. His hero is a young man aiming to turn his back upon small-town life and farm life and, as the faintly mechanical saying has it, "make something of himself" in the big city of Louisville. But he is halted in that enterprise by a river that has jumped its bed, sweeping along in its rage the wreckage of man's modest life, "great rafts of drift, barrels, bottles, sawlogs, whole trees, pieces of furniture," even "what looked to be the gable of a house, with what might have been a cat perched on top." The sight does not move Jayber to horror or despair, but rather to awe and reverence:

> And this is what it was like—the words were just right there in my mind, and I knew they were true: "the earth was without form, and void; and darkness was on the face of the deep. And the Spirit of God moved upon the face of the waters."

But it is not only the floods, and earthquakes, and electric storms that make nature strange to us. It is all wondrous and strange. When Elijah sought the Lord, he was not in the tempest, nor the earthquake, nor the fire, but in "a still small voice," that made the prophet hide his eyes in reverence. The poet Hopkins saw it as his special calling to see what he called the "inscape" in things, what makes them particularly what they are. We might think an ordinary flower just that; but to the mind made attentive to the works of nature, the most ordinary things are steeped in their own peculiar ways of being, and are mysterious. Here we find Hopkins describing bluebells:

> The bluebells in your hand baffle you with their inscape, made to every sense: if you draw your fingers through them they are lodged and struggle with a shock of wet heads; the long stalks rub and click and flatten to a fan on one another like your fingers themselves would when you passed the palms hard across one another, making a brittle rub and jostle like the noise of a hurdle strained by leaning against; then there is the faint honey smell and in the mouth the sweet gum when you bite them. But this is easy, it is the eye they baffle.

Not everyone is a poet, yet children come uneasily near to it in their natural fascination with anything at all. A child might take a stick to poke around a large mound of red ants, thousands and thousands of them, scurrying about their formicative business, without benefit of schooling, crawling up your shoes and socks if you step too near, to nip your ankles.

A few hundred feet behind the cemetery in the neighborhood where I grew up, water sprang up from some mossy hummocks, seemingly out of nowhere. Because it had no stream to feed it, we called it "the spring," though it was probably only water that had filtered through the topsoil and coal from a swamp a quarter of a mile away. Its pool was cold and clear, with red mosses in the bed, and a little trickling brook draining it at one end. That pool would have water in it even in the summer, when the brook would flow for a little while and then vanish, only reappearing now and then in a hollow downstream, as a muddy puddle. There were no fish there, only bugs. There I was free from school—and the television, and all the great troubles of life.

One way to neutralize this fascination with the natural world is to cordon it off in parks and zoos, and then to act as if only the parks and zoos were worth seeing. Persuade a child that a giraffe he sees once every couple of years is really impressive, but the wren on the fence post is only a drab little bird—though he warbles out a love song in the morning, cocking his stubby tail, and is in general one of the bravest and most cheerful of birds. Persuade the child that the Grand Canyon is worth seeing, or

Yellowstone National Park, or Mount Rushmore, or the breakers of the ocean on the Florida coast. But ignore the variations of hill and valley, river and pond, bare rock and rich bottom soil, in your own neighborhood. Children should be encouraged to think they have "done" rivers, or bird sanctuaries, or botanical gardens, in the way that weary tourists are proud to have done Belgium.

Attention to the small would only perplex a child with the unusualness of life. Here, for example, in the sort of writing that used to characterize children's books—wise, childlike, and precise at once—is a description of the praying mantis at dinner:

> The creature is not saying its prayers when it holds up its forelegs in that beseeching way; no, indeed! It is on the lookout for some unsuspecting insect on which it hopes to feed. When it catches sight of its prey, the mantis creeps to within striking range. Then, suddenly, those murderous forelegs shoot out like steel springs and the insect is caught on the sharp barbs. The mantis brings the struggling insect to its mouth and chews away heartily.*

And yet, the author adds, the carnivorous insects are among man's most useful allies, feeding on the bugs and beetles that devour our crops. A thought such as that—which opens the mind out to our humble dependence upon creatures so small and even so unpleasant—had better be politicized, to warp it into self-righteousness, or softened away with cuddles and cute smiles. I recently saw a large red fox at the side of a country road, with his dinner in his mouth: a fat, limp hare. Small children should at all costs not encounter the real and energetic enmity between fox and hare. Then, when they are older, they will have been too dulled by the sentimentality of "nature lessons" to care about it.

Finally, outside is dangerous because there you may meet a creature more threatening to your complacency than is any wolf or bear or panther. You may meet yourself. For one thing, the world without throws you upon your own resources. I have, for example, a friend which I bring in to my freshman class at the beginning of every year when we are reading the ancient Babylonian epic, *Gilgamesh*. My friend is a 150-pound rock. I found

---

* *The Book of Knowledge*, ed. E. V. McLoughlin and J. M. S. Careless. Toronto: Grolier, 1949.

it in a quarry and brought it home to form part of the border for one of our gardens. But once a year Rock comes to school with me, to illustrate the brute and blessed *incorrectness* of nature. Rock is no democrat. If a certain force is applied to Rock's base, it will oblige you by moving. If not, not all the political action committees in the world will cause it to move. It represents a world of excitement and risk and consequence. If you want that rock out of the hillside, you will have to dig it out. You or somebody like you will have to mine the ore for your picks and shovels. You will have to cut the wood to build the fire to melt the ore. And when you hew the rock, it will not simply materialize where you want it to go. You will have to carry it yourself. If you cannot, you will have to tame a horse, or a horsepower engine, to do it.

That struggle with brute nature is in fact one of the great themes of *Gilgamesh*. The hero Gilgamesh and his friend Enkidu have decided to undertake a quest that will win for them immortal glory, and that will redound to the benefit of their city, Uruk. Though they live in the plains of the Tigris and the Euphrates, they determine to go where people are not meant to go, far into the mountains of the north, to slay the monstrous guardian of the cedar forests, the giant Humbaba. And as they walk into those gloomy ravines, each man encouraging the other, we see in elemental form the old saga of man encountering what is beyond man, attempting to come to terms with it, or to master it, by cunning, and courage, and sweat. It is Ishmael drawn to the Atlantic shores, called by the mystery of the whale hunt, or Huck and Jim on their raft down the Mississippi. Sometimes we go into the depths to flee civilization. Sometimes we go there to build it.

A popular book when I was a boy, *My Side of the Mountain*, told the story of a young boy who left his mother at home—his father had died—to build for himself a small hut in the hills, where he would learn to fish and hunt for himself, to cook his own food, to stitch skins for hat and jacket, to bathe and keep himself clean, and to be at peace with himself and the world. An amiable man who stumbled upon the lad one day called him "Thoreau" and told him about the self-styled philosopher who retreated from town to live by himself in the woods. Neither the author nor the boy was interested in political lessons. The main thing—and this fascinated us who read the book—was his urgent need to prove himself against adversities, to become a man. The danger to our economy posed by even a small percentage of such self-reliant and resourceful people is not to be dismissed. What we need most of all is *need*—needy men and women, with money to spend, and vast structures of business and entertainment and government to rely upon.

But don't think that the principal danger of encountering oneself is that one will grow self-reliant. There are plenty of people now who take perfectly fine care of themselves by fitting neatly into the grooves of a business or bureaucracy, without ever being pestered by a single spark of imagination. Our universities are filled with them. The principle danger is that there will be a genuine self to rely upon. I know a young man whose parents took him and his sister to Spain every summer to live with their kinfolk, in the dry up-country outside of Seville. This lad, who felt out of place in his American school, and whose opportunities to be on his own outdoors were limited by suburbia and highways, for three months out of the year had the hills and plateaus of the Spanish countryside for his own. He'd eat a quick breakfast and set out for the day, not bothering to give anyone more than a general idea of his whereabouts, because he himself did not know exactly where he would end up. There he would be alone with his thoughts, growing in strength and cleverness, climbing the rocks and following the streams. When he came home in the evening, he would play his saxophone for the Spanish girls, and there would be something to play, because some of the lonely music of the hills would find its way into that horn, as it had already found its way into his mind and being.

Albert Einstein used to say that he had first begun to wonder about the speed of light when he was a boy, lazing about by himself upon the sunny mountains outside of Florence. He found there a clue that led him to the secret curvatures of the universe. Robert Frost found in the rugged hills of New Hampshire clues to that far more difficult maze, the human heart. So he recalls how the slender white birches, laced with icicles in the winter and bent over like girls washing their hair, would straighten again in summer, but would have enough springiness in them for boys to swing upon them, climbing them to the top, launching out and away, and making it gently to the ground, only to be carried up again. It is a silly pastime. But Frost, the hardened farmer, remembers that pastime and implicitly compares it against the emptiness of so much of what we serious and responsible adults do. The boy still lives within him. Says he, with the terseness of a New England judge: "One could do worse than be a swinger of birches."

Not to Be Found in the Rand McNally

"That is all very well," you may say, "but my children don't have to worry about that. They can play outside all they want, and it will never rouse their imagination. We live in the city."

But that confidence is unfounded. Have you ever seen a lovely, dead, blacktopped parking lot, spoiled by a crack running lengthwise? Give that crack a year, and it will fill up with windblown dust, and lush weeds will be poking their bold heads through. I cannot say that it is as dangerous for children to play outside in the city as in the country. The country presents to them a world of illimitable complexity, wild and yet orderly, like the spilling notes of a Bach fugue. The city, man's jumble of artifacts, cannot achieve that; and yet it will possess its own fascinations, and these must be averted if we want to kill the imagination.

A few years ago we had a big snowstorm in our town. We'd run out of milk, so I decided to walk—driving was out of the question—over the nearby bridge to Main Street, to see if the convenience store was open. Out on the roads that evening I had an experience that everybody used to have, and that almost nobody has had since the dawn of the automobile. I walked straight down a quiet Main Street, in the middle of the road, in zigzags if it pleased me, under the snowy night sky. It was as if all the boundaries of street and sidewalk had been whisked away. Italo Calvino describes the same experience in his series of tragicomic stories called *Marcovaldo*. A poor and usually bumbling workingman, one who never catches a break, suddenly finds himself with an empty city at his disposal, to crisscross at will. For a blessed day or two it is as if there never were such things as wealth or poverty.

The point is that children let loose in a town can have something like that experience all the time. I don't mean that they run out into traffic, or climb over fences with "No Trespassing" signs on them. But because they are children, they understand that certain adult proprieties do not so strictly apply to them. A grown-up cannot scramble down a fallen-in embankment to check out the river below, not without looking like a fool. Children can do it. A grown-up cannot poke around in a condemned building without looking like a thief or an arsonist. Children can do it. I recall from my childhood the best thing we had on what served as our "playground" for a few years: the gutted shell of a one-room schoolhouse, complete with graffiti I didn't understand, broken glass, crushed plaster, holes in the floor, and a fallen-in basement. I loved it there; but our baseball games made too much noise for an old lady neighbor, and soon the playground was no more.

In other words, for children there are Places of Interest and Secret Thoroughfares that do not appear on any map, along with Short Cuts and Ways to Get Underneath Bridges. Being outdoors gives them the chance to recast the map of their world. We boys who loafed in the woods tagged our landmarks and trails with names: Red Ash, Hamburger Rock, The Strippings. Kids in the city do exactly the same thing. A friend of mine, who grew up in center city Philadelphia a long time ago, said that he and his buddies would gather at a certain wall which banked a trolley line above it and a street at its base. They called this place, naturally, The Wall, and sometimes used the cover of The Wall to do mischief—as, for instance, taking a long stick and detaching the trolley from its electric line overhead, much to the annoyance of the driver.

Nor did they need playgrounds. Bill Cosby used to deliver a funny routine about growing up in Philadelphia, and stealing the wheels off baby buggies to furnish go-carts. I don't recommend something that requires as much dishonesty and ingenuity as filching the wheels of prams, particularly not when the babies are in them. But once the kids had their wheels they let their imaginations run with them. Each had his own "model" go-cart, with his own signature engine sound; Cosby's was the Flight of the Bumblebee, from *The Green Hornet.* Then they'd congregate on Dead Man's Hill, a straight drop of a bluff concluding in a freeway. With a wave of some kid's father's checkered boxers, they were off. Of course it's a comic exaggeration, but what do we suppose children did before playgrounds? One thing they did in New York was to invent stickball. In the version of that game that I know, you lob a rubber ball toward the batter, who tries to hit it on the bounce with a broomstick. The hit, if it isn't caught, is scored according to how many manhole covers it crosses. Evidently a good game of stickball could change the whole tenor of activity on a city street.

The responsible parent will, therefore, guard the child against the dangers of the city street. In this regard it is helpful to note that our cities have become genuinely dangerous to life and limb, not to mention full of opportunities for unspeakable moral squalor. We must suppress at all costs the fact that the causal arrows work both ways. As cities become more violent, good parents with children move away; but as good parents with children move away, cities become more violent. That is because children, roving over and across and under everything, will see what felons do not want them to see, as children are in many ways more observant than grown-ups. Preaching safety to the child, safety above all, safety always, world without end, has the considerable advantage of instilling in him the expectation that life should be provided with boardwalks and handrails. Such a child will never go for a walk in the woods if he lives in the country, and, even if our cities were better than sinkholes, will not walk down an alley if he lives in the city.

Virginia Woolf once wrote that a woman of Shakespeare's day could never have written such plays as the Bard wrote, because she'd have been denied the education to make it possible. More damning still, she would not have had a quiet room to write in. That is the gist of Woolf's essay, *A Room of One's Own*, standard feminist reading in colleges today. Now the odd thing about it is that, while other writers connected peace and quiet with the work of the imagination—Marlowe's Faustus brooding in his study, or Milton telling us that the Muse in his sleep would inspire "easy my unpremeditated verse"—Shakespeare never did. Our greatest writer, perhaps the greatest the world has ever seen, knew about dingy saloons, thieves on the highway, harlots in houses of ill repute, fights in the public square, processions and parades, and all the bustling humanity of city life. I have no idea whether the man, who was also an actor, director, and the manager of his theater company, had a room of his own. Maybe he did. What he certainly had was a city of his own. So did his friend and fellow playwright Ben Jonson, whose raucous portrayals of city life often teeter upon the brink of chaos. So did the young Samuel Johnson, wandering about London more than a century later, hardly a shilling in his pockets, cadging a meal here and a job there. What he learned on those streets eluded Virginia Woolf in her posh mansion with her posh literary friends. He learned about human suffering and endurance, and he never forgot the lesson.

If a child must go to the city, then, it should be with gates and barriers provided. He should be encouraged to believe that only certain sections of the city really count—the ones with high-toned coffee shops, for instance. Let him meet men of the road—what are now called, with insufferable condescension, the "homeless"—but only in sanctioned school functions, or at sanctioned philanthropic events, where everyone will give the expected response to the expected questions, and all the fear and degradation and sin and romance will be leached out. Encourage him to think that the over-schooled performers of high culture at the city amphitheater are the real urbanites, not the man who works for the bus company and lives at the back of a hardware store, or the old lady who sweeps the streets in front of the Lutheran Church. Let him "do" the city, but not wander in it, let alone really live there.

A New Thing in the World

We require such insulation from life. We are, as I've said, the first genera-tion of human beings who will spend most of their waking hours indoors. Whether this marks the next stage of our intellectual development as a spe-cies is doubtful.

My family and I spend every summer in a small fishing village on Cape Breton, in Nova Scotia. You cannot stand anywhere on our island, twenty miles in circumference, without looking out upon a cliff beetling above some crazy arm of a bay, or seeing the mainland like a shadow on the southern horizon, or hearing loons laughing above one of the inland lakes. There are places to explore everywhere: a little strip of land sometimes no more than a few yards wide continues from near-island to near-island for five miles, till it ends in the middle of a deep lagoon. You could go for a long walk on that; or over the rocky barrens facing the sea, where no trees will grow in the stiff cold breezes, but fuzzy gray ferns will grow, and blueberries, tea-berries, lingonberries, and bright golden lichen. We have sandy beaches and rocky beaches, coves where mackerel swarm, and shoals where mussels are left stranded by the tide, ready for picking. Or you can bike to an overlook and watch seals, or whales, or dolphins splashing in the waters off the harbor.

You can do all this, but why would you want to? Life, as we have con-structed it for ourselves, is spent within the walls of a house, a school, an office building, or a hospital, by way of preparation for the vault of an air-locked coffin. What this means is that the more we leave children to their devices outside, the more their imaginations will try to flap a little on the wing. They may develop into people who do not do as they are told, mean-ing that they will not buy what marketers want them to buy.

One day I had to duck into a local library to check my electronic mail. I'm not sure I ought to do that, but I did. It was a cool day in late August, the sun sometimes shining through clouds sailing along in a stiff breeze. Perfect for hiking, biking, playing touch football, or just getting lost, which is what I was aiming to do that afternoon. In the library were children taking part in an indoor summer reading program. A nice young lady was reading them a story about animals. Sitting next to me were two boys, soft-bodied and vacant in the eyes. They were watching video clips from professional "wrestling," the images of men overmuscled, stupid, and sleazy.

It seems too obvious a question to ask, but why weren't they outside wrestling themselves? If they had been, they would have introduced into their memories the spring of the wet grass underfoot, or how it feels when you grapple for a shoulder and lose the hold, or what happens when your leg gets hooked underneath your opponent's leg, or what grunts and laughs and growls you make when you are in a good fight with a friend. A couple of kids doing that, for a few minutes, are almost a world unto themselves, a world of good humor and sweat.

The thought of it reminds me of a scene from *Tom Sawyer*, where the great Mississippi River is the stage for both the world's traffic and freedom from the starched collars of the world. It is good that Mark Twain is seldom taught in grammar school now—too sophisticated, too boyish, too backward, all at once. There might be a riot. At one point in *Tom Sawyer*, the hero and two of his friends take a rowboat across to an island in the middle of a sluggish lagoon. There they strip and swim all morning, cook up some bacon they had toted along, and play at pirates all the afternoon, sometimes flopping down on the sand in exhaustion. Twain would have us understand that days like this were common enough in Tom's life. Tom does read—not his schoolbooks, usually, but novels of dash and daring that transport him to other scenes of the outdoors beyond his Missouri village. So he becomes the Black Avenger of the Spanish Main in his romp with his friends, and in *Huckleberry Finn* the boys forge oaths of loyalty by pricking themselves and writing their names in blood, just as good respectable outlaws do it in the books.

We shouldn't suppose that Mark Twain spun all that out of his own head, whole cloth. He wrote what he had seen and known himself. Plenty of people before our time saw and knew such things, too. The baseball historian Bill James wrote that Red Schoendienst, Hall of Fame second baseman for the Saint Louis Cardinals, had a Huckleberry Finn kind of boyhood, swimming with his seven brothers in the Kaskaskia River in southern Illinois. Plenty of kids had such days. My father did. We want to ensure that nobody has them now; more than that, we want to make such days unimaginable.

As I was sitting in that library, across the room came the cheerful sounds of the young employee, teaching the children how to say simple words in French. "Vache," she said to them. "Qu'est-que c'est que la vache dit?"

"Mooooooo," said the children.

A half a mile away there is a farm that grows strawberries and potatoes, with a little dairy on the side. Plenty of *vaches* browse on its hillside. What does the skin of a cow smell like? How is it to the touch? Is the hair stiff and bristly when you rub it the wrong way? How many times does the cow chew her plug of grass before she swallows it? Does she eat grass mostly, or does she poke around for something tastier? Will she eat berries? Clover? Thistles? What does clover look like? What is a thistle? Are cows as stupid as they look? Why is the bull penned up behind barbed wire? How much milk will a cow give in a day? Does it hurt them to have their udders so swollen like that? A child may ask a hundred questions about *les vaches*, just from being around them a little, not as part of some canned educational program, but just as part of life.

Such questions must be extinguished. If a child displays an unseemly desire to know something about cows, introduce him to an Internet Cow, giving Internet Milk, and leave it at that. Remember that information is to wisdom as a ceiling is to the sky. Walls are our friends. So are fences, guided tours, schedules, and signs that read "Keep off the Grass." We may no longer preach righteousness. We may no longer even believe in right. But if there is one right thing we should preserve at all costs, it is the right angle. Saint Augustine once said that the whole moral message of Christianity could be summed up in the command, "Love, and do what you will." People have misunderstood Augustine to mean, "Do what you please, and then call it love"—but that is another matter. We will modernize the ancient Christian. Let's not talk of love, that dangerous claim upon the soul. No, we will take our lesson from the empty forehead of the poor boy gaping at the hulks from the World Federation of Fakery. We will tell him he may do anything, so long as it is virtual and not real. That, and keep inside.

Method 2

Never Leave Children to Themselves

or

If Only We Had a Committee

An old trolley stop in my father-in-law's hometown in Pennsylvania has been refurbished and made into a diner. As you often see in such places, the owners have dug up a few wistful photographs of the village from long ago and placed them on the walls. One of them is dated 1939, and features two groups of men in baseball uniforms: the Kayser Athletic Association, which apparently fielded a baseball team called the Kaysers, who were about as local as it is possible to be, and the Philadelphia Athletics. The A's at that time had not yet become the decades-long door-mats of the American League. Indeed, there were several Hall of Famers on that team and in that picture. They included men who were among the two or three finest players ever to play at their position: catcher Mickey Cochrane, first baseman Jimmie (the Beast) Foxx, and the brilliant and ornery Moses (Lefty) Grove. And apparently in the middle of June that year the A's traveled the hundred miles north from Philadelphia to play the Kaysers in an exhibition game.

It hardly seems worth mentioning that such a photograph is unthinkable these days. Ballplayers might more likely be photographed posing beside their stockbrokers than beside any such locals. But the reason is not simply that today's ballplayers are millionaires many times over. It is that even if they had a hankering to play such a game, there aren't any local teams to play. The Kayser Athletic Association is no more.

And it isn't only the local ball club. Next to that photograph is another, of the local band, in uniform. There are twenty-nine men and boys in it, wielding drums, bugles, trumpets, flutes, trombones, and tubas. That would be twenty-nine, from a dusty little borough of fewer than a thousand people. I am told that some kind of a band is still in existence, with a few old men who play once in a while at a reconstructed bandstand in the local playground. The playground, by the way, is fenced off and locked during the off-season—winter. Children apparently do not play in winter.

For several years my daughter has sung in a Swedish choir founded by immigrants before the turn of the twentieth century. It began as a men's choir, and a few decades ago it adopted a women's choir too, but always with dispiritingly dwindling numbers of people who want to sing. Some of the men whom I have heard in the choir are over ninety and have been singing almost all their adult lives. Their songs, in Swedish and English, cover a nice range, from sad love lyrics to boisterous patriotic anthems, from the silly and sweet to the racy to the sublime. But young people will not join their ranks. It's not the sort of thing that young people do—though apparently it *was* the sort of thing that young people did, for almost a hundred years, until they stopped joining their elders.

If that's too high-toned a group for you, recall what the streets of Brooklyn and the Bronx were like in the summer, decades ago. Children, as I've noted, played in the streets. They did not need to be organized by adults. They fashioned their own games and chose their own teams. People told stories of how Willie Mays, then a young star outfielder for the New York Giants, would sometimes play stickball with the youths in the city—stickball, that beguilingly difficult game for kids with a narrow field and no decent equipment. No one taught kids how to play stickball. The necessities of the place suggested it, and the game was passed along from one generation of kids to the next, without a rule book, without umpires, and without adult supervision, save what the players got from the curious shop owners and passersby, some of whom might have liked to join them once in a while, to be young again themselves for a turn or two.

Stickball is gone. I live now in New England, in a place pocked with shallow ponds, perfect for ice skating and hockey. It is supposed to be a popular sport in New England. I have never seen any children playing it, not once. Some kids play it indoors, in the rinks—in leagues, organized by adults. New England is also supposedly wild about baseball. You can find Red Sox jerseys and caps everywhere, even in church on Sunday. And there are Little Leagues; not as many as there used to be, but still a few. But it has been at least ten years, possibly twenty, since I have seen a group of kids playing any kind of baseball game in a backyard or on a dead-end street.

People will blame indoor amusements, and certainly that's a large part of it. Television comes easy and deadens the brain. Electronic entertainment, too, is solitary and follows strictly delineated patterns. But that's not the whole of it, for we must remember that the premise of our educational system is that children need to be socialized into a managed world. We talk a great deal about independence, but we loathe it as much as we loathe the blessed freedom of nothing to do. Children no longer play because we have taken from them the opportunity and, I'll insist, even the capacity to play. And this, if we want to kill the imagination, is an altogether healthy thing.

If It's 8:47, We Must Be Learning about Atoms

We ought to rename our planet according to the bureaucratic shackles we place upon our children. We shall call it Tormentaria. It seems quite apt. The Tormentarians are a humane race. They don't favor harsh (though swift) punishment; they grow queasy if anyone mentions a whipping post or even a smack on the posterior. They prefer to work on the mind, patiently, interminably, beneficently. It is never their aim to settle things with a free and open fight. That would upset the blessed routine of Tormentaria. No, they direct all the machinery of their social systems to mold and squeeze the offender into the perfectly square hole he is destined to fill, for his own good and the good of his fellow Tormentarians.

The chief offenders of Tormentaria, or rather those who would grow up to be offenders if they were left to themselves, are the objects of plenty of molding and squeezing, for roughly twenty revolutions of Tormentaria around its sun. When they are hardly old enough to toddle about, they are wheeled away to what is called, in Tormentarian, an *asylo*, meaning "rainbow center," where they are attended to by paid professionals, usually of a kindly disposition, who will feed them at regular feeding times, nap them at regular napping times, give them regularly scheduled "activities" to keep them from rusting solid, and remember their names. The little Tormentarians learn to look forward to the *asylo*, because otherwise they seldom meet another of their own kind. Besides, the walls of the *asylo* are gaily painted with colors unknown to the flora and fauna of Tormentaria—gaudy blues to substitute for the sky and purples and oranges to substitute for fruit, and buds, and flowers. Children, the Tormentarians know, like that sort of thing, and the sheer blare of it all will make Tormentarian rivers and trees and bluffs dull by comparison.

In the *asylo* the children must be "tormentarianized" into predetermined games, never of a competitive nature, lest anyone should be hurt by real anger or disappointment, or elated by real victory. They also practice their alphabet, and the brightest among them learn to read drivel. That satisfies the vanity of their parents, who hope to send them to the finest penitentiaries on the planet. It also prepares them for their adult lives, when they will be reading newspapers and magazines. It has the added advantage of inducing what is called *burnout*. This is a fascinating phenomenon that warrants a closer look.

Every child born on Tormentaria possesses a network of filaments connecting various tissue masses in the brain, in the most incredibly tangled and luxuriant ways. That, the Tormentarians have determined, will not do. The task then is to work as few of these pathways as possible, and work them to death, so that the other pathways will close up, and the overused ones will burn out or be rendered useless for all traffic but the most ordinary. So let us say you have a child who does not want to learn the Tormentarian alphabet. He wants to learn instead, for example, what happens to a lump of pine resin if you leave it out in the sun. He does not want to spell SKY. He wants to go and look at it. The obvious thing to do with this child is to keep him from looking at the sky, while hammering the spelling of the word into him until he is sick of it. If his fellows are "ahead" of him in driveling out their letters, that's all to the Tormentarians' advantage, because then his *burnout* will be compounded with a belief that he is not very bright, when in fact quite the reverse may be true. After five or six years of this process, well before the child has matured, he will already "know" that he does not like to read, does not like numbers, is not good at science, and cannot make any sense of history. In other words, except for some minor social vices that may crop up later on—a propensity to drink or to get girls pregnant—he will be the perfect social specimen.

So much for the early years. But when he is a little older—let's say, a year or two before he would naturally be comfortable leaving his home and the person the more old-fashioned Tormentarians call his *mother*—the child is sent off to school. Here let us pause to note the impeccable Tormentarian social logic. In times past, when the Tormentarians had a hankering for physical discipline, the rich among them would send their boys or girls far away to a boarding school, to sleep in barracks, to be drilled in Old Tormentarian verb conjugations, to eat spartan fare, and to play rough games in the fields. The problem with this system was that, in spite of common cruelties and long stretches of drudgery, the children were thrown back upon their own resources, and developed their imaginations sometimes in spite of the school itself. They formed clubs for all kinds of things: singing, stamp collecting, chess. They fashioned their own laws and teams and hierarchies, and those, regardless of the bullying and worse, made them men and women almost before they knew they were real boys and girls.

The personal growth that was expected of such children can be divined from an excerpt of a letter from Tormentarian President Theodore Roosevelt to his son Kermit, at faraway Groton, evidently responding to a letter wherein Kermit has notified his father that he will be playing football. The president approves of the decision, and then adds, "I would rather have a boy of mine stand high in his studies than high in athletics, but I could a great deal rather have him show true manliness of character than show either intellectual or physical prowess; and I believe you and Ted both bid fair to develop just such character."*

It is clear from Roosevelt's correspondence that his sons had entered a world of its own, with great risks and greater rewards: a world wherein the other boys would esteem you according to your manly character. The experience was such as to rouse deep indignation or deep affection or both; and then too, there was the dangerous beauty of Old Tormentarian poetry lurking in the wings, ready to touch the barracks with gold.

That would not do. So the modern Tormentarians have devised a system that combines the virtues of the old elite schools with the virtues of the age of machines. The elites, they saw, had the correct instincts. They saw that it was good to remove children from their parents. But what good would that do, if they were going to form a republic of their own instead? The trick is to remove them both from their parents and from one another.

---

* Joan Patterson Kerr, ed., *A Bully Father: Theodore Roosevelt's Letters to His Children* (New York: Random House, 1995).

The old Tormentarians had a taste for inflicting drudgery upon their pupils. But unfortunately the drudgery they inflicted was too harsh in the beginning, and led to too great a result in the end. Better to sweeten the drudgery with saccharine, and make it lead nowhere.

So now the Tormentarian children sleep at home, but hardly live there. They get up very early in the morning to board a bus which stops every hundred yards to take on new passengers. This ensures that no child has very far to walk, and that the ride takes an hour or so in the morning and an hour or so in the evening. That will mean nearly two hours ripped out of every child's life, for no real purpose, day after day for twelve years—a significant achievement.

Then the child is shipped to what is called a "home" room—the Tormentarians have not lost all sense of humor. Here the child is numbered and checked off. An alarm rings, and all the children move from the "home" room to one of the classrooms, to be exercised in the alphabet, or whatever. Please note that this movement from room to room is of the utmost importance. It develops certain automatic responses in the child, useful for his adult life, when he will also move from room to room at the sound of an alarm. It is happily made necessary by the scale of the school, hundreds or even thousands of children crated and uncrated in one place every day, and hardly ever a single one lost. The anonymity of the place—since it is impossible for anyone to know everyone there by name or face—prepares the child for a world of anonymity. If the schools were kept small, there might be the great danger of a sense of home, and loyalty to it, with all the antisocial suspicions that home arouses: for instance, that the little girl sitting next to you is really quite beautiful. Children might come to suspect that a rational being conceals a universe of wonder. But when people are herded with general anonymity, as if they were freight to be moved from truck to loading dock to warehouse, that sense dies quickly.

Also useful in the Tormentarian regime is the partitioning of time into discrete segments. For instance, the child will learn that forty-five minutes is the correct amount of time to devote, at one sitting, to any subject whatsoever. Are you looking at pictures of butterflies? You should look at them for forty-five minutes. Are you reading a short story about a pirate? You should read it for forty-five minutes. But he is about to be hanged from the yardarm! No matter; let him wait till tomorrow. Are you leaning Tormentarian grammar? Probably not, but if you are, you should learn it for forty-five minutes. But you think you may have understood what a "participle" is for the first time in your life, and you want to test your theory out? Sorry, your forty-five minutes are up. Not to worry; the momentary excitement of discovery will pass, and tomorrow will find you as befuddled as ever. No matter whether the child's interest is as deep as the sea or as shallow as a rain puddle, and no matter whether the subject is Kings of Old or Being Nice to Animals, the organizing adults will make sure you spend forty-five minutes on it, all of you without distinction, no more, and no less. Every subject will be taken equally seriously, which means, in effect, that none of them can be taken quite seriously at all.

After six or seven hours of this—which cannot be called working at a "grindstone," because a real grindstone is a swift and lovely tool, and has the property of sharpening, whereas school is intended to blunt—after six or seven hours of this, I say, interrupted by a few minutes for cramming calories down to refuel the machine, the child is conveyed back to the bus, for an hour's ride to what is, again with delightfully wry humor, called "home." As no one is home waiting for him, he turns on a television to watch a program he has not the slightest interest in; this is called *homework*. So his life goes on, year after year.

Now, no one could endure the Tormentarian regime without what is called *down time*, lest the cables fray and snap and the moving parts wear thin. But the Tormentarians, master organizers that they are, parcel out that time most wisely. In the old days, before they had mastered the arts of human management, they simply squeezed school time into eight or nine months, and left the children otherwise perfectly free —generally in the summer, when the weather was best. Some scholars used to excuse the old Tormentarians for this lapse in judgment on the grounds that the people were agrarian, and children were needed for work in the fields. Of course this was nonsense. One plants in spring, and reaps in the fall. No, summers were left free because they were the best times for human beings to be together, as families and neighbors. But now, the Tormentarians have squeezed the summer holiday down to two months or even a month and a half, and have invaded it to boot with "enrichment assignments," guaranteed to ensure that every child will conceive a loathing for great literature, having had it turned into a spoilsport.

With a similar wise disdain for freedom, the Tormentarians have multiplied their "after school exercises." What all children once did on their own, without adults to manage their movements, now relatively few do, and under strict supervision. Parents themselves have taken their cue from the schools, and enlist their young charges in all kinds of drills: for dance or music or gymnastics or martial arts, until the schedule for a typical Tormentarian tot resembles the day's lineup for the executive of a large corporation. You may not, in Tormentaria, look up at the stars at night because you enjoy doing so; but you'll be admired and envied if your parents convey you to an Astronomy course, wherein you will do very little looking at stars and a lot of riding in a car, answering "present," looking at greaseboard drawings, and waiting in line to peer through a telescope. You may not, in Tormentaria, run off with your pals (boys only) to some swimming hole to strip naked and jump in and swim like happy fools. But you'll be admired and envied if your parents convey you to swimming practice, wherein you will have your weight checked on scales and your fat checked with calipers, your body shaved for streamlining, your times clocked, and your lungs filled with the sickly sweet odor of chlorine. You may not, in Tormentaria, holler for your friend from the street so that you can argue about which of your idols is the better ballplayer, but you will be admired and envied if your parents convey you to Debate Club, where you will sharpen your skills until, it is dearly hoped, you will be recognized by one of the Tormentarian Universities. Indeed, everything you do as a child must be geared—I use the word "geared" deliberately—toward that resumé which will gain you admission to Higher Blunting, followed by Prestigious Work, followed by retirement and death.

Anything Stuck in the Tree Is an Out

We can see how wise the Tormentarians are if we compare their children's schedule with that of a typical boy from a few generations ago:

Tormentarian Saturday:

8:00 AM: Gobble down breakfast.
8:15: Be driven to soccer.
8:30: Game.
11:30: Be driven to lunch at fast food joint.

11:45: Gobble down lunch.

Noon: Be driven "home."

12:15 PM: Down time. Video games. Television.

3:00: Be driven to martial arts lesson.

3:30: Martial arts.

4:45: Be driven "home."

5:15: Wait for dinner. Complain.

5:45: Gobble down dinner.

6:00: Pretend to be doing homework. Go on internet instead. Look at unusual pictures.

8:00: Do homework.

9:30: Watch seedy parts of television show or movie with parents.

10:00: Go to bedroom, chat with friends on internet. Do not write a single complete sentence.

11:45: Gobble down snack.

Midnight: Sleep.

Stan Musial's Saturday:

7:00 AM: Gobble down breakfast.

7:15: Do chores.

8:00: Disappear, with buddies.

7:00 PM: Reappear for supper. Gobble down supper.

7:15: Listen to radio with family.

7:45: Walk with father over to grandmother's house. Gobble down snack.

9:00: Do chores.

9:30: Sit on porch and gobble down another snack.

10:00: Sleep.

How irresponsible we once were, to allow our children such huge blocks of time to be themselves, outdoors with others of their kind, inventing things to do! Think of the trouble they got themselves into. Sometimes they went fishing. Sometimes they set off firecrackers in garbage cans. Sometimes they hopped trains. Sometimes they hiked through the woods and mapped out trails. Sometimes they rode their bicycles to nearby towns. Sometimes they climbed trees. Sometimes they declared war on one another. Sometimes they wandered off to a construction site to look at the backhoes and winches. Sometimes they formed secret societies with passwords and oaths and penalties of death, or worse.

All such things are to be avoided. Take for example one of the activities that seems most harmless: they got together to play ball. Do we not see how many things they needed to do in order to achieve that goal?

First, they needed players, and that meant rounding up the usual suspects, rousing them from bed, or cajoling them from their chores, or reminding them that they promised they would play and threatening them with ridicule if they did not. That already is a complex social activity: they had to organize themselves.

Then they needed a field to play in. Finding one was not always easy. You had to take what the neighborhood gave you—you had, most of the time, to "make" your field out of a half of a yard and a street, or a clearing beside a hill that wasn't too hilly, or the back end of a parking lot with a wall and fence on one side. That meant seeing how the game could or could not be played there. If you had a big tree behind what would be first base, you might declare anything caught in the tree to be an automatic out. Or, if there was a short wall in right field, you might declare anything that hit the wall to be in play, but anything over the wall to be out. If a barn is in center field, you might declare that anything hitting the roof is a home run, but anything missing the barn entirely is in play, even if it might have hit the roof had the barn been three feet to the left. You also need bases: an old shingle, somebody's volunteered shirt, the root of a tree. In all of this, you are using your imagination. You are envisioning what a good competitive game might look like, and are fitting your field with ground rules designed to make the game possible: steps, trees, fire hydrants, ditches, garage doors, garbage can lids, embankments, sidewalks, some old man's porch, the car parked across the street, all come into play, all become part of the world you fashion. None of this, it should be noted, is in the spirit of self-esteem and nebulous exercise that an adult-organized activity, say youth soccer, provides.

So much for the field, but you also need equipment. That too is not always the easiest thing to procure. Some fields aren't right for a hardball and bat. Others aren't even right for a tennis ball and bat. What to use? You use what is at hand, and alter the game accordingly: rubber balls, superballs, Wiffle balls, the dead core of an old baseball. If it's frayed or cracked you tape it up. You hit it with a wooden bat, an aluminum bat, a thin plastic bat, a big plastic bat, a broomstick, a Ping-Pong paddle, a tennis racket, a wooden plank, your arm and fist.

But how to play? The rules will have to depend upon the field and the equipment and the number of players. Here you'll see kids using all kinds of treacherous ingenuity. Is there an odd number of players? One will be the Official Pitcher for both sides. Are there only six players? Declare one outfield "closed": left field for lefty batters, right field for righties. Is the ball plastic or rubber? Call "hitting the runner," meaning that you can throw it at a runner advancing from base to base, and if you hit him when he's not touching a base, he's out. Are the bases too close? No leads allowed. Does the field slope away down a hill? Only one base on a wild throw. Is one of the players a lot bigger or older than the others? Declare that he must hit wrong-handed. Is there a flat wall for a backstop? Tape a strike zone on it and throw the ball hard. Would that result in too many walks? Declare that there will be no such thing as a walk.

But then, how do you choose the teams? Here we venture upon cat-walks and rope bridges—a false step, and the game is shot. When adults organize children, it is all taken care of, and usually inattentively. But to create a game that will be at all enjoyable, you have to consider who the big kids are, who can hit and who can catch and who can throw, how many girls there may be (distinguishing those who can throw from those who can't), who "needs" to be on the same team with someone else, and so on. If you are playing hardball and you have two lefties but only one glove, you have to keep them on separate teams. Same thing if you have two kids who will have to leave early. So you choose up sides. How do you do that? It depends. If the biggest kid is not evenly matched with the second biggest kid, then the second biggest chooses first. Perhaps he even chooses first and second. If not, you may come upon a fair way to choose players. You may play "rock paper scissors," or "odd or even." You may play "hand over hand" on an upside down baseball bat—last hand on the bat wins.

All this is well and good—all this, the mustering of players, the making of a field, the procuring or doctoring of equipment, the establishment of ground rules, and the choosing of sides. Now you actually have to play the game. You have to keep track of the batting order, or the downs, or the number of outs, or the fouls, or the score. Nobody is going to do it for you. But what happens when there's a disputed play?

Here again we see the wonders of organizing every waking non-electronic moment of a child's life. When adults are in charge, they will settle the dispute. Sometimes they do so preventively, by making sure that disputes cannot occur. That's what schools in Massachusetts did a few years ago, decreeing that for elementary school soccer matches, no one should keep score. What a remarkable teaching device that was! It prevented the children from using their wits to separate right from wrong. It shut off the opportunity for real appreciation of an opponent's case. It delivered the message, instead, that one's own feelings are paramount, and anyway, what difference does the score make, so long as everyone is having fun? Buried beneath the beneficence was the knowledge that the best of fun depends upon the pretense that a run or a goal actually means something; otherwise there is no real game at all. But even if score is kept, when the dispute arises, an adult steps in, splits the difference (which is usually an unjust split), and orders the kids to proceed in their maturation.

But boys from time immemorial have fashioned their own "rules" for meting out sandlot justice. The batter hits a ground ball to shortstop and says he has beaten the throw to first. The shortstop says he's out.

"I had you by a mile!" A mile, in sandlot parlance, means five or six inches, the distance of the foot as it is about to come down upon the base.

"Are you kidding? My foot landed before I heard the ball in the glove! You're blind!" This is the Counterargument with Evidence.

"You never heard the ball at all, you liar!" This is the Direct Attack on Personal Integrity.

"I'm not going to let you get away with it this time!" This is the Threat to Personal Well-Being.

"Well, go ahead and try something!" This is Calling the Bluff.

Usually matters don't go so far. The boys will argue, using evidence, and they all understand that it is in everyone's interest to respect evidence, since otherwise no game would be possible. If the evidence is indecisive, the next expedient is to summon the Nearest Uninvolved Person, a spectator perhaps, or one of the players known to be honest, so long as he had a good view of the play. If that doesn't work, you make an appeal to Worthy Opponents, those on the side of one of the disputants, who will admit that his teammate is wrong. And if that doesn't work, the boys will not go home in a snit. What would be the fun of that? They will not cry, like babies. They will not sue. They will use the supreme act of their moral imaginations. They will forgive the baseball universe. They will Pretend the Play Never Happened. Everyone goes back to where he was, and the play is done over—and everyone will accept the result, for better or for worse. Anybody who still harbors hard feelings about it is labeled a Sore Loser, and is looked upon with contempt by his fellows; it is a deep character flaw. But anybody who can engineer a quick solution acceptable to all sides is labeled a Good Sport, and of him great and glorious things are expected.

We should always remember that such a scene as I have described is the last thing we want. People who can organize themselves and accomplish something as devilishly complicated as a good ball game are hard to herd around. They can form societies of their own. They become men and women, not human resources. They can be free.

A Culture of Their Own

Am I exaggerating the danger of undulled and unsupervised children, coming together to form the rudiments of a community life? Mark Twain would not think so. Take for example another episode from the boyhood of Huckleberry Finn:

> Well, when Tom and me got to the edge of the hill-top, we looked away down into the village and could see three or four lights twinkling, where there was sick folks, may be; and the stars over us was sparkling ever so fine; and down by the village was the river, a whole mile broad, and awful still and grand.

Note, in passing, that Huck and Tom are out at night, under the vault of the sky, where the unlettered Huck's natural appreciation for beauty shines forth. Note too Huck's gentle glance toward the village far away, where he as the son of a worthless vagabond drunk does not quite belong, not yet. But he does want to belong somewhere. Soon other boys join them:

> We went down the hill and found Jo Harper, and Ben Rogers, and two or three more of the boys, hid in the old tanyard. So we unhitched a skiff and pulled down the river two mile and a half, to the big scar on the hillside, and went ashore.

Note that their adventure depends upon a flash of imagination that has caught fire from one to the next, so that in the hope of embarking on the imagined adventure they pull together, meeting at a certain place at a certain time, with a skiff ready nearby to use, to go to the place that Tom has designated as their hideout:

> We went to a clump of bushes, and Tom made everybody swear to keep the secret, and then showed them a hole in the hill, right in the thickest part of the bushes.

We see here another element in their union: the imagination conceives of a law and a means of securing agreement to obey the law. That prepares them to become a band of brothers:

> Then we lit the candles and crawled in on our hands and knees. We went about two hundred yards, and then the cave opened up. Tom poked about amongst the passages and pretty soon ducked under a wall where you wouldn't a noticed that there was a hole. We went along a narrow place and got into a kind of room, all damp and sweaty and cold, and there we stopped. Tom says: "Now we'll start this band of robbers and call it Tom Sawyer's Gang. Everybody that wants to join has got to take an oath, and write his name in blood."

Which they proceed to do, vowing to kill, with gruesome panache, anybody who divulges the secrets of the gang. Not just him, either, but his family too. That occasions the first dispute among the boys, because Huck Finn doesn't have any family that anybody can ever find. Huck's just at the point of being drummed out of the group, on the grounds that it wouldn't be fair to everybody else if he had no family to kill—he's at the point of tears, when happily he thinks of the good Miss Watson who has taken him in as an orphan. They could kill her. "Oh, she'll do, she'll do," say the boys, mercifully following the spirit rather than the letter of their law. They let Huck in.

It's true that most parents do not suffer the disadvantage of having the Mississippi River nearby, with its thousands of little islands, its oxbow lakes, its hiding-holes in the bluffs, its vast and majestic current, and its promise of lands far away. And no doubt Twain is having fun at the expense of Tom and the boys: they don't actually kill any people, as their boy-ish constitution declared they would. But the whole humor of the episode depends upon the reader's recognition: *that* is what he would have done, too, on the banks of the Mississippi, because in fact he was once a part of something like that, when he was a child. In other words, the episode is but a slight and romantic exaggeration of what people would have recognized as universal among children. Left to themselves, they simply will not remain alone. They will organize. They will establish their petty kingdoms, declare decrees, seat and unseat rulers, give one another new names, invent secret codes, build hideouts, and in general practice a rough sort of justice and mercy, all to fill the blessed long days of summer.

Here for instance is one man's reminiscence of a summer day in New Hampshire, when he and his friends got themselves together for an all-day jaunt of rowing, fishing, cooking their food, bathing, and in general being ridiculous:

> Immediately upon the closing of the schools arrangements were made for a combined fishing and bullfrogging excursion, to be prolific in huge strings of fish and vast quantities of frogs' legs . . .
>
> Early one morning the boys loaded [their boat] with a miscel laneous collection of supplies—a kettle, a spider, several dozen ears of green corn, a bag of potatoes, a piece of salt pork, a paper bag of meal, ditto of salt, ditto of sugar, a jug of coffee, several bottles of sweetened water, knives, forks, fishing tackle, butterfly nets, specimen cases, bottles of ether, etc., the latter articles belonging to the scientist of the expedition.

The author saw the most important thing about these days as not what they did, but that they did it together, on their own. He loved the river because that's where he and his friends fished and smoked sweetfern, together. Looking back upon it all years later, he is moved by that original bond of imagination, and casts himself, the least among his fellows, as a kind of chronicler for an army of better men than he:

> In the ancient forays of the Gauls, it was the custom to look to all the able-bodied men for actual warfare, and leave the old and sick and worn-out men to tend the camp. It happened that there was always

some man not old enough to shirk duty, but of no value in the rude sports, the forced marches, and the fierce conflicts of the time.

Such a one was usually employed to chronicle the events, to sing of the descriptions of battles and the prowess of heroes. This position was usually accorded him not because he was in any way better fitted for it, but because he was fit for nothing else. And so, perhaps for similar reasons, this position has fallen to Plupy's lot, and if his description pleases, he is indeed fortunate and grateful.*

It must be the object of an enlightened education to ensure that sentences such as those above will never again be written. It is not only that they are classically elegant. Nor that they bespeak a loyalty and humility which are really touching. It is that we want to produce children who could not conceive of the sentiments in that passage, because they have no experience of the sort of friendship and shared adventure the author describes. We want to produce children who have never known any other culture or community than the pasteboard substitutes we provide them for the real things. We want children for whom people like the author above are ten times more foreign than the Gauls were to him.

One thing to do is to point to the abuse of the good thing. We can do this with impunity, because reporters are not in the habit of thinking. People die in car accidents every day, yet nobody suggests that we abandon driving. People get drunk, yet nobody suggests (or not anymore) that we prohibit the sale of beer. Yet some young people form gangs and engage in more than pretended bloodshed. Therefore we must never leave children unsupervised. We must organize all their time, lest they lapse back into the beast.

There are several problems with this line of reasoning, and it will do well to analyze them, lest we be unprepared for the occasional sharp question. The reasoning relies upon what we might call the *Lord of the Flies* Syndrome. In that excellent novel by William Golding, a group of British boys are stranded on an island in the Pacific during the Second World War. Without any adults about, they form their own society. They have meetings; they elect a fair-haired leader; they enact the parliamentary rule that you can only speak at a meeting when you have the conch. But

---

* Henry Shute, *Reel Boys* (New York: G. W. Dillingham Co., 1905).

terrible fears and obsessions get the better of them. They seem to hear a groaning and creaking coming from the forest in the dead of night. It is a hanged parachutist, his lines tangled in the branches—but they don't know that. They believe it is some vague and terrifying beast. Soon one group of boys—actually, choirboys, with a bully for a leader—break away from the others. They become Hunters, they say; they are going to eat meat. And they do hunt, and revel in the killing, and dabble in sadistic initiation rites, and declare war against the others, and end up committing willful murder.

But what can we conclude from this —or from the violence of gangs in our cities today? The boys in Golding's novel are not unsupervised. They are absolutely alone. There is no home to go to, no school, no church. There are no adults to turn to, to allay their fears. Death looms nearby. Under such circumstances they naturally form alliances, and those, so far as they are acts of the imagination, are good and natural things. The same may be said for the city gang. It is not that these boys spend too much time outside of the home. It is that they have no genuine home to spend time outside of. They have, for one, no fathers in those flophouses. They have no groups of men to emulate, keeping order, getting together for sport or the hunt or protection of community. Churches have collapsed into hobby houses for girls and old ladies. The schools are huge and anonymous. Sports teams are, consequently, relatively few. Institutions that used to minister to troubled youths, in groups, have become day-care asylums or exercise clubs for middle-class families.

In other words, the problem is not that children, by themselves, will destroy things. It is that, in such circumstances as we have provided them, when youths gather (and they do not often gather), they will gather to destroy. We opponents of the imagination must bury that fact. We must say, over and over, "Children need to be supervised," even though this "need" has only arisen in its current virulent form because of actions we have taken to make the supervision necessary.

People who worked with youths in the past understood this dynamic, and so they organized them into groups that would, so to speak, also organize themselves, collecting dues, enforcing rules, determining what activities to pursue, and recruiting new members. They believed that the true solution to the gang was not the obliteration of childhood or of the natural human impulse to form communities. They believed that they needed to provide the genuine article, for which the gang is a perversion or a counterfeit.

Here for instance is advice from one of the most prominent leader in the boys' movement in the early twentieth century, one Father Kilian J. Hennrich, a Capuchin friar, found in *Boyleader's Primer* (1930). He understands that boys simply will not develop their characters if everything is always kept perfectly safe for them, and so, even though the activity he describes is organized by an adult, the leader leads with a gentle hand:

> Team play is one of the highest forms of play. Do not make the games too serious but get as much fun out of them as is consistent with order and propriety. Encourage timid boys to take risks and see to it that the selfish boys do not get the lion's share to the detriment of others who are less forward. There is no need to treat boys as if they were made of glass. They ought to be able to bear a few falls, knocks, and bruises. It's nature's way of teaching them to take care of themselves.

Scouting encouraged a similar initiative and camaraderie among young people. You cannot have everything done for you when you are hiking in the wilderness. You must pitch tent, secure fresh water, catch fish, build a fire, keep yourself clean, and a dozen other things—besides amusing yourselves with songs and games and conversation.

What a dangerous world for the ingenuity did young people once dwell in! For such self-reliant children, on those times when they *are* organized into teams or troops, can do things that show they are well on their way to maturity. Colonel Theodore Roosevelt Jr. was on a scientific expedition in the cold plateaus of Tibet, inaccessible except by crossing the Western Himalayas. He and his entourage were stationed in Leh, a village that it took him and his men two and a half weeks to reach, on horseback and on foot. "What was my surprise yesterday," he writes, "to find a Boy Scout troop drawn up for my inspection. We are nearly 12,000 feet above sea level, and as far as I know, this Boy Scout troop is the 'highest' in the world." The boys, he goes on to say, prove to be of great help when the caravans come in from Turkestan and India. Sometimes the men "get on sprees and leave their animals loose. Then the Boy Scouts . . . catch the animals, see they are unloaded, and are of real assistance."

Boat-building was apparently a common hobby among a branch of the Boy Scouts, called the Sea Scouts, with over 400 councils in the United States as of 1932. The Scouts would sell do-it-yourself plans for sailing skiffs, V-bottom sloops, and round bottom scows, up to sixteen feet long, for fifty cents or a dollar. Or they encouraged the boys to go on hikes that involved a great deal more than trudging after an adult leader, as in the "Hare and Hounds Hike":

> Two Scouts are the hares. Give them a head start of about thirty minutes. They carry the cooking utensils and the grub for the whole Patrol and lay a trail with regular trail marks for the rest to follow. From time to time they separate and make two branches of the trail, then come together again. If not caught before arriving at destination, the two hares build a fire and start to cook the Patrol meal. The object, as far as they are concerned, is to have the meal ready before the others reach them.*

We should prefer to raise children who cannot round up animals, do not know how wood is hewn and planed, cannot lay down or follow a trail, or cook a meal—or, more to the point, children who would never desire to do any of these things, because what little they have done has been overseen and overmanaged by the dullest of all creatures, the bureaucratic adult.

Belonging to Another World

But I have not yet mentioned the greatest threat that children, left to their own inventive devices, pose to a state that wishes to snuff out the fires of the imagination. It is that such children, still partly independent of the technocratic machine, remind us of a life with genuine sorrows and joys, untouched by adult concerns. As Shakespeare's King Polixenes puts it in *The Winter's Tale*, thinking of the days he enjoyed with his friend when they were young:

> We were, fair Queen,
> Two lads that thought there was no more behind

---

* The Scouting references are from various *Boy's Life* magazines from the 1920s and '30s.

But such a day tomorrow as today,
And to be boy eternal.

And the very presence of his own son now wakens his good cheer to life, especially when his thoughts turn to age and melancholy:

If at home, sir,
He's all my exercise, my mirth, my matter;
Now my sworn friend, and then mine enemy;
My parasite, my soldier, statesman, all.
He makes a July's day short as December,
And with his varying childness, cures in me
Thoughts that would thick my blood.

If we have children around us, and we let them be children, they will not miss entering our world. That will come soon enough, and indeed their play is in part a preparation for the adult world, for better or for worse. As Saint Augustine in *Confessions* puts it, "Yet we loved to play, and this was punished in us by men who did the same things themselves. However, the trivial concerns of adults are called business, while such things in children are punished by the adults." The real danger is to ourselves: that we will look upon their world, a fallen world no doubt, but a world still touched with wonder and gratitude, and choose to allow those childlike virtues to enter our hearts. "Suffer the little children to come unto me," says Christ, "for of such is the kingdom of Heaven." Which He might have rephrased, and did rephrase, thus: "He who would save his life must lose it."

For it is a *world* that children dwell in, or used to. We think we teach children how to speak, but the fact is they also teach one another, and us too. Children are a tremendous source of new words, and a storehouse of old ones, the latter not always taught to them by their parents, but passed on from one generation to the next, happily skipping the grown-ups in their career. When I was a boy, the children in Pennsylvania had the perfect word for what you do to snow to pack it solid and smooth for sled runners. You "pank" it. I have no idea where that came from, but it sounded right. When my cousins called out to a group of kids in another yard, they often used a pronoun that normal English speakers had long dispensed with: "What are *ye* doing?" They adopted for themselves the privilege of

Adam, and named not only beasts but rocks and streams and one another: Smacky, Ding, Lippy, Frano, The Bounds.

When I was a kid, television had already marched like Sherman to the sea, cutting a wide swath through a child's day, with hardly a twisted railroad track or a burnt barn to show for it. We still had some games, which we passed along to the younger kids when they grew old enough to play. No grown up that I recall ever sat us down to teach us the rules. These were apparently invented and altered by kids from generations past—in some cases from centuries past: Hide and Seek, Red Rover, Dodgeball, Jump Rope, Cops and Robbers, King of the Hill, Jailbreak, Crack the Whip, Leap Frog, War. Some were improvisations of one of the recognized sports: Five Hundred, Home Run Derby, Hit the Bat, Pepper, Pickle (baseball); Horse (basketball); Two-Hand Touch (with delayed rushing the quarterback; football). Probably someone thirty or forty years older than I might remember ten times as many games. These constituted a thread of memory linking the ages. Now, let us all thank the totalitarian school and electronic entertainment, most of these games are forgotten. A former student of mine, a retrograde Eagle Scout, told me that his Boy Scouts lacked the capacity to get up a game of anything; they didn't know how to organize themselves, and they didn't know any games to play.

Or songs to sing. This too comes as a surprise, but children used also to sing, in the days before the specialization and compartmentalization of everything—and before the three-tone compression of popular music had left most of them so tone deaf that "Happy Birthday" sounds to them as complicated as Chopin. Even the schools cheerfully enough encouraged it. The amiable reminiscer Harry Shute recalls his schoolmaster teaching the children "Annie Lyle," "What's the News," "We Love to Sing Together," and "Speed Away." Laura Ingalls Wilder recalled how her father would of an evening take down his fiddle and play "The Arkansas Traveler" or "Sweet Betsy from Pike." Thomas Howard has written of the natural virtues that such perennially remembered songs would encourage. Which virtues? Howard enumerates quite a few: innocence, duty, domestic contentment, fidelity, purity, soundness of mind, courtesy, sacrifice, joy, peace, plain goodness, and, most strange to us now, "hesitant delight in my lady":

'And 'twas from Aunt Dinah's quilting party / I was seeing Nellie home.' What the boy wants seems very restricted indeed: merely the delicate, nay fragile, venture of accompanying her to her door. The delight anticipated in such an austere pleasure puzzles imaginations cauterized by debauchery.*

Philip Sidney in *Apology for Poetry*, affirming the power of poetry to move us to virtue, thinks first of all of ballads sung by the homeliest of peasants: "Certainly, I must confess mine own barbarousness; I never heard the old song of Percy and Douglas that I found not my heart moved more then with a trumpet; and yet it is sung but by some blind crowder, with no rougher voice then rude style." At Saint Gregory's Academy, a Catholic boys' high school in Pennsylvania, everyone sings old ballads of courage and unshakeable friendship. "I shall never laugh again," cries the refrain of one of the most haunting of them, mourning the loss of a comrade on the battlefield.

Not all such songs were taught in any formal way. I suspect that most of them the children picked up from overhearing their elders, or from other children. Some of them seem to have been made up by children, like the notorious song of Dunderbeck, coming out of New Orleans in the nineteenth century, and occasioned by a gruesome scandal:

Oh Dunderbeck, oh Dunderbeck, how could you be so mean,
To ever have invented the Sausage Meat Machine?
Now all the neighbors' cats and dogs will never more be seen,
For they've been ground to Sausage Meat in Dunderbeck's Machine.

Same thing for playing of musical instruments. Granted, many children learned how to play the piano or the violin by paid instruction. Most, however, did not: they could not, because there weren't hundreds of thousands of music masters hanging about looking for work, and their parents hadn't thousands of dollars to throw at them, either. So children learned to play music by watching, and hearing, and trying an instrument out for themselves: and this is attested to by accounts of people who played music but could not read it. The old Celtic fiddlers of Cape Breton did not read their thickets of arpeggios from a sheet. They heard them, remembered them, in their very arms and fingers, and passed along the memory to others who

---

* "The Oldies Record," *Touchstone*, October 2008.

took up the instrument in turn. These things too formed no small part of a young person's life. I don't know who it was who invented the cigar-box banjo or the kazoo, either, but I'll wager it was not Rachmaninoff.

We could go on in this vein for a long time. John J. Audubon roamed the woods as a lad and watched birds. He was a crack shot, and collected specimens. Many lads were crack shots. Some of these were taught by their fathers. Others taught themselves. Grown-ups did not take kids out for Slingshot Lessons. Maybe they taught them how to make a fish trap, or how to bait a line with a worm. Maybe they did not need to do that, because older brothers or neighbor kids had done the job already. Children collected butterflies, coins, stamps, arrowheads, feathers, rocks, and insects. They bought magazines and traded them with one another. They traded baseball cards. They played rummy, poker, pinochle, and cribbage. They mapped the woods. They learned bird calls. They foraged for nuts, and mushrooms, and berries. They jumped off bridges into streams. They rode freight trains. They needed no committees. They were alive.

Method 3

Keep Children Away from Machines and Machinists

or

All Unauthorized Personnel Prohibited

Thomas Edison did not last long in school. When his family moved to Michigan, they put the eight-year-old Tom in the local elementary school, where he proceeded to torment the teacher by asking the simple question, "Why?" When it became clear that the teacher had neither the capacity nor the willingness to answer that question, and that Tom would be punished for asking it, his mother (his father, alas, thought he was a dunce) removed him from the school and taught him his lessons at home.

Not incidentally, he became the greatest inventor America has ever known. That's because when his lessons were over—and it shouldn't take too long for a bright child to learn how to read—Tom would potter about the barn or the toolshed, experimenting. Once when he was a small boy he asked his mother why geese squat on their eggs. When she replied that they do that to keep them warm, so they might hatch, Tom decided it was time to experiment on his own, and curled up with a clutch of goose eggs in the neighbor's barn, waiting for them to hatch. But that was just like the boy: "As soon as he could run down the hill, at the age of three or four, he would go [to his father's shingle mill and lumber yard] and play with discarded shingles and chips, making plank roads or toy buildings for hours on end."* He tried to produce an electric current by "vigorously rubbing

---

* Matthew Josephson, *Edison: A Biography* (New York: John Wiley & Sons, Inc., 1959).

the fur of two big tomcats, whose tails he had attached to wires." He gave a gas-producing powder to a friend "reasoning that the gas thus generated might set the boy flying through the air." Sulfuric acid from the wet-cell batteries he cobbled together in his bedroom ate through the furniture and the floor.

He was especially fascinated by the telegraph, and longed to learn how to transmit and receive code. That came about when, as a teenage porter for a railroad based in Detroit, he took up a side business selling newspapers. This was during the early years of the Civil War. Edison would go to the composing room at the *Detroit Free Press* to see what headlines they were going to put up. One day he learned that the paper would be reporting news of the terrible massacre of Union troops at Shiloh. Edison instantly conceived the idea of telegraphing the news to all the railroad stations in the vicinity, and to chalk up a bulletin in the depots, before his train arrived. He took a thousand copies of the paper that day, five times his usual number. He saw the power of the telegraph, and determined to become a telegrapher. He got his wish after he had saved the child of a stationmaster from being struck by a train.

It's hard for us to remember it now, but there was a time when Americans were fascinated by machines. It's easy to decry the pollution and the ravaged landscapes left in the wake of the first machine age in the nineteenth century. Yet people knew, by physical experience, how hard it was, for instance, for a woman to wash clothes in a tub and scrub out the dirt on a washboard, before wringing them out and pinning them on the line to dry. They knew too the immense labor involved in procuring things we now take for granted. How do you have ice in the summer? Before refrigeration machines, you had to procure it in the winter, from frozen ponds. Indeed, newspapers in the nineteenth century would sometimes warn of winters that were unfortunately *too warm*, with the result that there would be a shortage of ice in the summer. People wanted that ice for cool drinks, certainly, but hospitals needed it too to help tend their feverish patients; in a hospital, ice grew to be considered a necessity. But how do you get the ice from frozen ponds? You take teams of men and boys out with ice saws, hooks, and tongs. You cut the ice into neat blocks, pry it out, carry it with the tongs (which are reverse-levers with *negative* mechanical advantage, so that a fifty-pound block might feel like well over a hundred pounds), and load them onto sledges, for storage in the icehouse, each block insulated and separated from the others by layers of sawdust (which would have to be saved up just for that purpose). So, quite naturally, when iceboxes and then heat-pump refrigerators came around, people took notice.

The county where I grew up had the world's richest deposit of anthracite coal: hard, shiny, slow-burning, and hot. The early miners wanted to sell that coal to the big markets of New York and Philadelphia. That meant getting the coal to the Delaware River, across the humps of some tall ridges, about sixty miles away. From the river, barges could float the coal down to Philadelphia, or to an old canal dredged between the Delaware and the Hudson, and then down the Hudson to New York. But getting the coal across the ridges would have been too expensive, had the engineers not thought of a unique solution. It was called the Gravity Railroad, because it worked by gravity: the full cars at the top of one hill would go down while empty cars, connected to the full cars by pulleys and cables, would be drawn in the opposite direction to the top. The engineers had the whole stretch rigged so that the momentum of the downswing would be just enough to get the cars to the top of the next ridge. In a few places the gravity wouldn't suffice, so teams of mules were hitched to pull the cars along.

Nothing remains of it now but a few bare train beds and some Gravity Streets, but it was something of a tourist draw in those days. If you look at postcards from that time and even much later, you can see many things of that sort, which if not picturesque had yet piqued the imaginations of people come to visit: grain elevators, loading docks, strip mines, coal breakers, bridges, viaducts, railroad roundhouses, factories.

And ingenuity was perfectly encouraged, if not in the schools, then certainly in hobby magazines, books marketed for young Edisons, radio kits, and so forth, well into the middle of the twentieth century. You can still order many of these items from a retrograde outfit called Lindsay Publications. Here is a part of what their booklist has to say about Alfred P. Morgan's *The Boy Electrician* (1940):

You might start with a cork and needle compass, but before long you'll
be building a Wimshurst machine, powerful batteries from scratch,
galvanometers, voltmeters, ammeters, telegraph keys and sounders,
a telephone, a high-voltage induction coil, a step-down transformer,
wireless telegraphy with a crystal set receiver, vacuum tube receivers

including a regenerative, motors and generators, an electric train, a device to convert heat into electricity and even a Tesla coil!

That was only one book in a series; Morgan also wrote *The Boy Carpenter* and *The Boy Engineer.* One H. H. Windsor, for his part, published an enormous two-volume work called *The Boy Mechanic: 1000 Things for Boys to Do.* The book, whose language for richness and precision soars many miles above even the best newspapers of our own day, includes a dizzying variety of projects, such as how to weave and use snowshoes, growing strawberries on the surface of a board, siphoning away acid with a tube and a Bunsen burner, building an electric incubator, and constructing a wireless telephone set. The instructions for the latter include a long and careful explanation of how a magnetic field established in a coil of wire through which passes an electric current will cause a similar magnetic field in a second coil, with electrical pressure directed opposite to the current in the first coil. Since a telephone transmitter sends an electrical current that varies according to the fluctuation of the sound waves of the spoken voice, a coil connected to a diaphragm on the receiving end will cause that diaphragm to vibrate in unison with the one in the transmitter. If the Boy Mechanic constructs the wireless set, he will not only know how to do that; he will have learned how the translation of sound into electrical current and back again makes telephones work. And he will have learned it from reading such passages as this:

> Pressing the button K at the transmitting station, closes the transmitter circuit and removes the shunt from about the secondary winding of the induction. Any vibration of the transmitter will cause a varying current to pass through the primary winding P, which in turn induces an electrical pressure in the secondary winding S, and this pressure causes a varying current to pass through the coil A. The varying current in the winding of the coil A produces a varying magnetic field which acts upon the receiving coil, inducing an electrical pressure in it and producing a current through the receiver at the receiving station.

None of this, of course, will do. First of all, it is not safe. A child might be buzzed by a 20-volt battery. He might cut his finger with a handsaw. He might have to call a hobby shop to purchase a condenser. He might poke himself in the eye with the arrow of the weather vane he's making. He might fall off the garage roof where he is trying to place the weather vane. He might hammer his thumb while he's trying to nail up the scaffold for the pulley for the well he's digging. He might fall into the well.

Worse still, it encourages the wholly undesirable virtue of self-reliance. Remember that while we do want to raise children who are alienated from deep affection for their nation, their town, their heritage, their neighbors, and even their families, that does not mean that we want them to know how to do things for themselves. Just as we want them to be herded up with others of their kind, yet essentially alone, so we want them to consider themselves already competent at doing anything important, yet unable to change a doorknob.

Most damaging of all, though, is that a fascination with machines is entirely in the spirit of play. Here we might do well to compare that against the wisdom of what are now called science museums. A child winding a coil of copper wire around a spool, and tracing it left and right with a thin metal strip serving as a tuner, is engaging in all kinds of experiments at once. He's seeing from how far his rudimentary radio can pick up signals. He sees just how much room there is for error in his tuner—what distance he needs to travel before the station fades out. If he moves his body while he is doing it, he will have a physical memory of what it is like to *be* an antenna! He will do these things wholly on his own, in quiet, with maybe only a few written instructions to lead his way. Now the science museum, by contrast, won't have anything you can actually do that might lead to things breaking (or bones breaking). But the science museum, like science classes in school generally, is not about the business of stirring the imagination. It is instead about persuading the child to Believe the Right Things about Science. One had to believe, a few decades ago, that the world was cooling, and that we were in a fair way to find glaciers advancing upon Boston. Now one must believe that the world is heating up, and that we are in a fair way to find the ice caps melting and swelling the sea to wash Boston off the map. One must believe in recycling, the safeguarding of habitats, the descent of the politician from the ape, the goodness of furry mammals, the badness of man, and so forth—not because these beliefs spring from an active imagination coming to grips with the evidence, but because they are part of the scientific catechesis.

Mechanics, and play in general, don't fit in so easily. It's hard to be thinking about politics when you are trying to invent a catapult out of a couple of rocks, a young tree, a reel for a garden hose, and a spatula. So mechanics are out; physics and electronics too; but biology, or rather ecology, is in. That is because the subject allows for a great deal of political preaching. At all costs we must encourage our children *not* to be fascinated by the actual habits of whales, or by the design that makes it possible for them to be underwater mammals. We must encourage them to believe that Whales Must Be Saved. It hardly matters here what the correct position is; that is not the point. We might as easily turn science courses and museums into political programs affirming that Whales Must Be Destroyed, Whales are a Threat to Our Humanity, Captain Ahab Was Right, and so on. The point is to keep wonder far away—and never let children play with the elements of the world.

Safety Kills

The quickest way to prevent children from developing their ingenuity is to keep them away from adults who know how to do things. We can do this the more readily by repeating to ourselves the truism that Safety Kills. Michelangelo did not sculpt the *David* in a padded cell. In fact, he had to hang around with the rough stone quarriers in Carrara to learn what marble was really like, from inside, so to speak, when men cut it out of the mountain. Had he been told to wear a helmet all his life, he would never have gone to Carrara in the first place.

The young geologist Louis Agassiz grew up among the glaciers of France and Switzerland. He hiked and climbed mountains all through his youth. Had he waited for parks commissions to put up convenient fences and elevators, we would never have heard of Louis Agassiz. The boyhood of the Norwegian explorer Roald Amundsen was more rigorous still. He was enchanted by stories of the explorers who had tried to find a northwest passage from the Atlantic to the Pacific, and even gnawed on his boots to see if he could survive on the same terrible rations that Sir John Franklin's men had suffered. He wandered about the wilderness, toughening his muscles and his resolve, pursuing his fantastic dream of exploration:

During the months when the weather was fiercest, from November through April, he was rarely home on his days off from school. He went out, usually alone, to traverse the craggy mountains that ring Oslo. He preferred to be alone, for he wanted to test himself against the rugged terrain and the elements without having to explain to a school chum why he was doing so.*

Christopher Columbus, the daring man who sailed west to go east, writes thus of his youth among the sea-dogs on the Genovese coast, men who had been places and who knew things. Consider this entry from what passed once for children's reading in *The New Wonder World Encyclopedia*:

> I do not recall anything special about my boyhood except my love of the sea. Our home was not far from the water, and if ever I was missed, my brothers were sent to look for me along the quays, where I was sure to be found listening to the sailors or studying the white-winged caravels, which I knew every one by name, if it belonged to our port of Genoa. My father wanted me to be a weaver, but it was of no use. I was born for the sea, and was like a fish out of water until fourteen, when I shipped for my first voyage.

You never got to be a master mason in the Middle Ages unless you had gone through years of apprenticeship first, doing the lowly work nearby while the master showed you how to dress a stone to be set atop an arch. You might well get hurt, working around a cathedral while it was going up—asked to carry supplies up ladders and scaffolding. But the men and women of the Middle Ages did not know of our dismissal of mere manual labour. So writes the art historian Emile Male in *The Gothic Image*:

> In the cathedrals, where all mediaeval thought took visible shape, knowledge and manual labour are given a place of equal honour. In the church where kings, barons, and bishops fill so modest a place we find representations of almost every craft. At Chartres and Bourges, for example, in the windows given by the guilds, the lower part shows

---

* J. Alvin Kugelmass, *Roald Amundsen: A Saga of the Polar Seas* (New York: J. Messner, 1955).

the donors with the badges of their trade—trowel, hammer, wool-carding comb, baker's shovel and butcher's knife.

So we can use the threat of one danger to conceal from sentimentalists the threat of the other danger. We can stress to such an extraordinary degree the safeguarding of Johnny's knee or pate, that we can leave his imagination wholly undeveloped. We don't, you understand, *really* value Johnny's physical safety, or otherwise we would not build the vast institutional schools we build, and we would not smile complacently upon the destruction of Johnny's family life. But we can use the one possibility of injury as a lever to shut down the other possibility that Johnny might ever be among electricians, carpenters, or mechanics.

Nor should we forget about Johnny's sister, Jane. I'll concede that Jane probably has little desire to handle a jackhammer and see what happens to the sidewalk underneath. But Jane used to hang around women who knew how to do things, and she learned a great deal from them. What do you do with the sour milk in the refrigerator, other than throw it out? What are those little crab apples on the ornamental tree in the yard good for? How do you cut the armholes out for a vest? What kinds of flowers or vegetables will grow in that sandy soil? Can you propagate your quince bushes by cuttings? What is a quince bush? What is a cutting?

There were thousands of things that women about the home knew how to do, involving all kinds of ingenuity—a home with a good woman in it was always a work of the imagination. Laura Ingalls Wilder recalled in *Little House in the Big Woods* how her mother used to make butter. Even so simple a thing as an appealing color called upon ingenuity and practice:

> After she had put the cream in the tall crockery churn and set it near the stove to warm, she washed and scraped a long orange-colored carrot. Then she grated it on the bottom of the old, leaky tin pan that Pa had punched full of nail-holes for her. Ma rubbed the carrot across the roughness until she had rubbed it all through the holes, and when she lifted up the pan, there was a soft, juicy mound of grated carrot.
>
> She put this in a little pan of milk on the stove and when the milk was hot she poured milk and carrot into a cloth bag. Then she squeezed the bright yellow milk into the churn, where it colored all the cream. Now the butter would be yellow.

My grandmother, I remember, insisted that the only thing for cooking tomato sauce in was a big cast iron pot; something of the salty smell and taste of the iron would give the sauce a special bite. She put vanilla flavoring into her yellow egg-based Easter cookies; my other grandmother used less egg, and flavored hers with anise. She for her part made her own french fries, chopping the potatoes rather thick, quick-frying them in a skillet, and then putting them in the oven to turn brown on the edges. They tasted like homemade potato chips, if potato chips could taste like potatoes. Late in her life, when she was losing her memory, my sister asked her for her recipe for chicken soup—since she never wrote anything down, but did everything by long experience. "First you wring the chicken's neck," she said.

It is true that craft shows abound on the less-traveled television channels, but it should not be too difficult to keep Jane away from them. Teach her—the schools will certainly assist you in this—that all the many things her grandmothers did were nothing but mind-numbing drudgery. Never let on that it might be fun to figure out what to do with forty gallons of cranberries. Canning is drudgery. Never suggest that it might be a real delight to make for yourself, or for a friend, a scarf or a sweater; or that even setting up a loom, let alone working it, requires a mechanical expertise that would impress an Edison or a Graham Bell. Weaving is drudgery. Never breathe a word of what Tolkien had to say about gardening: that his ideal hobby would be to farm exactly three feet square of land and do it perfectly. All that is silly.

The Girl Scouts nowadays understand the principle behind this. Let us say that you like to look up at the sky and scout out the planets. There are the easy ones to find: bright Venus, like a steady torchlight in the west, visible before even the brightest stars come out, or Jupiter, also big, not quite as bright as Venus, usually, but still brighter than any star. Then there is Mars, the red planet, usually like a reddish orange star showing up where it doesn't belong, rarely as bright as Jupiter, but still bright enough, and the medium yellow Saturn, and, once in a very long while, on a cloudless evening when the horizon is free of obstruction, Mercury. He's bright enough to mistake for a star, if you don't know that the light you see that never twinkles is a planet.

Now suppose you are fascinated by the stars. You want to learn about the constellations: why that one is called Cassiopeia, the one that looks like a W in the northern sky, and what she might have to do with the horse Pegasus, or who Orion was, and why they call the stars that follow him his dogs. Besides being outdoors, all at once you are running the danger of delving into mythology, or of looking things up in an encyclopedia, or of buying a star chart or a small telescope of your own, to see if you can train it on Saturn, and what will show up if you do. That's what I did when I was young, and I can still recall the shiver of discovery when I pointed the telescope at what I thought was Saturn, then peered through the objective, turning the wheels of the viewer ever so slightly to pull it into focus, occasionally nudging the lever that turned the scope on a swivel, to keep the object in view. And I saw, slowly swimming across the field of the lens, that small and beautiful picture of an alien world, with icy rings aslant around it, and a small white "star" nearby, which I guessed was the moon, Titan, a moon with volcanoes and an atmosphere. Or the time I took the scope out into the parking lot at college, careless of the curious stares I was getting from everyone else, and pointed it low in the western sky at a sort of gleaming smudge. It was Halley's Comet. In the lens it looked like every child's drawing of a comet I have ever seen, with long trails of light, like flowing hair. That's what the ancient Greeks thought of it, and that's why they gave it the name they did, *cometa*.

Had I continued with my hobby, I'd have found other hobbyists of like mind, and they'd have taught me where I could get a better scope, and what nebulae I might be able to see, and other items of curiosity, thousands of them, across the night sky. One amateur, a Charles Messier (1730–1817), with a telescope no more powerful than mine would be, did nothing but record every single object he saw in the sky that was not a star, and to this day astronomers honor the hobbyist by numbering those objects accordingly: M1, for example, is the Crab Nebula, the remains of a supernova, with the M standing for Messier, who first saw it, by playing with a machine, and the sky.

The Girl Scouts, though, encourage none of that. For the Girl Scouts, hanging around someone who knows things has been transformed into hanging around someone who has made a career out of what might just be starting to interest you. The object is to learn how to make a career out of it yourself. Indeed you cannot earn your "patch" in the modern Girl Scouts without researching how your interest might be made into a career. Fortunately the Girl Scouts offer no patches for kissing. It is enough to snuff out the fire of love, which is, of course, precisely what killers of the imagination want.

It has not always been so, with the Girl Scouts. Here is a typical paragraph from an old guidebook, evincing the playfulness and excitement of taking up a hobby:

> Some people like to collect live insects—two or three kinds at a time, build homes for them out of boxes, jars, screen wire, and so on, and watch them over a period of time. When we do this, we really learn about them, because, first of all, we have to discover what they eat in order to keep them alive.

The same book recommends that girls ask for permission to poke around for rocks in a quarry, for collecting minerals; or that they carry first-aid equipment on a hike, including, among other things, ammonia and zapharin chloride; that they learn lashing with twine or rope when hammer and nails are not handy; that they learn how to use a rope and board to save a girl who has fallen through ice, and so forth.

So it is all right to encourage young people to see "careers" everywhere, as they are unlikely to learn anything from tagging along after people in their usual "professional" rounds. But it is most unwise to encourage them to tag along after people actually accomplishing something requiring real craft, or brute strength, or years of careful observation. Let me give some examples of things to discourage.

No Work with Big Machines

Harry Truman used to say that he enjoyed the horse-drawn plow better than a diesel-powered tractor, because he could think all day long while he was working. Be that as it may, neither one of them is beneficial to our purposes. It usually means that a young person will drive a tractor before he will drive a car, and that will encourage an independence of spirit that can lead to all kinds of mischief. For instance, most of the weird age-ruining of the schools will be lost. The young man sitting on a tractor for the first time will be both the child he is and the man he is going to be. That is, he will have to learn from someone who knows just how the engine is turned on, what a "choke" is, why the machine sometimes stalls in tall vegetation, what "four wheel drive" means, how to take slopes along the side rather than straight up or straight down, what to do if the machine gets stuck in a muddy rut, what the gear shift is all about, and so forth. He will, in other words, feel like the child whose world is opening out into adventure. On the other hand, he will be participating in something tangible and important and a bit risky: he will be doing some of the work on the farm. And while he is doing it, and obeying his teacher, he will be puzzling out the hows and the whys, as he will see and hear and feel directly before him and beneath him the rightness of the rules of his instruction. The closer the machine is to what the machine is working upon, the more it will appeal to the whole of the human mind, working in its turn upon it too: and this principle applies all the more powerfully when the machine works outdoors. Consider Wendell Berry's loving and whimsical description of one of the tasks on his farm, done by machine and by hand:

> Just a few days ago I finished up one of the heaviest of my spring jobs: hauling manure ... My labor-saving equipment consists of a team of horses and a forty-year-old manure spreader. We forked the manure on by hand—forty-five loads. I made my back tired and my hands sore, but I got a considerable amount of pleasure out of it ... And, since there were no noises, fumes, or vibrations the loading times were socially pleasant. I had some help from neighbors, from my son, and, toward the end, from my daughter who arrived home well rested from college. She helped me load, and then read *The Portrait of a Lady* while I drove up the hill to empty the spreader.*

We forget, as we sit comfortably in front of a computer screen, how fascinating a large machine can be. Take for example a horse-treadmill hitched up to a saw, to cut logs into manageable blocks. Let's not sniff at this sort of thing as if it were primitive, a machine fit to be run by hayseeds. There are all kinds of practical problems to solve in conceiving such a machine, and practical necessities to observe if you are going to run it right. Why does the treadmill have to be tilted slightly upward, and what

---

* Wendell Berry, *The Gift of Good Land: Further Essays Cultural and Agricultural* (San Francisco: North Point Press, 1981).

should the angle of incline be? What kind of harness should the horse be hitched up with, to relieve undue pressure on his neck? At what speed should the main axle of the treadmill turn in order to swing the saw's arm with enough force to cut the wood? What kind of blade should the saw be provided with? What materials should all the parts of the machine be made out of, and why? Are there any parts that need to be oiled? Are there parts that might slip if you gave them too much oil? Which parts wear out the soonest? How many men at once does it take to work the mill? Then, when you have mastered the principles of that machine, you can use your expertise for humbler or more whimsical tasks. I have seen an old dog-treadmill hooked up to a butter churn—and to a baby's cradle, to rock the child to sleep!

You will say now, "Thank goodness there aren't machines like that still around, ready for children to look at and learn from." But of course, there are. They are not, to be sure, popular destinations for school field trips, because they'd involve going to an infernally hot foundry or a noisy machine shop, or to a factory where People Who Have Failed in Life are working. Or they might involve approaching a real work site, with back-hoes (what is a backhoe, and why is it called that?), or pile drivers (what is a pile driver?). Learning a little bit about such machines may also stir some curiosity about the past. The Romans, without diesel engines, built highways, bridges, aqueducts, palaces, and stadiums. How did they manage to sink a bridge's piers into a riverbed? What recipes did they use for their concrete? Did they have different recipes for different purposes? If they had pile drivers (and they did), how were they constructed? What did they use to pound the pile down?

And then there's the machine right outside everyone's house—the car. You could ask a thousand questions of it, if you were moved for once to pay attention. In some ways it is not all that different from the horse treadmill. It uses the energy of ignited gasoline in chambers called "cylinders" (and why would they be cylindrical?) to push sets of pistons alternately (why alternately?), to produce reciprocating motion. Then this motion is trans-lated by various devices to produce the rotary motion of the drive shaft. That rotary motion, going at right angles to the car, is then translated into rotary motion in a perpendicular direction, to turn the axles. What kind of gear-mechanism turns rotary motion in one direction into rotary motion in another? What do car mechanics mean by the "universal joint"? Why do the pistons need to fire "in time"? What does the timing chain have to do with that? What causes the gasoline in the cylinders to ignite? What is a spark plug? Why does the battery in the car take so many years to run out? How does an alternator work?

Even so simple a thing as turning a car involves machines of magnificent ingenuity. For example, if while you are turning the car the outside wheel turned with the same speed as the inside wheel, it would drag along, because the outside wheel must cover more ground than the inside wheel, in the same time. So cars use a device called the "differential," a geared mechanism attached to the drive train and, by separate shafts, to each of the two wheels, to allow the outside wheel to roll at greater speed.

A young fellow who could answer such questions about cars would then be able to see how the same kind of engine could be rigged up to other sorts of machines, to do other kinds of work. I once met a man who built his own farmhouse from lumber he had cut himself and milled by a saw hitched to a Chevy engine. He had cut every piece of the house to size first, complete with dovetails and tenons, before getting a team of his friends to auger and peg them into place, without using a single nail. The same man produced and stored his own electricity by way of a windmill on top of a tower, with the wires hooked up to a series of storage batteries, each weighing over a hundred pounds, which he had salvaged from the phone company and which he housed in an old barn. Any kid who grew up on that farm, and who didn't know essentially how all our electricity is produced, whether by windmill or a falling river or coal-powered steam or a large hamster on a hamster wheel, must not have been paying attention.

No Making Friends with Craftsmen

In *The Swiss Family Robinson*, the mother and father and their four sons manage to secure provisions from their wrecked ship off the coast, build a waterproof house twenty feet off the ground to keep themselves safe from wild beasts, and rig it up with rope ladders and outbuildings and windows and all kinds of fascinating and practical contraptions. Here, for instance, the father directs construction of a winding stairway—within the hollow of an enormous tree:

We began to cut into the side of the tree, toward the sea, a doorway equal in dimensions to the door of the captain's cabin, which we had removed with all its framework and windows. We next cleared away from the cavity all the rotten wood, and rendered the interior even and smooth, leaving sufficient thickness for cutting out resting places for the winding stairs, without injuring the bark. I then fixed in the center the trunk of a tree about twenty feet in length, and a foot thick, in order to carry my winding staircase round it. On the outside of this trunk, and the inside of the cavity of our own tree, we formed grooves, at which the boards were to be placed to form the stairs.

It goes without saying that you will want to keep your child away from the book—which, as it proceeds from bad to worse, is also a story featuring a brave young man who falls in love with and marries a gracious and resourceful young lady. But you will also want to keep your child away from people like Herr Robinson—and there are still a few around.

Laura Ingalls Wilder tells of how her father one winter carved a wooden bracket for a Christmas present for his wife, just using a couple of whittling knives and sandpaper. He festooned it with stars and moons and curlicues, she said, and there's no doubt that he hadn't taken a single Course in Whittling at school. He only learned it by watching, and by doing. Amish boys are taught trades from the time they are very young. They will be working the bellows in the blacksmith's shop, maybe pounding out a hot iron bar for something easy like a spike or a hook, till finally they are men and can work the complicated curves and loops of an iron railing. The greatest violins in the world have been made for centuries by one or two Italian families, passing down their knowledge, literally *handing* it down, from one generation to the next.

A few miles up the road from me lives a man who restores Victorian houses. His own home is a showcase. I've watched it from the outside as he has fitted his porch and his eaves with marvelously turned finials, newels, and spindles, painted in a three-color plan. He is a master, and, if our schools wanted to encourage the love for beautiful and imaginative work—for his house, though obviously a Victorian house, looks like no other house in the state—they would troop their young carpenters up to his place to check out the lathe. They do no such thing, thank God. The purpose of schooling is to make young people proud of their supposed originality and their differences, while being all as predictable as hamburger.

In old days, people entertained themselves, or expressed their joy, their sorrow, their friendship, or their devotion, with a thing called "music." It involved the cunning arrangement of sound, sometimes made by the human voice, and sometimes produced by the craft of a musical instrument. Young people learned how to play them by watching and listening to someone else, someone who had mastered the art. Sometimes it involved a deliberate program of instruction. More often (especially among the common people, and for nearly everyone before musical notation was invented) it was simply picked up, tried out, practiced, investigated, worked; an art, like pottery or painting. Your "school" in learning such a thing was no school at all but leisure—which is what the Greek word *schola* originally suggested. You had some time and you were at ease, so you went to that kind of work which is hard to distinguish from play.

There's a great Greek sculpture that reveals this space for the imagination. It's of the satyr god Pan, leaning against a rock and showing a youth beside him how to hold the pan-pipes. The lad is concentrating intently on the musical instrument. For all they care, there might be a war going on two miles away; it wouldn't matter. The art is what fascinates. When a young person is in the company of a master artist to work at the art, and there are no car horns to alarm him about school starting, time itself seems suspended. The young Johann Sebastian Bach, when he was but a boy, got leave from his father and mother to travel alone over hundreds of miles of country to meet the great organist Buxtehude, who had come to Leipzig. What did the inconveniences of the road matter? He would finally sit in the reechoing cathedral and hear the master play.

No Playing with Maps and Blueprints

Recently, the Claymation artist Nick Park has made the Rube Goldberg machine (and the artistry of great old film noir movies) the heart of his Wallace and Gromit short films. Wallace the inventor (and the real genius of the household, his dog Gromit, who spends his spare time knitting and reading *The Republic,* by Pluto) has rigged his house with every child inventor's dreams. His bed swivels upward at the touch of a button so that he can

slide off into his trousers, after which he drops through a trap door down
to the kitchen, where his toast pops out of the toaster and into the air just
in time for—smack!—a catapulted wad of jam.

"They're Techno-Trousers!" says Wallace to Gromit, who is suspi-
cious of the gigantic mechanical pants he is about to be given as a birthday
present. "Ex-NASA! Great for walkies."

You will suppose that watching the antics of Wallace and Gromit can
do no harm to a child's mediocrity. You suppose wrong. Consider the fascination of another inveterate cartoon inventor, Chuck Jones's scraggly and
pathetic coyote. Here is a cartoon employing not a single word, except
sometimes for labels on parcels coming from the Acme Company, or for
freeze-frame mock-Latin names for the species and genus of the coyote
and his quarry the roadrunner: names like *hungribus ravenus* and *speedi-
bus maximus.* There's a background orchestra of jaunty classical strings,
and sound effects (for when the coyote is flattened like a metal spring, for
instance). Other than that, there's nothing. All the interest of the cartoon
comes from the strategic use of machines. What will happen if the coyote
ties small rockets to the back of his roller skates? What will happen if he
puts iron pellets in the birdseed, and then cranks out the gigantic magnet?
What will happen if the coyote cuts the rope of his rock-hurling catapult,
which looks like a gigantic spatula?

Jones was, for my money, the greatest genius in the history of cartoons.
His love of the abstract idea—the blueprint of a machine, especially if the
machine could never really exist—was a persistent feature of that genius.
For the question, "What would happen if the coyote tied rockets to a pair
of roller skates?" required not only the blueprint of rocket-powered skates,
but the blueprint, so to speak, of the whole cartoon. It was in his mind
similar to the question, "What would happen if Elmer Fudd is hunting
Bugs Bunny on a windy autumn day, and a truck full of theatrical hats hits
a bump in the road and the hats go flying, and every time a hat falls on
Elmer or Bugs, he *becomes* the character associated with the hat?" The mere
idea is a stroke of madcap genius, but it then inspires the blueprint or plot
of the cartoon, which moves from one comic surprise and reversal to the
next, until finally a top hat falls on Elmer and a bridal veil falls on Bugs,
and he carries "her" down the aisle into the sunset.

The blueprint is imaginary, with all kinds of clever application to our
world of rocks and streams and trees, and people going places and buying

things. You don't want your child to imagine an open bedroom at the peak of a tall house with cathedral ceilings, accessible only by rope ladder. You'd better not then bring him anywhere near drafting materials. Charles Dickens, before he actually wrote a word of his novels, had them mainly planned out, as his notes to himself in his working plans show:

> *Chapter XXIX.*
> *The Young Man.*
>
> Mr. Guppy waits on Lady Dedlock. She finds that Esther is her child.
>
> Guppy to bring Krook's papers from the old portmanteau
> Richard? No
> Caddy Jellyby's marriage? Yes.
> Brickmaker's family?
> Charley's illness? Yes.
> Dawn of Esther's
> Krook's death? Yes
> Miss Flite? Yes. Carry Allan Woodcourt through, by her
> Connect Esther & Jo? Yes.
> Mrs. Snagsby?
> Esther's love must be kept in view, to make the coming trial the greater and the victory the more meritorious.

He arranged his wild horde of characters as the intricately ordered parts of a living thing. If you don't want your child to write long novels wherein each character plays an orchestrated part to bring about the effect of the whole, you should keep him away from abstract structures generally. Best to sit him in front of a piece of paper and ask him to write about what he feels. Self-expression is the finest antidote for a perky imagination ever invented.

The Brontë sisters, when they were girls in the gloomy parsonage where they lived with their father, passed the time by drawing maps for their imaginary land of Angria. J. R. R. Tolkien did much the same thing. It was not as if he conceived of his tales of Middle Earth and then provided them with geographical and linguistic blueprints. It is rather that those blueprints had always been at the heart of his imaginary creations. God, says the author of the Book of Wisdom, made the universe "in measure, weight, and number," and all the artists of the Middle Ages and the

Renaissance paid heed; they too, in what Tolkien would call their "subcre-ations," or what Philip Sidney called their "foreconceit," would draw up their worlds so ordered. Edmund Spenser went so far as to build the lati-tude and the calendar date of his wedding, not to mention the days, weeks, months, and seasons in the year and the hours in the day, into his marriage hymn, *Epithalamion*. It was meant as a gift for his bride. It was, in its intricate order, like a little universe.

So we sniff at the humble art of the draftsman. But we should take a cue from it nonetheless. Tolkien was a great lover of the earthy things God made: trees and animals, the sea and the shore, well-sparred sailboats, snug little houses. The man who seemed most detached from anything real was apparently quite a hand at gardening and flying kites.

It's a combination to detest. As I've argued before, we very much want to keep young people away from sand and sea, and all the mysterious reali-ties of the world. But we don't want them then to pore over imaginary con-structions of worlds, either. We want them neither to work with machines, nor to invent new products from the Acme Company for the coyote to buy. We want them to be fumblers with both the hands and the brain. The answer, thanks to technological development and social degeneration, is near. We take them from both the real and the imaginary, and fix them in the unreal or the anti-real.

It is one thing to design a car by hand, drawing it out on paper. You have to get the proportions right. If it's going to be a real mechanical blue-print, you have to draw blowups of the moving parts: here is the engine, here is the drive train, here is the brake system, and so on. That requires concentration and trouble, and maybe quite a few crumpled up papers tossed across the room. It is another thing to try to put the car together—or even to put a go-cart together, using the model you have drawn up. Wood won't always do what you want it to do. Sometimes it is crooked and needs to be manhandled into position. Sometimes it threatens to split when you hammer a nail into it. Sometimes you will know where you want all the pieces, but you will see that they have to be put together in a certain order and no other, because otherwise there won't be any room for you to fasten the last ones in.

But it is another thing entirely to work neither with the drawing nor with the bumpy materials. That is what I mean by unreality. The finest thing to do is to sit your child in front of a video game which involves the manipulation of something on a screen—a gun, often enough—and then to pretend that the manipulation, following the tracks of the game's design, is somehow imaginative. It really is not, and you know it is not, but then, that's not why you sit the child in front of the video game. You do it because you know that when he is there doing that, he is not elsewhere doing something else. As, for instance, living.

Make Sure Arts and Crafts Are Just for Decoration

Here you need to be careful. Decoration is, after all, an appeal to the beautiful and the orderly. You do not want your children to learn to paint intricate flower-designs in oil on enamel. You do not want them to learn to knit a winter cap. They might end up asking for an easel and a palette for Christmas, or, heaven forbid, a loom.

But if you do engage in the arts, make sure they are puny and merely pretty, and by all means keep things as petty as possible. I remember when I was a boy handing in a drawing of a grapevine for my seventh-grade teacher. I wanted the grapes to be big and full, so I drew them that way, even exaggerating the size. The teacher failed the assignment, on the grounds that the grapes were too big.

So keep everything small and safe and dull. There's an old rock quarry a few miles from my house that has filled up with clear, clean water. I'm told that it is 150 feet deep in the middle. I believe it, because the "shore" on one side is only the part of a steep embankment that happens to be above water. Right at the water's edge stand a couple of tall birch trees. Some boys evidently climbed to the top of two of them, tying a cord between them and then tying a rope to the cord, so as to make for a rope swing. That seems not to have worked well, so they climbed up the tallest of the trees and attached to a strong upper limb a hempen rope in a complicated tangle of loops and knots. You grab that rope and carry the end thirty feet up the embankment, then pull tight and fling yourself forward. The swing launches you high in the air and about thirty feet from shore. I first saw it seven or eight years ago. It is still there, and it still works beautifully.

That rope swing is an emblem of the daring use of a mechanical imagination. It alters the face of nature, and gives us something exhilarating, or impressive, or comfortable, or bold. It is far from what are called "arts and crafts," because its object is too big for that. It makes its mark upon the world.

Or think of the mischief a good shovel, an ax or chain saw, and a mattock can do. If you teach your kid how to use them, they might—use them. They see a stand of scrub trees in a vacant area of your yard. They cut the trees down and grub up the roots. Then with the shovel they might clear a parcel for planting vegetables. That would show the dangerous virtue of initiative. In New England, you can hardly clear any land at all without digging up enough rocks to make a nice wall or border. They might build one of those, too.

No Hunting. No Raising Animals

You are to eat your food from carnifaction factories: horrible warehouses where animals are force-fattened and stuffed with growth hormones, then slaughtered and sliced and packaged to market. This is what is known as enlightenment.

Deer hunting was a popular pastime in the rural Pennsylvania where I grew up. People who know nothing about the subject suppose it is for beer-drinking men who want to show off their prowess. Encourage that bigotry in your children.

Do not let on that you know that hunting requires actual knowledge of anything, which a young person must learn from someone who is proficient. You have to know how to clean and take care of a rifle; what the difference between one gauge and another is; what "trajectory" means. You have to coordinate your efforts with those of your fellow hunters, sometimes flushing the game, sometimes waiting, with numb fingers and aching knees, for the quarry to come. You are, at best, pitting your skill and your strategy against the animals, appreciating their strange ways, and not at all taking them for granted as creatures of strength and speed and keen instinct. A teenage lad may learn to hunt alone for small game, like woodcock or pheasant, and then he has to remember their roosting grounds, or set up a blind for himself, and maybe rig up some boots and leggings to keep his feet warm while he stands or crouches in the bog.

Here is how the naturalist and essayist Farley Mowat describes a morning of mallard shooting with his father in *The Dog Who Wouldn't Be*

(1957). They and their dog have driven more than two hundred miles up to a brackish pond in the flats of northern Saskatchewan, and have stationed themselves in the mud while it is still quite dark, knowing that the ducks will begin to rouse themselves and take off in the morning:

> Somewhere far overhead—or perhaps it was only in my mind—I heard the quivering sibilance of wings. I reached out my hand and touched the cold, oily barrel of my gun lying in the straw beside me; and I knew a quality of happiness that has not been mine since that long-past hour.

Better to tell your child that rifles and all the other implements of hunting are simply evil. Best to do this while your mouth is full of a cheeseburger from McDonald's. Sating the appetite with what is cheap and easy is the rule in this regard, as in so many others.

No soldering kits, no ham radios, no transformers, no catapults. No big drills, no routers, no table saws, no axes. No shovels, no tillers, no mattocks, no hoes. No engines to take apart, no car innards, no automobile batteries. No acetylene torches, no hammers, no hacksaws, no pipe wrenches. No fly rods, no sandbags, no cinderblocks, no wheelbarrows. No bags of concrete mix, no fifty foot long ropes, no ladders, no chopping blocks. No tire irons, no sailboats, no paddles, no inner tubes. No rollers, no crankshafts, no crazy glue, no cement. No vacuum tubes, no motherboards, no Bunsen burners, no sledges.

No hunting, no trespassing, no fishing, no working on cars in the driveway, no laying tile, no demolition of dead barns, no bonfires, no outdoor cooking, no bird traps, no pigeon cages, no telegraphs, no rope ladders, no crow's nests. No painting initials on sides of cliffs, no riding bicycles into ponds. No drawing up master plans for the invasion of Russia, no invention of the machinery of language. No screwdrivers to the back end of a telephone to see what is inside, no cutting of wax records, no wicker dumbwaiters, no Morse code.

No rabbets, no dadoes, no fluting, no dovetails, no finials. No dies, no drill presses, no clamps. No hot iron, no hot copper, no hot glass. No gears, no sprockets, no axles, no cranks, no swivels. No clock pendulums, no flywheels, no springs, no spools. No trades, no gear, no tackle, and no trim.

What will your children be good for, you ask, if they have neither deep reading nor an imaginative encounter with the natural world nor the cleverness of eye and hand? Why, then they might be just right for government work. Someone, after all, has to govern the dulled and dependent masses, and why not a person just as dulled and dependent as they? It's what our own blueprint, the Constitution, is all about.

Method 4

Replace the Fairy Tale with Political Clichés and Fads

or

Vote Early and Often

In *Marcovaldo*, Italo Calvino writes a series of vignettes about a working-class man of that name, his harried wife, and their children. Marcovaldo is the essential sad sack; not a particularly good man, but not a bad man either, simply struggling to catch a break here and there in a hard life.

There they are in their flat in the attic of a tenement one hot summer night, trying to look up at the stars in the sky. But their view is interrupted at intervals by a blaring neon sign reading GNAC, part of the lettering for SPAAK-COGNAC, shining off and on for twenty seconds at a turn. When the GNAC is out, "the moon suddenly faded, the sky became a flat, uniform black, the stars lost their radiance, and the cats, male and female that for ten seconds had been letting out howls of love, moving languidly toward each other along the drainpipes and the roof-trees, squatted on the tiles, their fur bristling in the phosphorescent neon light."

Marcovaldo and his family think different thoughts, also at intervals, depending upon whether the GNAC is shining. His teenage daughter Isolina, for instance,

> felt carried away by the moonlight; her heart yearned, and even the faintest croaking of a radio from the lower floors of the building came to her like the notes of a serenade; there was the GNAC, and that radio seemed to take on a different rhythm, a jazz beat, and Isolina

thought of the dance-hall full of blazing lights and herself, poor thing, up here all alone.

Her teenage brother sighs for the pale face of a girl he can only just see beyond the curl of the unlit G, a girl whose sight he loses entirely when the sign lights up. The smaller children feel one moment as if they are in a warm, dark forest full of brigands, while under the influence of GNAC they turn their fingers into pistols and play at shooting each other. Marcovaldo's wife one moment feels like a mother protecting her little ones, wishing to shoo them off to bed; when the GNAC comes on, everything again is "electric, outside and inside," and she feels as if she were "paying a visit to someone important." Marcovaldo one moment is trying to teach his children the names of the constellations, and the next is swept up in thoughts of commerce and enterprise.

I will return to the GNAC shortly—it is a helpful symbol of what we can do to keep people from a deep engagement with reality. But first let us consider this modern fairy-tale, for that is what it is. Calvino's writing, when it is not in the style of a philosophical game, always partakes of the folk tale, with characters immediately recognizable for their types. Marcovaldo is the poor soul, the born loser; he is Ralph Kramden the bus driver, Italian style. His daughter Isolina, literally "the poor lonely girl," is the fair maiden of passionate heart, who yearns for a youth to love her. The elder brother Fiordiligi is the sighing poet, ineffectual, who sees beauty where no one else can. That these are types makes the story at once not only comprehensible but resonant. We come upon the members of the family and we say, "I have seen that person before." Had we met them a hundred years ago, or a thousand years ago, we should have said much the same thing.

It has been a great victory for the crushers of imagination to label such figures "stereotypes," and add a sneer to it, as if people who used them in their stories were not very imaginative—or, sometimes, as if they were downright narrow-minded and wicked. The youth, the lonely maiden, the ineffective father, the doting mother, these are all *types*, because they are true to life; it is how they came to be types in the first place. Such characters are like a child's palette of colors: bold blue, and green, and yellow, and red, and white. Of course they simplify: as the towering marble pillars of the Parthenon simplify, or as the tonic chord in a Bach chorale resolves all the preceding complexity into the perfectly expected and harmonious simplicity of the right ending.

Fairy tales and folk tales are for children and childlike people, not because they are little and inconsequential, but because they are as enormous as life itself. The original story of Aschenputtel (English "Cinderella") features a stepmother and two horrible stepsisters who reduce the girl to a mere slave. Her mother, from her grave in the garden nearby, appears to her to help her, giving her the dress and the glass slippers and the coach that will take her to the ball, to dance with the prince. He falls in love with her, as he must—for in fairy tales, someone has to see beneath the surface of things, and glimpse the beauty that everyone else overlooks. When the prince and Cinderella finally marry, the envious sisters, marching down the aisles as bridesmaids, have their eyes pecked out by some very helpful little birds. It is altogether the right ending. Right, that is, if you want to stir the imaginations of your children. No such thing will ever have happened in the history of the human race, if by "happen" you mean that such events would occur as they are told, helpful birds and all. But such things do happen, all the time. We have met the characters in Cinderella, too.

And those characters dwell in a moral world, whose laws are as clear as the law of gravity. That too is a great advantage of the folk tale. It is not a failure of imagination to see the sky as blue. It is a failure rather to be weary of its being blue—and not to notice how blue it is. An appreciation for the subtler colors of the sky will come later. In the folk tale, good is good and evil is evil, and the former will triumph and the latter will fail. This is not the result of the imaginative quest. It is rather its principle and foundation. It is what will enable the child later on to understand *Macbeth*, or *Don Quixote*, or *David Copperfield*.

If you do not want a child to paint, you take away his palette. If you do not want him to use his imagination to conceive of archetypal stories, you take away his narrative palette. You take away, or corrupt, or subvert all his types. That you will do most efficiently if you deprive him of folk tales. You will have all kinds of excuses for doing so. Some of the tales are terribly violent: Red Riding Hood's grandmother is ripped out of the belly of the wolf by a handy woodsman with an ax. Others are hopelessly rooted in old-fashioned beliefs (based upon thousands of years of observation) about men and women, mothers and fathers, good children and bad children, good rulers and bad rulers, sheep and wolves, and so forth. Mrs. Midas just *had* to whisper the secret about King Midas's donkey-ears to the reed at the shore, and then word got about on the wind. Robin Hood is the leader of his merry men not only because he can cleave their arrows in half when they hit the bull's-eye before him, but because he gives gifts with a manly and cheerful freedom. So when the Tinker fights him to a draw with fists and staves in Howard Pyle's *The Merry Adventures of Robin Hood*, Robin does not wish vengeance upon him, but likes him all the better for his high spirit and invites him to join them:

> "Nay, touch him not," said Robin, "for a right stout man is he. A metal man he is by trade, and a mettled man by nature; moreover, he doth sing a lovely ballad. Say, good fellow, wilt thou join my merry men all? Three suits of Lincoln green shalt thou have a year, beside twenty marks in fee; thou shalt share all with us and lead a right merry life in the greenwood; for cares have we not and misfortune cometh not upon us within the sweet shades of Sherwood, where we shoot the dun deer, and feed upon venison and sweet oaten cakes, and curds and honey. Wilt thou come with us?"

In any case, when you starve your child of the folk tale, you not only cramp his imagination for the time being. You help to render vast realms of human art (not to mention human life) incomprehensible. Prince Calaf travels to China incognito, where he learns of a beautiful but cruel princess, whose suitors must answer her riddle correctly or else be put to death. The advisors to her father, the king, try to persuade the young man to leave, and not burden their consciences with yet another death, but it won't do; he has fallen in love. He takes up the challenge, the bold youth, and succeeds in answering the riddle, much to the Princess's rage. Then he proposes a riddle of his own: he will agree to be executed in the morning after all, if the Princess can answer *his* riddle.

"What is that?" she asks, smoldering.

"My riddle is simply this," he says. "*What is my name?*"

In the end, after her furious attempts to torture it out of Calaf's handmaiden (who gives up her life for the man she loves in vain), she will yield herself defeated. But meanwhile, something is happening to her, something has touched her icy heart. On the morning when she must guess, the

Prince himself reveals his name to her, whispering it into her ear. If she wishes him to die, he will gladly die.

"I know his name!" cries the princess to the King and all the court. "His name—*is Love.*"

That's the plot of Puccini's opera *Turandot.* If you have no heart for the folk tale, you must wave goodbye to Puccini. And to almost all the other great operas. And to the romances and comedies of Shakespeare. And to *Macbeth, King Lear,* and *Richard III.* And to Homer. And to the whole idea behind Dante's *Divine Comedy,* that a man might be so inspired by the love of a beautiful woman as to find in it a clue to the mystery of the universe. And to all the works of William Faulkner. And to Flannery O'Connor's macabre fairy tales of sin and redemption, set in the rural south. And to *The Twilight Zone.* And to *Star Wars.*

By now the reader sees the danger. If you don't want your child to have a mind capable of falling in love with the music of Puccini or the poetry of Dante, you had better see to the folk tales. How do you do that? I think the GNAC in Calvino's story can give us some clues. You drown the stories, or you flatten them into homogeneity, just as all the stars and the moonlight disappear when the GNAC comes out. You sneer at any connection with the timeless: just as the GNAC is all about business, here, right now, in the only time that means anything. Finally, and most important, you turn all stories into a bald, brazen sales pitch, preferably a political pitch. The GNAC comes on to sell booze; our tales must come on to sell, sell, sell more potent stuff than cognac.

GNAC Says: Buy This, It's the Same as Everything Else

Once upon a time there was a man who married a beautiful but weak and simple wife. She tried to remain true to him, but one day a youth from far across the sea came through town. Her husband was a grave and serious man, but the youth was cheerful and talkative. Her husband tried his hardest to live by the law of his faith, but the youth was carefree and wild. His hair was black and glossy as the raven's down. His eyes were black, and his complexion dark. One night when her husband was away, he came to her and pleaded with her so persuasively that she gave in to him, and loved him. She had a child by him, of dark skin and glossy hair.

But her husband had to travel in winter across the mountains to the city of the king, and the youth went with him. He was so wild, and so foolish, with the mind of a boy, that the husband pitied him. Then one night they had to take lodgings in an empty stone hut, a hovel for hunters and trappers passing through. There the youth challenged the husband, and said that he loved his wife and she loved him, and he would have her, no matter what the husband thought. At which the good and upright man took an heirloom he carried with him—an ax—and smote the youth through the brain. But never from that moment till the day he died did the husband enjoy peace in his heart, for he did not want to embarrass his wife or disinherit his son, whom he tried, and often failed, to love. He carried both her sin and his, silently, like an acid corroding him from within, till he lay on his deathbed—and perhaps beyond.

That is story of Sigrid Undset's tetralogy, *The Master of Hestviken*. It is full of the great elemental motives of human life, large and simple, and as profound as the sea. We can as soon tire of them as we can tire of humanity itself. None of the three characters I have named is wholly good; none is wholly evil. But good and evil remain unchanged, and against them we judge the wife's failure, the husband's jealousy, the youth's seduction and arrogance; and, conversely, the wife's simplicity and loneliness, the husband's self-sacrifice, the youth's frankness and vitality. It is a stunning and dangerous work of the imagination. We read, and we come to know these characters. They become parts of our moral universe, or rather they are lights to shine upon what we have seen and known, to reveal what may have lain hidden from our understanding.

Therefore, such a work should be kept far from our children. Not because there is violence in it—though that may serve as a convenient excuse. No, we nod and smile at violent banality all the time, on television and in movies. Consider what happens to people whose night skies are spangled with constellations like *The Master of Hestviken*, or *Moby-Dick*, or *The Brothers Karamazov*. These people are hard to fool. They are also hard to enlist in pursuit of the trivial and ephemeral. It is as if we had given them a powerful telescope atop a high mountain, and shown them how to use it, and directed their attention to the Orion nebula, and once they had learned to do so and to love the beauty they found there, expected them to look at light bulbs on a marquee. Or, if not a telescope, a magical device for seeing deep into the human heart; and then expected them to watch *American Idol*, or to be impressed by the maunderings of the latest political hack.

No, we must turn on the GNAC. First we turn on that blaring sign to homogenize the story—to reduce it to the even blare of its surroundings. How do we do that? We reject everything that is archetypal and real, and replace it with one of the four or five stock one-dimensional figures or flat motifs from mass entertainment. Let's see, then. The husband is a quiet but strikingly handsome man, keen-sighted and thoughtful. Obviously that won't do. That sort of character is not on the menu at McNovel's. He must be made a bit ugly, or dumpy, or old, or simply mean. That will provide the wife a convenient excuse for her infidelity, and will allow the audience to know that the sin is really correct after all. So it is in Kate Chopin's *The Awakening*, a novel that replaces intelligent probing into the human heart with a feminist manifesto. Undset's hero, the troubled husband, though jealous (and understandably so, given the outcome), genuinely loves his wife. That too must go. We don't actually want our young people to encounter the mysteries of love anyway; best to keep them preoccupied with the tedium of lust instead. The husband notices his rival's youth and is moved by it; almost draws back from the murder he has in his heart. No, we'll have to have him planning it coldly all along. The wife is frail. No, women are never frail. We'll have to have her put her husband in his place, with her fist if need be. She knows exactly what she is doing, bless her. The youth is amoral. No, he comes to liberate her with his love.

You see, it is all the difference between a fundamental truth and a cliché. The things we tire of hearing are those that poor novelists, movie directors, and composers repeat only because other novelists, directors, and composers have used them before. They are good for a cheap, automatic, superficial, and temporary response. The joke is not really funny or new, but we laugh anyway, because all the cues direct us to laugh. The wicked deed does not really reveal anything about the dark corners of the human heart, but we don't care about that; we just file the deed into its automatic mental slot labeled "wicked," and go on watching the show, pretending that we care what happens. The fundamental truths, by contrast, require a real response: they cause us to brood over the mystery of this life, even when we recognize the great characters—the disappointed husband, the lonely wife, the interloper. But a real response requires silence, and patience, and thought. It's not easy. Clichés are easy. So we bring up our children on clichés.

Everyone knows that men are beasts and that religious people are bigots. Run with those clichés and you have Margaret Atwood's *The Handmaid's*

Tale. I might add that it's a great book to assign to young people, if only for the imbecilic prose, in the poseur's style of Thoughts Too Great for Complete Sentences:

> Without a word. Both of us shaking, how I'd like to. In Serena's parlor, with the dried flowers, on the Chinese carpet, his thin body. A man entirely unknown. It would be like shouting, it would be like shooting someone. My hand goes down, how about that, I could unbutton, and then. But it's too dangerous, he knows it, we push each other away, not far. Too much trust, too much risk, too much already.

The lust, which is in its own right just a tad dangerous, is here used with real care: it is the sugar-coating to make the clichés go down. We may think of the same use of bare skin in movies and television shows. People complain about it, but if it weren't for that skin, who on earth could bear to sit through anything so banal for twenty-five minutes? It would be like having to *talk* to a Playboy bunny.

So that turns up the GNAC. Or take Nathaniel Hawthorne's fascinating romance of sin and judgment, *The Scarlet Letter*. In the book, the cold-hearted husband, Chillingworth, leaves his wife Hester and lives for a time among the savages—the Indians, where he can indulge his baser appetites. This apparently is exactly what some people in the Massachusetts Bay Colony did; and when we read about it in Hawthorne's novel, we are meant to sense the pull of the dark forests beyond the small and vulnerable clearing of civilization we have struggled to win for ourselves. It is not that the Indians in the book are evil, but that the heart of man is deeply divided, and it requires all our learning, social custom, law, and personal courage to keep ourselves from lapsing back into that forest. Now obviously we cannot have that. We cannot encourage our young people to glance into their own hearts. So we turn up the GNAC.

We make a film version of the novel (Roland Joffe, 1995), call it an "original" adaptation, and then replace every subtlety with current platitudes. Chillingworth is evil, certainly; husbands generally are a bad lot. But the Indians, they have to be good. They are always good. They are In Touch With Nature. And the strictures against fornication and adultery that the foolish Puritans live by, why, they are bad, just as religious people generally are bad, or at least narrow-minded and contemptible. So we will have Hester Prynne never repent of her adultery—that would be a change of heart, and that would require a heart to be changed. No, she will ride off triumphant into the forest with the Indians, perhaps to set up a shop selling herbal medicines to tourists, and lobbying for the political rights of single mothers. How the GNAC does shed light upon all things!

Homogeneity is the rule. All television shows must look alike. All hamburgers must come from vast fast-food franchises, and taste alike. States should mandate curricula for all their schools. Washington should dictate in turn to the states. Department heads should choose all the books for their teachers. Textbook manufacturers should flatten out all the peculiarities of authorship. Newspapers should all read alike, and, if we can manage it, they should all be owned by only a few media conglomerates, and should hash out the same articles from three or four wire services. The language of the articles should be reduced to the blank stupidity of the old Dick and Jane readers. The Congress passes laws. Oh, pass laws, pass many laws! All little children should attend state supervised day-care centers and watch public pablum on the television. Do not look at the stars. GNAC is everywhere.

New! Improved! GNAC!

The wizard Prospero and his daughter Miranda have lived for almost her whole life on a rocky island in the Mediterranean. He is about to reveal to her that he is the banished Duke of Milan, and that she is therefore a princess. But first he is curious to find out how much she remembers from when she was but a small child, in the days before they were cast out of their city. She seems to recall that she had a few nursemaids who attended her. He then asks, "What seest thou else / In the deep backward and abysm of time?" thinking of time as a profound and mysterious source of riches. And sure enough, Shakespeare's *Tempest* is a moral fable, a tale of rights restored and sins forgiven. Time is of the essence in the tale, because time is the working out of the timeless designs of Providence.

The most pernicious works of art, though they are the products of their time, transport us from our own time not only to theirs, but to a realm that embraces all times. We call Shakespeare timeless, but what we mean is that he is not shackled to the particular age from whence he arose—though he could have arisen in no other age but that one. The story of Aladdin's lamp could only have come from the Middle East, a world where men prayed to Allah on beautiful carpets, but where they also believed in the *djinn*, the usually malignant spirits of the desert. It was a world of extravagance and luxury, with old Baghdad known for its gold, silks, and spices; a world of great beauty and cruelty, ruled by despots who were sometimes enlightened and sometimes barbaric and sometimes a little of both. And yet to read the tale of Aladdin is to mount that same flying carpet with him, and travel not only to faraway Baghdad, but to a land of permanent things: of the brave and noble youth; of the beautiful and pure maiden he loves; of the lowly exalted to glory, and the arrogant reduced to nothing. If there should ever arise on earth beings who could not understand and cherish the story of Aladdin, we must conclude that they are not our sort of beings. They could not be human.

Herman Melville wrote a good many brainy and finely crafted works, and some of them bear the mark of their time, and are therefore of less interest to us. *The Confidence-Man* is about a swindler who boards a ship steaming down the Mississippi, and who uses the greed, anxiety, and egotism of his fellow passengers to win their "confidence" in him, selling worthless potions to the sick and dying, selling worthless stock to speculators, and dunning the sentimentalists to support a worthless charity for Seminoles in Florida. It is a good novel, but it is hard to understand it without placing it in the context of late nineteenth-century industrialism. That is not the case with *Moby-Dick*. As long as there are men who know the joy of uniting in death-defying purpose—the joy of war, or of the hunt, of laying their lives on the line at a throw of the dice, of daring fate, even after they have known the terrors of the deep—then they will read and understand *Moby-Dick*.

> His three boats stove around him, and oars and men both whirling in the eddies; one captain, seizing the line-knife from his broken prow, had dashed at the whale, as an Arkansas duellist at his foe, blindly seeking with a six inch blade to reach the fathom-deep life of the whale. That captain was Ahab. And then it was, that suddenly sweeping his sickle-shaped lower jaw beneath him, Moby Dick had reaped away Ahab's leg, as a mower a blade of grass in the field.

It goes without saying, then, that if we want to smother the child's imagination, then we should not allow it to stray off into timeless realms of fable. J. R. R. Tolkien wrote a dangerously pleasant story about just that. In "Smith of Wootton Major," a young boy is chosen by the faeries—who are not Tinkerbell-like creatures with sparkling wands, but beings of fearful power and wisdom, rather as angels were once conceived—to wander away into their land, and have adventures, and return to his world where something of the reality behind the everyday, something of the true faery world beneath the false world of ordinary appetites and selfishness, will be passed on. In every generation, he is told, there is one person so graced, that the door to the real world of the imagination will not be shut forever.

Then let us mire the child in the inanities of his own time and place. The GNAC cries out, "Buy me now! I am here! This moment is all! You need a drink! I am new, I am improved! GNAC!" So should children's literature also be.

Let's suppose we have children who live in the tenements of that devastated city, Detroit. Because they are human children, with imaginations yearning for the timeless, they will want to read about magic lamps and genies, or about men going down to the sea in ships, or about a boy who steps into a different world. They apparently want to read, by the millions, about a boy named Harry who attends a sorcerer's school and does battle against the evil magician Voldemort. They used to want to read, by the millions, the swashbuckling novels of Rafael Sabatini—about how Captain Blood was wrongly sentenced to exile, and how he set himself up as the commander of an island in the Caribbean, and how he finally saved the beautiful daughter of the old governor and, after a few terrific battles, won back his good name.

Children will bear out what Emily Dickinson said about the power of imaginative literature that is manifestly *not* about ourselves. A book is like a great ship taking us to lands unknown. And it does so almost at a nod, as if one of Arabia's *djinn* had swept us off to the Dome of the Rock, where Mohammed claimed to have his vision of paradise:

How frugal is the chariot
That bears a human soul!

Our children will want to ascend that chariot. So we will give them instead stories about Detroit. Those will be "relevant" to them. The odd thing is that stories about Detroit could be of greatest interest to children who have never been near anything like Detroit—say, Eskimo children on the frozen banks of the Mackenzie River, whose clearest idea of a city is a few government shanties on a couple of blacktopped streets, with a liquor store and a gas station. And even at that, such a story could only rouse the imagination if in some way it did not matter that it was set in Detroit.

I remember a tale from my youth about a teenage boy, fatherless, who had moved with his mother to a rough neighborhood. He ran into bullies, who dragged him by force to the top of a high building. There they laid a pole from the roof of their building to the roof of another twenty feet away. The pole had about two feet to spare on either end. And they forced him at gunpoint to grab the pole and hang over the nothingness between the buildings. Then they left him, to fend for himself. I cared nothing about the city, except insofar as it was strange to me; I cared nothing about the problems of juvenile delinquency. The story was about an innocent person outnumbered by evil people, and the drama was in seeing whether he would survive.

So we must be careful here. In giving our children what is "relevant," we want to ensure that it is rooted in this time, this place, these platitudes. If you can, give them books so caked with topical references that they won't be understandable in thirty years. Such works, calling for automatic responses, are often little more than political propaganda with a little bit of a story line—more about those soon. If you don't have those, though, you can still rely on the flood of books that don't rise above the ephemeral. Romance novels will do. You can read ten of them at a clip without being disturbed by a single thought to open up the shell of your mind. Some years ago, the romance novels were populated by women dying to swoon away in the arms of Dangerous but Gentle Men, who only needed a Loyal Woman to bring them back into Decent Society. Now what they need is a Strong Woman, a Lady Lawyer, or an Adventuring Careerist—the clichés will shift from decade to decade, but the dullness will remain.

Remember to foster banality. Since the contemporary novelist and poet wears banality like a badge of distinction, you should not have far to search. Here, for instance, from Lorrie Moore's *Anagrams*, is writing utterly boxed into the cramped little world of the graduate student or the professional-to-be:

"Trouble in Newton-land," says Eleanor. Newton is the biochemist she's been seeing for over a year now. "He's having an affair with someone. He says he feels rejuvenated with her."

"Oh, Christ. What is she, another biochemist?"

"No," sighs Eleanor, stacking up dishes in the kitchen. "She works for AT&T."

Sympathy is important at a time like this. "God," I finally say, "I'm so glad I have MCI."

How very droll, and how self-important. "See," say the characters in the story, neither of whom you can really care about, "how intelligently bored I am with everything."

Coming to the Aid of the Party

G. K. Chesterton once wrote that the trouble with people who do not believe in God is not that they then believe in nothing. It is that they will believe in anything. And the biggest anything around for people to believe in, in our day, is the State. We might put it this way. We should substitute for the wonder of imagination the irritable flush of political partisanship. We should accept the maxim that all human endeavor is ultimately about power. Therefore education is about power. So is art.

Some decades ago, a genuine madman took control of a large European state, and enticed people into elevating The Folk to the status of their national idol. All art too was to promote the glory of The Folk. Since his vision involved a caricature of masculinity, what the Germans under Hitler produced were sculptures of brave warriors with ridiculously bulging muscles, their jaws set, their Waffen im Hand, ready to defeat the enemies of the Reich, na ja! The politics may change, but the principle is the same. Art must be placed in the service of a clear and present social program. We are selling GNAC, remember.

Sex sells, the advertisers tell us. So in the politicization of everything in a child's library (which should be small anyway), we ought to use sex whenever we can. A school district in Illinois has done just that, requiring students to read *Angels in America*, a piece of unbearably ridiculous propaganda for homosexual rights. If you can think of a political cliché that is not in this work, you should send word to the author, that he might supply it in a revised edition. Sexually repressed Mormons are in it. A bored housewife is in it. Global warming is in it. Vietnam is in it. The villain Ed Meese is in it. "Who is Ed Meese?" the student asks, rolling his eyes. Why, he was the attorney general for the Reagan administration.

"What was the Reagan administration?"

"That was a time of great evil in America."

"And who is this Roy Cohn?"

"He was the evil lawyer who prosecuted people during the McCarthy Era. But he was also a homosexual who died of AIDS. Ronald Reagan didn't care if people died of AIDS, because," and you see how it goes. All the fascinating corrugations of history neatly smoothed flat, so that students will be prepared to give the planned response to all questions. They will, to boot, be fooled into thinking that they are thinking, just because they will have adopted the correct position on matters they know absolutely nothing about.

The school in my own district decided it would be nice to abandon great art altogether, and have students read, for English class, a screed against both traditional manhood and gun ownership, called *Give a Boy a Gun*. The rationale was the book's relevance. What with the terrible school shootings that have plagued our nation for the last twenty years, we should compel students to "rethink" America's fascination with firearms. Note that we should not compel school administrators to rethink their commitment to large anonymous institutions, nor social service agencies to rethink their commitment to the disintegration of the family. In any case, all disputes about the causes of school violence aside, it is the assignment of the book that is more important than the book itself. The assignment delivers this message: Reading is all about the adopting of the correct position. We are not about working the imagination. We are about working the precincts.

In this enterprise we can indulge ourselves, a little, in what might otherwise be a healthy admiration for heroes. We might even tell stories once in a while. Take, for example, Joy Hakim's *A History of US*, a series of quite popular history books for the elementary years. Miss Hakim, a native of Great Britain, manages to tell the story of the United States with some verve; she *likes* the country, it seems. The textbooks are, of course, written for beings whose minds have been blasted by electronic jitters and cannot concentrate on a sentence or a thought of any complexity. The layout of the books capitulates to, and contributes to, this jitteriness by being peppered with pictures, boldface print, insets, cartoons, anything but sophisticated words. But these are other matters. Time and again, Miss Hakim—who is by far the best of a weak lot—is out to teach students that the Story of Us is reducible to the Story of the Triumph of the Correct Way to Think about Everything. So we are told about Harriet Tubman, the black woman who was one of the most important players in the Underground Railroad, that she "was stronger than most men." Now this, simply, is nonsense, and is politically motivated nonsense. Not to take anything away from her courage and endurance, but Harriet Tubman was only five feet tall, and a woman, in the days when every man but the feeble and the more effete aristocrats did physical labor. Any farmer or road worker or lumberjack will tell you that a six-foot-tall lad, no matter how well built he is, is going to have a hard time holding his own against grown men.

But what is important about the comment is not its veracity, but its clear political motivation. Miss Hakim is a feminist, as will be clear even to her young readers. If you feed children enough of what is politically motivated, regardless of the direction of the motive, you will insinuate into their minds that all the humanistic subjects they study, and some of the scientific ones too, are power games and nothing more. So, for example, when Hakim discusses Jefferson's Declaration of Independence—a tract she sincerely admires—she pretends not to know what Jefferson meant by the statement "All men are created equal." "He didn't mention women," she notes, despite admitting that "we do know that in the 18th century the words 'men' and 'mankind' included men and women." What could have opened up the possibility for a real flight of the moral and political imagination is thus rendered ineffectual. Instead of assuming that Jefferson knew what he meant, and that he *still*, for instance, did not believe in the universal franchise, and then wondering how he could reconcile his belief in equality with his denial of the vote to women, we take the easy way out, declaring that the ideas in the Declaration have "take[n] on meanings that go beyond what the writers intended," namely, meanings that we ourselves approve of, and so do not have to think about. Again, it does not matter from what direction the political stance is taken; all that matters is that politics, finally, is all that matters.

Charles Dickens, to take a surprising example, wrote *A Child's History of England* precisely to counter what he believed was the dull, dry, uninspiring historiography to which children would otherwise be exposed. It was, for him, a work of the imagination, and he too tells his stories with verve. In fact, he does make events and personages come alive, and his prose is anything but banal. Here he begins his description of Henry VIII:

> He was just eighteen years of age when he came to the throne. People said he was handsome then; but I don't believe it. He was a big, burly, noisy, small-eyed, large-faced, double-chinned, swinish-looking fellow in later life (as we know from the likenesses of him, painted by the famous HANS HOLBEIN), and it is not easy to believe that so bad a character can ever have been veiled under a prepossessing appearance.

Now that is vigorous prose, by all means to be avoided in our textbooks. Note the teasing personality of the author, whispering confidentially into our ear. Note the bravura of that list of adjectives, cranking up to the climax in "swinish-looking." Note the parenthetical bit of information, opening the child's awareness out into a world of art, that Henry was painted by Holbein.

In short, there's a lot to be wary of here, if we want to keep our children's minds as dull as butter knives. But, fortunately, Dickens in this work cannot help himself. He must play the political partisan. Once you read a few pages of it, you must begin to suspect all the rest. Or you give in to it, because you understand that one political game is pretty much of a piece with any other. Here is Dickens's account of the beginning of the Reformation:

> There now arose at Wittemberg, in Germany, the great leader of the mighty change in England which is called the Reformation, and which set the people free from their slavery to the priests. This was a learned Doctor, named MARTIN LUTHER, who knew all about them, for he had been a priest, and even a monk, himself. The preaching and writing of Wickliffe had set a number of men thinking on this subject; and Luther, finding one day to his great surprise, that there really was a book called the New Testament which the priests did not allow to be read, and which contained truths that they suppressed, began to be very vigorous against the whole body, from the Pope downward. It happened, while he was yet only beginning his

vast work of awakening the nation, that an impudent fellow named TETZEL, a friar of very bad character, came into his neighborhood selling what were called Indulgences, by wholesale, to raise money for beautifying the great Cathedral of St. Peter's, at Rome. Whoever bought an Indulgence of the Pope was supposed to buy himself off from the punishment of Heaven for his offences. Luther told the people that these Indulgences were worthless bits of paper, before God, and that Tetzel and his masters were a crew of impostors in selling them.

The King and the Cardinal were mightily indignant at this presumption; and the King (with the help of SIR THOMAS MORE, a wise man, whom he afterwards repaid by striking off his head) even wrote a book about it, with which the Pope was so well pleased that he gave the King the title of Defender of the Faith.

Dickens was, as I've suggested, at cross purposes when he wrote *A Child's History of England*. He wanted to rouse their imaginations, and so he employed his considerable wit to do that. No one now would dare so bracing a splash of cold water as his comment about Henry's repayment of Thomas More. No one likewise would dare give students the dramatic irony of a monk suddenly discovering that, after all, the New Testament does exist. And yet there is much to learn from Dickens's method here. Because he writes with GNAC in mind—though a rich and flavorful GNAC, like good hearty Victorian sherry—he must reduce his figures to caricatures. As there is no mystery in Joy Hakim's cartoon superheroine Harriet Tubman, so there is no mystery in Dickens's Luther, or the Pope, or Henry, or Thomas More. Furthermore, the reduction of people to politically motivated cartoon figures entails the reduction of history to a comic book story. And that means that almost every sentence you write will embroil you in nonsense.

It was, for instance, not true that Henry was granted the title Defender of the Faith for defending the doctrine of Indulgences. Nor that the doctrine simply stated that you could buy off the punishment for your sins. Nor that priests had suppressed knowledge of the New Testament. All Dickens would need to do, to write ably for our children now, would be to adopt a somewhat different political stance, turn his prose into an amalgamation of childish chatter, bureaucratic puffery, and political sloganeering, and allow his politics to determine what he was going to illustrate and what he was not.

The reader may now object, "All histories are written in this way!" On the contrary, they are not. Some come dangerously close to a fair, thorough, and thoughtful examination of the past, united with the artist's desire to bring to life the people who lived then, with their great successes and their failures. Sir Walter Scott did for Scotland what Dickens tried to do for England: he wrote a history meant to be read to children, *History of Scotland.* Here he is describing an event in the rebellion of William Wallace against the usurping English under Edward I. The English have fled into the chapel of the garrison of Dunnottar, built upon a precipice over the sea, with the chapel on the very brink. The Scots put the chapel to the torch, causing the English—including women, children, and priests—to flee from the building only to be slaughtered at the point of the Scottish swords, or to throw themselves into the sea and swim to the cliffs, where they cling like sea-birds, says Scott, crying for assistance.

Scott is a thoroughgoing admirer of Wallace, and a Scottish patriot. But his honesty, and his artistic desire to paint a human scene in all its complexity of light and darkness, will not be overridden by his politics:

> The followers of Wallace were frightened at this dreadful scene, and falling on their knees before the priests who chanced to be in the army, they asked forgiveness for having committed so much slaughter, within the limits of a church dedicated to the service of God. But Wallace had so deep a sense of the injuries which the English had done to his country, that he only laughed at the contrition of his soldiers—"I will absolve you all, myself," he said. "Are you Scottish soldiers, and do you repent for a trifle like this, which is not half what the invaders deserved at our hands?" So deep-seated was Wallace's feeling of national resentment, that it seems to have overcome, in such instances, the scruples of a temper which was naturally humane.

There you have it, what we must never allow. Scott levels moral judgment upon a man whose politics he supports. He sheds a tear for Wallace's shortcomings. He does not deny that he was great. He does not detract from his portrait for political reasons. Instead he sees that there is a universe of good and evil that can never be reduced to politics, just as the real vault of heaven powdered with stars cannot be reduced to the plaster dome of a planetarium. And, paradoxically, unlike the dopey upstart that Dickens unwittingly makes Luther out to be, and the butch field-hockey captain that Miss Hakim unwittingly makes Harriet Tubman out to be, Scott's William Wallace emerges for the child as a fundamentally good man, scarred by his desire for vengeance.

Likewise, the old McGuffey Readers, long ridiculed for their unabashed championing of what used to be called the virtues—among them the four cardinal virtues of temperance, prudence, courage, justice, and the three theological virtues of faith, hope, and love—are not simply boiled-down political sloganeering. For one, the literature they include won't allow for it. Consider the authors included in McGuffey's *Sixth Eclectic Reader.* First, many have to do with politics only in the broadest and most humane sense, as the study of man's dealings with other men. So we find nine selections from Shakespeare, and many another from poets and novelists as diverse as Pope, Dryden, Milton, Wordsworth, Coleridge, Goldsmith, Irving, Scott, Milton, Addison, and Byron. Liberal abolitionists are well represented, by Channing, Everett, and Sumner. But then so are conservatives, by Samuel Johnson, Edmund Burke, and Benjamin Disraeli. Daniel Webster delivers his famous Reply to Hayne, defending the national government against the idea that individual states in their sovereign capacity entered into the federal system of their own will and could likewise secede from it. But then Hayne himself is given an opportunity to defend the patriotism of his native South Carolina. Immorality, indecency, and stupidity are, however, not to be found.

Here is an example of the care for the imagination which we must reject. McGuffey includes an excerpt from a novel about the expulsion of the Moors from Granada. Nowadays, that would invite the selling of GNAC: we could turn the Christian Spaniards into villains, especially King Ferdinand, and the Muslims into the unappreciated victims of Spanish bigotry. But McGuffey could have peddled a different flavor of GNAC back then, had he chosen. He could have found a novelist or an essayist who portrayed the event as the crown jewel of Christian conquest over the evil Muslims. Behold instead how the minds of the poor students of old were encouraged *not* to fold in upon automatic political slogans. The Moorish king, Boabdil, has taken a noble and bitter farewell of Ferdinand and Isabella. He has been mocked, gently, by the Spanish king, but has not returned the jest. Now he rides to join his people at the coast, from which they will sail, never more to return to the land they have called home:

> Boabdil spurred on at full speed, till his panting charger halted at a little village where his mother, his slaves, and his faithful wife, Amine—sent on before—awaited him. Joining these, he proceeded without delay upon his melancholy path. They ascended that eminence which is the pass into the Alpuxarras. From its height, the vale, the rivers, the spires, and the towers of Granada broke gloriously upon the view of the little band. They halted mechanically and abruptly; every eye was turned to the beloved scene. The proud shame of baffled warriors, the tender memories of home, of childhood, of fatherland, swelled every heart, and gushed from every eye.

I don't claim that Edward Bulwer-Lytton, the author of the piece, was a great writer. His prose gives "purple" new meaning. But the editor has included this account regardless of politics. For the moment, his students will be suspended in a realm where kingdoms come and pass away, and only what is truly human remains. They will feel with the Moorish king "in vain seeking to wrap himself in Eastern pride or stoical philosophy." They will not therefore want to join a Moorish Reconquest Society. They may be less likely, indeed, to place ultimate hope in any political program, pro-Moor or otherwise. They will have tasted something better than GNAC.

Many years ago, I attended a panel discussion on whether my college ought to curtail its program in Western Civilization. One of the panelists was a feminist theologian, a former nun, who taught in the program and disliked it intensely. When it was her turn to speak, she began with her slogan, "Teaching is a political act." That was on my mind for the rest of the evening, till I asked another of the panelists, a young lady who felt aggrieved for having had to take the course for two years, why we read Virgil's *Aeneid*. I expected her to say something of the political sloganeering sort. We read Virgil to confirm the patriarchy. We read Virgil to confirm Western hegemony. We read Virgil to breathe life into our racism. Her answer stunned me. "I don't know why we read Virgil," she said, petulantly.

I proceeded then to defend reading the Romans on practical political grounds. If you read Livy, I said, you will have real insight into what John Adams and other federalists were thinking when they put together the machinery of our government. You will see also that the authority of the father in ancient Rome is by no means morally unambiguous. If you want to be subversive, I said, you can hardly do worse than to look into the darkness behind the patriotism of Virgil's *Aeneid*.

"I don't know what you're talking about," she replied.

I see now that the reduction of art to politics is intended to produce just that perfect response, "I don't know what you're talking about." For if you had to choose between art and the slogan, or between history and the slogan, you might as well choose the slogan and have done with pretending even to care about art or history. We do not want students who will reduce everything in art or history or religion or human life to a political slogan. Those students will still be in an intermediate state of stultification. They will still maintain some connection to art and history and religion and the fascinating drama of human life. And as long as they maintain that connection, no matter if it be as thin as the filigree of a spider's web, they may one day notice that Virgil's *Aeneid* is *not* a piece of Roman propaganda for the Augustan empire, nor a piece of reaction against that empire; that it is the West's great epic of loss, of a good man in a confused world, trying to do what he believes is right, gaining nothing but sorrow and toil for it, and presented in the end with an insoluble moral dilemma. He trusts in the noble virtue of piety, and yet whether he slays his enemy Turnus in the final scene of the poem or whether he spares him, he will seem to have sinned against piety. His paganism ends in despair. The student may notice that, if he keeps reading long enough.

No, the result we are aiming for is well captured by that student's response. The reduction of all things to politics must reduce them, in their own right, to irrelevance. Homer who? Why should I care about Michelangelo? I don't know what you're talking about. Pass the GNAC, please.

Method 5

Cast Aspersions upon the Heroic and Patriotic

or

We Are All Traitors Now

When I was a boy, my cousins and I would get up early in the morning on Memorial Day to catch the men in uniform as they made their way up the steep hill to the Protestant Cemetery. There, with the day's parade still gathering below, banked by the woods behind, these soldiers of old, looking stern in the eye, with their bellies sometimes lapping a little over their belts, would commemorate their brothers in arms who had died.

We watched in silence, not understanding the half of what was going on. The commander barked out an order. Clock clock, went the rifle bolts. Fire! And again, and again, a salute of twenty-one guns. Then, amid the curling smoke, and the boom still reverberating in our eardrums, and the birds frightened into flight, came the lone plaintive call of Taps. I never knew that it was a night hymn for the army, for which you could sing the words:

> Fading light dims the sight
> And a star gems the sky, gleaming bright.
> From afar drawing nigh,
> Falls the night.
>
> Day is done, gone the sun
> From the lakes, from the hills, from the sky;

All is well, safely rest;
God is nigh.

Then goodnight, peaceful night;
Till the light of the dawn shineth bright;.
God is near, do not fear,
Friend, goodnight.

You didn't really need the words. For as we boys stood there, listening, we suspected that something of dreadful importance had gone on, something that had to do with being a man, and even more, with belonging to a nation, our nation.

But the solemnity of the day brought with it a real joy, and a lot of boisterous fun. That is, in fact, one of the purposes of solemnity, which we, the interminably informal and drab, have forgotten. For as soon as the men had brought their rifles back to the marching position, and turned in formation to proceed down the hill, we scampered after them, eager to be the first to hop a ride on one of the fire trucks. From there we picked up school bands, with their braying trombones and bear-grunting tubas, their tinkling glockenspiels and twittering flutes, all happily off key and making up for their clumsiness with sweat and good will. We picked up the Knights of Columbus in full regalia, their crested helmets nodding in the breeze. We picked up cadres of majorettes, flashing their batons. We picked up Boy Scouts and Girl Scouts and Cub Scouts and Brownies. We picked up Ladies' Auxiliaries of outfits we had hardly heard of. We picked up the glad-handing mayor in a fancy car, and other politicians, and policemen, and more fire trucks. And the town came out to watch, as we snaked our way through our rubbly old streets clear to the mountain opposite, where our parade stopped for an hour at the Catholic cemetery.

Solemnity again; the priest said mass; hardly audible to the crowd in the open air. And when that was done and the people were dismissed, it was back to the fire truck for one last fling, on to the American Legion—a venerable stone watering hole—for doughnuts and orange juice.

It wasn't, I suppose, much of a parade, but it was something. My town has not had one in at least thirty years. I have a picture of my town celebrating the end of World War I. An old Irish priest in a derby hat is marching in front, followed by all kinds of guilds and leagues and societies, boys and girls, men and women, young and old. They're marching down Main Street, and the line must be a mile and a half long. I have another picture of an event in town. It's of a crowd gathered in a large open area next to the parish hall, with streamers and bunting, and a raised platform for the speakers, one of whom is the city solicitor of Philadelphia, come from two hundred miles away to assist in the celebration. The event? The dedication of a small playground.

That playground no longer exists. It's part of a parking lot next to what was once the parish hall, then was my grade school, and now are the borough offices, with a small lockup for drunks and unlicensed druggists. The Knights of Columbus had a building next to the playground. It is gone, as are the Knights. So are all the leagues and guilds and societies that made up the old parade. So is the borough high school, a stone building resembling a church, or a town hall with a belfry. It used to stand opposite that parish hall. It is gone, in favor of a sprawlingly ugly brick complex far enough away to require that almost all the students be bused. Not that it is the town's school, either. It houses students from a "region," thus taking from the borough the principal reason for its existence in the first place.

My town also boasts the largest Glacial Pothole in the world. You may well ask what a glacial pothole is. Glaciers, though they are ice, often behave like streams or rivers; they sometimes make whirlpools as they retreat back to their lairs in the north. When such a whirlpool strikes a core of soft rock surrounded by a harder "shell," the ice will gouge it out, leaving a smooth cylindrical hole in the stone, a "pothole." The one in my town is about eighty feet deep and forty feet across. An old miner discovered it over a century ago. In the 1950s they proudly made a little state park out of it, and I have pictures of the finned battleships of those days, Buicks and Fords, lined up at the park, as people took lunches to poke around in the woods nearby, have a picnic, and talk. It was, I suppose, a part of who we were. All that is gone. Well, the pothole is still there, and there's a chain link fence around it, to keep fools from falling in. Broken bottles and fast-food trash litter the pit. If there's a car in the lot, the person inside is waiting for something illegal.

One of the most anthologized stories in the old readers was Edward Everett Hale's "The Man Without a Country." In that story, a heedless young supporter of the traitor Aaron Burr—and note, it was taken for granted that the students would know who Burr was and why he was a traitor—cries out to the judge at his sentencing, "I wish I should never hear the name of the United States of America again!" With that request the judge complies. The man, Philip Nolan, is sentenced to life custody on one American ship after another. He is given every courtesy, provided with good food and comfortable quarters. He is even, after many years of remorse, treated with genuine respect. But he may not see a single American flag. He may not read a single American newspaper. He may not hear, from anyone, the name of his nation. No one will say "God bless America" in his presence. He dies on board a ship, an old man full of sorrow, before his friends can persuade Congress to commute the sentence. But he dies a repentant patriot.

I might write that we are all Philip Nolans now. It would not be true. First, there are still plenty of Americans who love their country. As I write these words, some of them are fighting in her cause overseas; among them are a few young men I myself have taught. And yet even their patriotism has been hamstrung, hobbled. Few people honor them for it; in the common life of an American, in the life from day to day, there is little sense of the holy place, or the holy day. Our holidays are not holy. They are extensions of the weekend. Our birthplaces are to be escaped from as soon as we free ourselves from our parents. Hale opens his story with a quote from Sir Walter Scott:

Breathes there the man with heart so dead,
That never to himself hath said,
"This is my own, my native land!"

Indeed there are such men and women. We are legion. Not the American Legion, mind you.

When Dante and his guide Virgil are climbing the lower reaches of the mountain of Purgatory, they reach an isolated ledge and are no longer sure which way to go. Dante points out a solitary soul in the distance, watching them closely, like a lion, moving his eyes but not his head. To this soul Virgil comes, asking the way. But the soul has a question of his own. It turns out that in his heart he is not solitary at all:

Virgil approached the spirit nonetheless
and asked of him to point us the best way

to climb the mount, and he made no response
But to inquire about our native land
and who we were in life; and the sweet guide
began with "Mantua," when that desert shade
Rose up from where he'd stood so firm in place—
"We share one country, you of Mantua!
I am Sordello!"—and the two embraced.

It is a moment we cannot now imagine. What might the modern man cry? "Yes, I too was born in that subdivision, on the northwestern side of the surveying line that separates Jefferson Township from the Plainfield Regional District." For just as we have nearly lost the capacity to weep a tear of gratitude at our nation's birthday, so have we lost the local geography of life. In every sense of the word, from the homestead to the town, from the state to the nation, from the distant past to the last lights darkening in the west, we do not *honor* our father and our mother.

And that deadens one very dangerous region of the heart. It used to be thought that the purpose of the school was to stir patriotic feeling to life and give it noble expression. It is now the school's purpose to dampen that feeling—and at the same time to give students the smug impression that to interpret one's national history in the least charitable light, to go out of one's way to find one's native land in the wrong, to sniff at one's local and national pastimes in favor of the fashionably foreign, is to drag that ignorant old country into the light where she belongs, to do her a favor against her will. We must produce people who could never write the following verse from *America*, nor sing it without rolling their eyes in impatience, because they could not conceive the feeling it describes:

I love thy rocks and rills,
Thy woods and templed hills;
My heart with rapture fills,
Like that above.

Kill the Fathers

If you comb through old schoolbooks, or the books that were marketed to boys (many a publishing house had a complete Boys' List, something that in our more enlightened time is unthinkable), you will find plenty of tales that appeal to the heart by calling it to acknowledge, in gratitude and wonder, what we have been given by the fathers of our nation. One anthology includes a story about a new boy in the countryside who promptly gets into a fight with one of the locals at a fishing hole. When they dust themselves off and start talking, the local boy invites the newcomer home, where Grandma is bound to have something good to eat. There he plies Grandma for a story about the man who first cleared out that land, Daniel Boone.

The old lady, sitting on the porch, tilts her head back and tells the tale of the Battle of Boonesborough. Now it is clear that the boys have heard of the battle before—and that only whets their appetite. She tells of how the Indians had, during the siege of the palisaded village, kidnapped three of the young women. Boone and several men then had to sneak into the Indian camp, at imminent risk of their lives, to slay their captors and set them free:

> "At last Boone gave a signal. The four men fired and rushed forward instantly. The remainder of the party bounded down the hill, yelling as loudly as they could. The savages nearest the girls, who were huddled together 'tattered, torn and despairing' at the foot of the tree, were killed at first fire. The others were for a brief but sufficient instant paralyzed by surprise. All but one. He leaped across the fire, his tomahawk upraised over the head of Jemima Boone. But before it could descend, its wielder collapsed, a knife in his throat.
>
> "Mr. Burnett was always very skillful at throwing a knife," stated the old lady.*

The new boy cries out that this is the most wonderful thing he has ever heard. But more wonders are in store for him yet, for the fourth girl saved in

---

* "Daniel Boone's Rifle" from *The Young Folks' Shelf of Books* (New York: P. F. Collier and Sons, 1949).

that raid was to be the wife of said Mr. Burnett, and is in fact the old woman herself. Then Grandma, having had enough of the storytelling, dismisses the boys, but not before showing them the Captain's rifle, and letting them take it out to shoot with. The boys, of course, will be friends, bound together not only by the fight, but by a shared honor for the great man. Their friendship, in part, will be knit by the imaginative embrace of the past.

The past is dangerous, not least because it cannot go away. It is simply *there*, never to change, and in its constancy it reflects the eternity of God. It presents to the young mind a vast field of fascination, of war and peace, loyalty and treason, invention and folly, bitter twists of fate and sweet poetic justice. When that past is the past of one's people or country or church, then the danger is terrible indeed, because then the past makes claims upon our honor and allegiance. Then it knocks at the door, saying softly, "I am still here." And then our plans for social control—for inducing the kind of amnesia that has people always hankering after what is supposed to be new, without asking inconvenient questions about where the desirable thing has come from and where it will take us—must fail. For a man with a past may be free; but a man without a past, never.

That is why, in George Orwell's *1984*, the workers in Big Brother's Ministry of Truth send photographs and articles and other bits of evidence of a genuine past down the "Memory Hole," to be shredded into oblivion. It is also why J. R. R. Tolkien provides his worthy hobbits with a veritable chronicle of great deeds, glorious and disastrous, stretching all the way back to the dawn of the world. It is one of the delights of the good in his works, never the evil, to enjoy a jug of beer, a good smoke, and a story of the old days, when Feanor forged the rings of power.

For to honor the past is to dwell richly in time, since you assume that those who come after you will, if you are worthy of it, honor you in turn. In one of the quiet moments of Tolkien's *The Two Towers*, Sam Gamgee encourages his friend and master Frodo, reminding him that the troubles they are suffering through, even the dreariness and loneliness of their journey, might well also have been part of what actually happened between the verses of the stories they grew up hearing. In the noblest of stories, the ones that really mattered,

Folk seem to have been just landed in them, usually—their paths were laid that way, as you put it. But I expect they had lots of chances, like us, of turning back, only they didn't. And if they had, we shouldn't know, because they'd have been forgotten. We hear about those as just went on—and not all to a good end, mind you; at least not to what folk inside a story and not outside it call a good end. . . . But those aren't always the best tales to hear, though they may be the best tales to get landed in! I wonder what sort of a tale we've fallen into?

Sam's heart is formed by those old stories, and that gives him the capacity to see himself, now, as taking part in a chapter of the saga of Middle Earth, so that one day hobbits may put their feet up by the fireside and tell the story of Sam and Frodo, and their fight against the Dark Lord.

It is perfectly natural in man to do this. Sir Walter Scott opens his novel *Old Mortality* with an account of a wizened wanderer, an old Scottish Calvinist, who spends the last years of his life journeying from cemetery to cemetery, brushing the dirt and mold from the headstones of his comrades in the lost fight for Scottish independence. Though the man is not in his right mind, and though the cause itself was by no means wholly good, Scott holds the example up to us as something to honor. It is what he himself did as a writer, returning again and again to the stories of his people.

The Muses are daughters of Zeus and the goddess of Memory. The epic tale of Gilgamesh, the hero-king of Babylon, is engraved in stone on the walls of his city, Uruk, where all may read it. Herodotus, that father of historians, begins his great work with words that take for granted that it is good to remember:

> These are the researches of Herodotus of Halicarnassus, which he publishes, in the hope of thereby preserving from decay the remembrance of what men have done, and of preserving the great and wonderful actions of the Greeks and the Barbarians from losing their due meed of glory.

"Let no one sing bad songs about our prowess!" cries Roland to his men in the *Chanson de Roland*, as they fight a hopeless battle against a far larger Saracen army that has taken them by surprise in the narrow ravines of Roncesvalles. "I in my turn, after carefully going over the whole story from the beginning," writes Luke the evangelist, "have decided to write an ordered account for you, Theophilus, so that your Excellency may learn how well founded the teaching is that you have believed." "Do this in remembrance of me," says Jesus.

A child in republican Rome grew up under the eyes of his household gods, the waxen figurines of his forefathers, looking down upon him from the hearth. They and their example instructed him in what it meant to belong to that family, as the legends of the early days of Rome instructed him in his duty to his country. Those duties were presented to him dramatically, with a bodily immediacy that grasped him from beyond the centuries. So he would hear of how one lone soldier named Horatius stood upon the bridge against the advancing Volscians, ordering his men to burn and topple the supports behind him, lest the enemy cross into Rome. Or how, when the Gauls first burst through the walls of Rome, they found the city nearly empty—for the common people and the women and children had all retreated to the citadel atop the Capitoline hill. But here and there, in their houses, were seated the august old senators in their togas, impassive, contemptuous of the Gauls, quietly awaiting death.

Those were pagans, but the ancient Christians had their own stories. They remembered Lawrence the deacon, condemned to die by being roasted on a gridiron. "Turn me over again," said Lawrence as he lay dying, "I am not done on the other side." Or they remembered Polycarp, the aged disciple of the apostle John, condemned to die by fire, calmly awaiting the flames, singing praise to God, and blessing Him, "because Thou hast seen fit to bestow upon me this day and this hour, that I may share, among the martyrs, the cup of Thy Anointed and rise to eternal life both in soul and in body."* Even in our flights of fiction we want to create rich histories, worlds of imagination within worlds of imagination. When Tirian, the last King of Narnia, finally enters Aslan's Country, he sees that immortality includes the past, never lost. For he is led, ever "further up and further in," deeper into what was and is and is to come, till he sees in an orchard two thrones, and in those two thrones a King and Queen so great and beautiful that everyone bowed down before them. And well they might, for these two were King Frank and Queen Helen from whom all the most ancient Kings of Narnia and Archenland are descended. And Tirian felt as you would feel if you were brought before Adam and Eve in all their glory.

---

* "The Martyrdom of Saint Polycarp," from *The Diduche*, trans. James A. Kleist, SJ, (New York: The Newman Press, 1948).

Or as Dante felt, when his sight is suddenly restored in Paradise and he sees a light before him, a soul whom his holy guide Beatrice identifies:

"He dwells within that radiance," she replied,
"and looks on his Creator lovingly,
who was the first soul whom the First Power made."
And as the crowning branches of a tree
bow in the passing wind, and then arise
by their own power that lifts them naturally,
So while she spoke to me I dropped my eyes
in wonder.

It is all a part of our duty to obey the commandment, "Honor thy father and they mother." That does not mean, necessarily, to whitewash thy father and thy mother. It might surprise us to see how honest the old textbooks were in treating of the faults of our ancestors. So *The Making of Our Country* by John C. Winston (1921) delivers this rousing account of a confrontation in Congress just before the Civil War:

In 1856 Charles Sumner, a radical free soil senator from Massachusetts, made a speech on "The Crime against Kansas" in which he attacked the South in the most abusive and insulting language. The southern members were wild with fury. Two days later Preston S. Brooks, a representative from South Carolina, assaulted Sumner with a cane as he sat at his desk in the Senate chamber and beat him into insensibility. The people of the South declared that Brooks had given Sumner only what he deserved. To the antislavery men of the North the assault upon Sumner seemed an act of the basest cowardice.

But the same text honors the courage of the men who fought for the Confederacy. Consider this description of one memorable fight in the battle that saw the Confederacy's last hopes for victory dwindle away:

Lee had failed in his attacks on both wings of Meade's army. On July 3d he tried to break its center on Cemetery Ridge. About one o'clock in the afternoon a hundred Confederate guns opened fire upon the center of the Union line. The Federal guns replied, and for two hours the earth trembled under a terrific artillery duel. Then fifteen thousand men of the South, led by Pickett with his division of Virginians, charged the Union center. There was no more heroic feat of arms during the whole war. With undaunted courage Pickett's men came on in the face of a withering fire, and a handful of them under Armistead surged over the stone wall which marked the Union line. But they were too few to hold what they had won and were soon beaten back with awful slaughter. The cause of secession here reached its high water mark and began to recede.

This book, fittingly enough, has a picture by Millais of two boys in Renaissance wear, listening—one of them has his chin in both palms—to a bearded and barefoot Scotsman telling a story of the land beyond the seas. The picture is entitled *The Boyhood of Raleigh.* The idea is impossible to miss. Just as the lad Raleigh was fired to adventure by the stories of old, so the young reader of this textbook—which was written *for the sixth grade!*—will be fired by the stories of his country.

And that is the last thing we want. The Canadian travel writer, naturalist, and novelist Farley Mowat was (and still is) an atheist with little good to say about the Western world. But he owed his independence to a man of prodigious imagination and contempt for the new-fashioned stupidities of his day: his duck-shooting, boat-sailing, librarian father. *My Father's Son* is Mowat's tribute to that man. And so long as people have such a figure towering in the vistas of their imaginations, they will prove difficult to manipulate. In Wendell Berry's *Jayber Crow*, the impudent Troy Chatham looks with contempt upon the old-fashioned and artful ways of his farmer father-in-law. Troy's a man for machines, and up-to-date thinking, and scientific methods, and debt, and a loveless marriage, and bankruptcy.

The task, then, for us who wish to destroy the imagination seems clear enough. We should kill the father and the mother. We have not yet been able to kill the mother, but we have done almost as well, by removing her from the imaginative lives of her children, whom she sees far less of than her mother saw of her, and by rendering her simultaneously needy (she is a prodigious relier upon mass-fed government programs) and free of the burdensome leadership of men. We have succeeded much better at killing the father. In most of our large cities, it's rare to find a child living with his father; and our mass-entertainment derides fathers as unnecessary, boorish, and dull. This killing of the father shuts the child off from a world of significance. "My old man used to say," begins many a man's reminiscence, long after the father has returned to the dust. We are raising the first children in the history of the world who will, by the millions, not know what that sentence means.

"*You* are the cursed polluter of this land!" cries the blind prophet Tiresias to the even blinder Oedipus, king of Thebes. He will learn, as Sophocles' play draws to its terrible climax, that his father was not Polybus of Corinth, the city he fled so as not to fulfill the oracle which told him that he would kill his father and marry his mother. No, his true father was Laius of Thebes, whom he slew unwittingly, when the king and his men assaulted him in the highway. When Sophocles wrote *Oedipus Tyrannos*, it seemed to some in Athens that they had, in their radical democratic reforms, also killed their fathers. The danger, as Sophocles saw it, struck to the heart of the social order. To ignore tradition—to despise the past, to "kill the father"—is to set oneself above those laws that have no past, because they apply to all men, everywhere, at all times. So says the Chorus:

> I only ask to live, with pure faith keeping
> In word and deed that Law which leaps the sky,
> Made of no mortal mould, undimmed, unsleeping,
> Whose living godhead does not age or die.

We should prefer instead of Sophocles the spawner of modern public education, John Dewey:

> Education has accordingly not only to safeguard an individual against the besetting erroneous tendencies of his own mind—its rashness, presumption, and preference of what chimes with self-interest to objective evidence—but also to undermine and destroy the accumulated and self-perpetuating prejudices of long ages.*

It is to Dewey's credit that he saw that you cannot destroy those old prejudices while continuing to expose pupils to the literature of the classical past. Oedipus killed Laius, but he did not know it. Dewey killed Sophocles, and he did know.

---

* John Dewey, *How We Think* (New York: D. C. Heath & Co., 1910).

What we want are not exactly traitors. A courageous traitor we may loathe and yet respect. We want instead citizens that are not really citizens, whose rejection of their country is too ordinary, lackluster, and thoughtless to rise to the level of treachery. Whatever region of the heart beats warm with piety, we want to still it. And this we can do by spreading abroad three untruths. *The patriot is narrow-minded because he is attached to a single place. The patriot is narrow-minded because he is bound to the past. The patriot is dangerous because he cannot understand people who fight for countries besides his own.* If we can cause children to accept these untruths, we will not only have dulled their imaginations. We will have made them morally obtuse, to boot; and that is no small achievement.

The Piety of Place

Children are enthralled both by what is small and near, and what is far, far away; it is that great jumble of highways and office buildings in between that loses their interest. And this is entirely natural.

In *The Back of the North Wind*, George MacDonald turns an ordinary hayloft into a scene of wonders. It's the place where his hero, a little boy named Diamond, goes to sleep every night, winding his way through a maze of haystacks before finally burrowing into his small bed, huddling under the blankets. Diamond's family are poor, but the boy could wish for no better room than this place in the stable, with the horse sleeping quietly below, or munching his hay, and the cold north wind whistling mysteriously outside. Even the chink in the thin wooden boards behind his head looms important in his nights, because through it the wind first comes, calling to him to join her. That he will do, and she will bless his adventures with his father, a cabman in the dingy streets of London, and will take him far away too, to the land of happiness beyond the North.

The Welsh novelist Richard Llewellyn, in *How Green Was My Valley*, recalls what to anyone else might have been only a poor patch of the Welsh uplands, scarred by coal mines, whose people were hardworking but powerless, devout but ignorant. But it was in that place and there alone that he learned of eternal and universal things. So, a grown man now, he thinks of his beloved father, and of the simple pieties that raised simple men not only to delight in a home and a hot meal and the love of a good wife, but to praise God too and to sing for their country, whether it deserved their full devotion or not:

> Did my father die under the coal? But, God in heaven, he is down there now, dancing in the street with Davy's red jersey over his coat, and coming, in a moment, to smoke his pipe in the front room and pat my mother's hand, and look, and O, the heat of his pride, at the picture of a Queen, given by the hand of a Queen, in the Palace of a Queen, to his eldest son, whose baton lifted voices in music fit for a Queen to hear.

Or we can turn to the poet William Butler Yeats, for whom the mountains and lakes of Ireland were ever a source of poetic inspiration, as if he could only feel again the spirit of his fathers by returning to the place where he was a boy. Yeats was no man to shun the heat of politics. But when he sought the balm for his mind, he returned to the holy places he loved, places on no tourist brochure. He loved them for their own sake, small, local, Irish, and beautiful. His love for them is one with his love for oppressed Ireland; they were the nurses of that love. In the following poem he writes at the time of Queen Victoria's death, on his hopes for freedom at last for his country, but also, and more important, on his love for one place far from the bustle and the news:

> "In the Seven Woods"
>
> I have heard the pigeons in the Seven Woods
> Make their faint thunder, and the garden bees
> Hum in the lime-tree flowers; and put away
> The unavailing outcries and the old bitterness
> That empty the heart. I have forgot awhile
> Tara uprooted, and new commonness
> Upon the throne and crying about the streets
> And hanging its paper flowers from post to post,
> Because it is alone of all things happy.
> I am contented, for I know that Quiet
> Wanders laughing and eating her wild heart
> Among pigeons and bees, while that Great Archer,

Who but awaits His hour to shoot, still hangs
A cloudy quiver over Pairc-na-lee.

We see, then, that this devotion to place is heady alcohol for the young
mind. It is as potent a liquor as strong family love, with which it is closely
bound. Consider what it has done in the arts alone. Shakespeare, in his fanciful *A Midsummer Night's Dream*, sends two pairs of crossed lovers out into
the woods beyond Athens, and promptly throngs the woods with an English sprite named Robin Goodfellow and a ragtag company of craftsman,
straight out of an English country town, who have come out there to practice an English-style skit on Pyramus and Thisbe, with all the silly devices
and bumpy meter of a local morality play put on by your neighbors Harry
and Ned. Shakespeare is smiling there, but we can hear the true strains of
patriotism in John of Gaunt's famous speech in *Richard II*, as he lies dying,
worrying that the land he loves will fall prey to faction and violence:

This royal throne of kings, this scept'red isle,
This earth of majesty, this seat of Mars,
This other Eden, demi-paradise,
This fortress built by Nature for herself
Against infection and the hand of war,
This happy breed of men, this little world,
This precious stone set in the silver sea
Which serves it in the office of a wall,
Or as a moat defensive to a house,
Against the envy of less happier lands,
This blessed plot, this earth, this realm, this England.

In Flannery O'Connor's short story "A Good Man Is Hard to Find,"
the grandmother tries to engage her grandchildren's imagination as they
travel through the hills of northern Georgia. Because she loves her homeland, with a crotchety pride but also a certain innocence, she can take real
pleasure from the things she sees out of the window, things that could
never make it to a flashy tourist brochure:

She pointed out interesting details of the scenery: Stone Mountain;
the blue granite that in some places came up to both sides of the

highway; the brilliant red clay banks slightly streaked with purple; and the various crops that made rows of green lace-work on the ground. The trees were full of silver-white sunlight and the meanest of them sparkled.

But the children can't be bothered. They have been trained up on the flashy, the immediate sensation. They have no love for their land, and no patience even to behold its beauty:

The children were reading comic magazines and their mother had gone back to sleep.

"Let's go through Georgia fast so we won't have to look at it much," John Wesley said.

"If I were a little boy," said the grandmother, "I wouldn't talk about my native state that way. Tennessee has the mountains and Georgia has the hills."

"Tennessee is just a hillbilly dumping ground," John Wesley said, "and Georgia is a lousy state too."

"You said it," June Star said.

We see here the products of easy cynicism. Learn to despise the place where you were born, its old customs, its glories and its shame. Then stick your head in a comic book. That done, you will be triple-armored against the threat of a real thought, or the call of the transcendent. Some people have no worlds for God to pierce through.

When the playwright Sophocles was a man of ninety, soon to die, he looked back upon his beloved city of Athens and the errors that had led her into the long and disastrous war against Sparta. Before he left his country-men forever, Sophocles wanted to give them his last word on the mystery of man's suffering—for he knew that his fellow Athenians had been humiliated, and that they were struggling to find a way to explain their fate. He did not outline a political program. He did not say, "Despise your country." He did not encourage them to "think globally," if that is even possible. He did not shrug his shoulders and ask what difference the loss of civic liberty meant, anyway. Rather he returned their attention to the small, and old, and venerable; of things that ideology cannot touch. In his imagination, in his final play *Oedipus at Colonus*, produced on stage by his grandson after his death, Sophocles described, with all the gentle lyricism of an old and wise poet, the little rural village of Colonus, just outside the city, where he was once a boy. So the chorus of Colonians, old men too, welcome the aged and suffering Oedipus, who is seeking a place where he can die at peace:

> Here in our white Colonus, stranger guest,
> Of all earth's lovely lands the loveliest,
> Fine horses breed, and leaf-enfolded vales
> Are thronged with sweetly-singing nightingales,
> Screened in deep arbours, ivy, dark as wine,
> And tangled bowers of berry-clustered vine;
> To whose dark avenues and windless courts
> The Grape-god with his nursing-nymphs resorts.

The thought of that small village somehow, because it was so close to Sophocles' heart, more powerfully struck him with the mystery of being than did all the philosophers and political power brokers among whom he lived all his life. Piety nurses the imagination, because it places us in both greatness and smallness, in the stillness of a single moment, and in the long sweep of the generations. Ideology digs many graves, but tends not a single stone.

We can feel the same pull at the heart even in the best fantasy literature written for young people. Tolkien begins his sagas of Middle Earth not by describing some vast geopolitical organization, but by ushering us into a snug, well-stocked hobbit hole, in a lovely and rather provincial place called The Shire. The hardy hobbits who dwell in the Shire don't puzzle their heads too much about great doings far away. They like gardening, eating hearty breakfasts, enjoying a good harvest of barley for beer, celebrating their holidays with raucous dancing and fireworks, and telling stories of the notable hobbits of old. So powerful a hold does the Shire take upon the imagination, that Tolkien provides us with maps to the place because naturally we'll want to know who lives where. Somehow that Shire becomes a part of our world, too, as if we ourselves grew up there, or wished we had.

The trouble with this kind of piety is that it produces real patriots. Chesterton once wrote, only partly in jest, that if local patriotism and even local wars were said to have paralyzed civilization in medieval and Renaissance Italy, "we must at least admit that these warring towns turned out a number of paralytics who go by the names of Dante and Michael Angelo, Ariosto and Titian, Leonardo and Columbus, not to mention Catherine of Siena and [Francis of Assisi]."* But we want no patriots. Therefore we want no lovers of their own place. The very purpose of what is miscalled multiculturalism is to destroy culture, by teaching students to dismiss their own and to patronize the rest. Hence the antidote to love of *this* place is not only a hatred of this place, but a phony engagement with *any other* place. Multiculturalism in this sense is like going a-whoring. Pretending to love every woman you meet, you love none at all. Nor do you genuinely get to know any of them, since it never occurs to you that there are any depths to learn to appreciate. If there's nothing to claim your devotion in north Georgia, what should there be to do so in South Wales? We will raise, at best, the mildly interested tourist, who collapses everything he sees into the two dimensions of a social fad. They will rack up places they've seen just as callous safari hunters rack up skins and horns, only without the danger that might awaken the heart. Or they will stay home, since one place will be as dull as the next.

Let me give an example of really effective destruction of the capacity for wonder at a place, near or far. Here, from an old history textbook— G. W. Botsford's *A History of Greece*, is a description of the special atmosphere of the games of ancient Greece:

> Modern athletic competitions bring home to us in some measure the intense energy of the contestants, the glory of victory, and the irresistible waves of enthusiasm in the audience at Olympia. But we miss the beautiful bare forms of the Greek athletes, the artistic and religious setting of the games—the splendid temple and the multitude of statues; we miss, too, the Greek sky, the national interest, the historic associations, and the grand triumphal music of the Pindaric ode which greeted the victor on his stately entrance into his native city.

Compare that now with this description of the effect of Greek geography upon the ancient culture:

---

* G. K. Chesterton, *St. Francis of Assisi* (New York: Doubleday, 1957).

Geography played an important role in the evolution of Greek history. Compared to the landmasses of Mesopotamia and Egypt, Greece occupied a small area, a mountainous peninsula that encompassed only 45,000 square miles of territory, about the size of the state of Louisiana. The mountains and the sea played especially significant roles in the development of Greek history. Much of Greece consists of small plains and river valleys surrounded by mountain ranges 8,000 to 10,000 feet high. The mountainous terrain had the effect of isolating Greeks from one another. Consequently, Greek communities tended to follow their own separate paths and develop their own way of life. Over a period of time, these communities became attached to their independence and were only too willing to fight one another to gain advantage.*

You will note in this passage an utter numbness to the sense of place; the beauty of Greece, which inspired the poets and sculptors and architects, is reduced to quantities, and those are only interesting insofar as they influence the politics of the land. As for the politics, that too is given a smug chiding. We are told, no doubt, that the independent Greek communities surely did flourish in "unique cultural expressions," whatever that vague phrase is supposed to mean, but alas, they were not so wise as we are, because it would all be devastated by their foolish penchant for fighting. The discussion does not improve as the chapter continues. Of Greek sports, the author says next to nothing, but he does manage to focus on how badly women were treated, and how easy it was for a homosexual to find objects of his desire. All things must be seen in the context of our own political concerns.

In such texts it doesn't matter, for instance, that George Washington and John Adams and the rest of the founding fathers bequeathed to the world a new way of life—in Lincoln's ringing words at Gettysburg, "government of the people, by the people, for the people." Nor that they did so in the teeth of opposition from their foreign overlords and loyalists at home. Washington's indomitable courage we overlook, but we do note that he was only a fair tactician, and that he held slaves. Meanwhile, we make much of Abigail Adams, not because she exerted any great influence upon the events of the day, but because she makes a convenient mascot for our

---

* Jackson Spielvogel, *Western Civilization* (Belmont, CA: Thompson Wadsworth, 2006).

contemporary team. Such passages do not return us to hallowed places. They are intended to *expose* those places—such places as cannot be ignored entirely.

Living in the Past

Now there are those who believe that all this cherishing of the noble past is helpful in squelching the imagination, because the past is always the same, whereas the imagination reaches out to the New and Improved. Do not believe it.

The past is like a secret room in an old house, filled with dust and cobwebs, but also rays of light cast upon ancient armor, and odd tools whose use we have forgotten, and books recalling the words and deeds of men and women who once walked the earth, and whose bones now rest in their graves. It is a chamber that strikes one with the sense of holiness, because we come into the presence of those who once were as we are, and who now are as we will be.

I am looking at a coin. It isn't very old, as such things go: a little silver dime dated 1916. It is creamy white, and rings like a bell when you spin it on a table. On the front of the coin is a bust of Miss Liberty, with a winged helmet. She is delicately beautiful, but her lips are parted as if she were determined to speak. The wings, we're told, represent Freedom of Thought, something that might have seemed in peril in 1916, when the First World War was turning Europe into a vast cemetery, and the new republic in Russia was teetering on the brink of communism. On the back of the coin we see the Roman *fasces*, a bundle of rods tied up in cords; behind the bundle is an ax. The Fascists in Italy had not yet given the old Roman symbol of strength-in-unity an evil name. Near the rim on the reverse, under the fasces, stands a small "D," denoting that the dime was minted in Denver.

There's a lot to read in a coin like that. It was, for one, a serious coin; not an advertisement for tourism. It featured no portrait of any particular person. In fact, no American coin had done so, until the Lincoln penny debuted in 1909, the centennial of the president's birth. Liberty, apparently, was more important than personality. The people who minted and who used the coin were expected to know a little bit about history in their own right—otherwise the fasces would have made no sense. Even their nickname for it, the "Mercury Dime," is at least a classical mistake. In some way that small coin speaks eloquently about the world of a people that we Americans no longer are. And because they were Americans, but they were not like ourselves, they appeal to the imagination. They say, "Countryman, look again at the things we saw! Listen to what we have to say."

In the *Aeneid*, Virgil takes his readers to the wooded hills that, centuries later, would become the site of Rome. It is not an exercise in sentimentality. He begs them to imagine not simply what that place was like before all the temples and palaces, the narrow streets with their tenements, and the pillared walkways of the Forum. He wishes also to revive in them a sense of the old piety that united the Romans and made them great. So the progenitor of the Romans, Aeneas, walks with the Arcadian king Evander to a mysterious grove, a place full of portents:

> "Some god," he said, "it is not sure what god,
> Lives in this grove, this hilltop thick with leaves.
> Arcadians think they've seen great Jove himself
> Sometimes with his right hand shaking the aegis
> To darken sky and make the storm clouds rise
> Towering in turmoil."

We see in Evander's description of the hills a kind of mysterious connection from one generation to the next, and a reverence that rings true. His name means simply "good man," and if we look at what he says and does, his goodness consists largely in his loyalty. He honors Aeneas because he remembers that his father once honored Aeneas's father. He honors Hercules, because he remembers that the demigod once dwelt on a nearby hillside and cleansed it of the thieving monster, Cacus. He honors the gods, because he has received from them a land of peace wherein to dwell. Virgil suggests that Evander's loyalty is related to the simplicity of his life, which is not the same thing as the relative poverty of his village of huts, Pallanteum. Evander is not too high and mighty to remember.

Livy had a similar object in mind when he wrote his phenomenal *History of Rome*. It was not to be a bare chronicle, but an exercise in the moral imagination. For now, he says, we Romans have grown vicious along with our luxuries. We have been conquered by those we have conquered, forgetting our virtues but adopting foreign vices, until we have become so sick that we cannot even endure the cure for our diseases. Nevertheless, says Livy, it is good to look back upon the deeds of our forefathers, deriving from our memorial the comfort that such stories cannot fail to bring, and perhaps the strength to revive their virtues in a better day to come.

And Livy tells his stories with terrific panache. Take for instance the meeting of the wily middle-aged general Hannibal, nemesis of Rome, with the young Scipio, on the plains of Zama in North Africa, at the end of the devastating Second Punic War.

Now Hannibal was perhaps the greatest military tactician who ever lived. His frontal retreat at Cannae, followed by flanking actions that shut the Romans in a ring of death, is still textbook strategy at military schools. Once, at Lake Trasumenus, he lured his Roman pursuers into a narrow defile between a mountain ridge and a lake, then turned on them from the front, while reserves placed in ambush on the ridge cut off their retreat from the rear. Thirty thousand Roman soldiers fell on that day—half the number of Americans who fell in the entire Vietnam war. Another time, when Hannibal was being harried by the armies of Quintus Fabius Maximus, who earned the nickname "Cunctator" or "The Delayer" by his shrewd refusal to engage Hannibal in a pitched battle (which he knew the Romans would lose), he waited till the dead of night and tied flaming torches to the tails of cows in his cattle train, driving them in a panic across the fields. The Romans thought that Hannibal was breaking camp, so they pursued the lights, while Hannibal and his army slipped away in another direction.

It is this Hannibal, then, who steps forward at Zama to persuade Scipio to accept the terms of a cease fire. Hannibal does not apologize for his lifelong hatred of Rome. He admits that ever since he was a child he had been Rome's enemy, and he reminds Scipio, as if in passing, of how close he came to breaching the walls of the city. "What I was at Lake Trasumenus, and at Cannae, you are today," he says, adopting the strategy now of suggesting that there is no certainty in human affairs, and that the man on the top of fortune's wheel must expect decline. "Better and safer is a certain peace than a hoped-for victory," says Hannibal, "for the first is in your own hands, but the second in the hands of the gods," and the gods, as we know, are not to be trusted. "We will not refuse you—indeed we will concede as yours everything for which you went to war: Sicily, Sardinia, Spain, and all the islands in the sea between Africa and Italy," and as for the Carthagin-

ians, they, so long as the gods are pleased to allow it, will be shut within the
boundaries of their empire on the African mainland. The finishing touch is
a master stroke. To understand it, we must understand human dedication
far beyond the personal desire for gain. We must understand, even in an
enemy, that there are things worth fighting for, even dying for. Any patriot
can understand a Hannibal; even Livy, who portrays the man, unjustly, as
cruel and bloodthirsty, cannot help but show us now a man worthy to be
the enemy of Rome. "I am Hannibal who seeks peace, I who would never
seek it unless I believed it to be of profit, and for that profit I will keep the
peace I seek. As through me came the war at first, wherein I shone until
the gods began to envy me, so be not displeased now if through me comes
peace" (translations mine).

We can see in this tense moment the pride of the man, indomitable, as
he yet bows to necessity and attempts to negotiate, for the sake of the country he undoubtedly loves, a peace that scalds him in every cell of his being.
But Scipio makes short work of the appeal. He does what our young people
must never do: he remembers. He recalls how Carthage dealt treacherously
with Regulus in the First Punic War. He recalls that Carthage, as Hannibal himself has just admitted, began the Second War by attacking Roman
allies in Sicily and Spain. He does not gloat; he is in Livy's account as he
was in life, a philosophical young man. "As for what pertains to me," he
says, "I am mindful of the weakness of man and I respect the power of fortune, and I know that all that we do is subject to a thousand chances." But
he knows well that had he not taken his fleets to Carthage, Hannibal would
never have left Italy on his own. Therefore he feels no shame in proceeding
to war. "Prepare for battle," he says, "for you never have been able to suffer
peace" (translation mine).

What was the use of hearing such stories? Hannibal was possibly not
quite so shrewd as Livy portrays him—though we have no evidence to
cause us to doubt it. Scipio was possibly not quite so noble, though we have
plenty of evidence to support his temperance and humanity, some of it
coming grudgingly from his enemies in Rome. But the lad who heard these
stories could bring such beings, larger than life, into his own life. He could
know what the implacable and largehearted enemy looked like; he could
recognize too the young, severe patriot.

It is no good argument to say that we do not meet such people every
day, in that shadow world which shallow thinkers call "real life." Philip

Sidney for one fully admits as much in *Apology for Poetry*, and says that that is why poetry is superior to a bare chronicle of events as they happened. For the poet wishes not simply to create an Aeneas or a Cyrus the Great on the pages of his work, but also in the expanding heart and mind of his young reader:

> Nature never set forth the earth in so rich tapestry as divers poets have done, neither with so pleasant rivers, fruitful trees, sweet smelling flowers, nor whatsoever else may make the too much loved earth more lovely. Her world is brazen, the poets only deliver a golden.
>
> But ... go to man ... and know whether she have brought forth so true a lover as Theagenes, so constant a friend as Pylades, so valiant a man as Orlando, so right a prince as Xenophon's Cyrus, so excellent a man every way as Virgil's Aeneas. . . . Which delivering forth [of the poet's ideal] so far substantially worketh, not only to make a Cyrus, which had been but a particular excellency, as nature might have done, but to bestow a Cyrus upon the world, to make many Cyruses, if they will learn aright why and how that maker made him.

The imagination seeks out the ideal, and beholds its beauty. In doing so it penetrates farther to the truth than does the sloth of cynicism. Anyone may see a wart or a mole; faults abound in every man; the grime of life tarnishes us all. But the imagination forgives the blemish and attempts to see beneath the grime. When we apply its wisdom to our country, whatever that country may be, can we grow to love her enough to wish to correct her, as Virgil and Livy wished to correct their Rome, and as Sidney wished to correct his England.

But if we want to ensure that our young people grow up with the cramped imagination of the cynic, we should, if we cannot ignore the past completely, at least magnify the tarnish on those who came before us. We should emulate God's creation of man in His image and likeness, but in reverse, as through the wrong end of a telescope. We should make everything small—like ourselves. That will leave us with quite a sense of moral and intellectual superiority. And that's more deadly to the imagination than were the spears of Hannibal's soldiers to the Romans at Cannae, centuries ago.

Method 6

Cut All Heroes Down to Size

or

Pottering with the Puny

It is the cold and quiet time before the dawn. An old king enfeebled with age and sorrow approaches the tent of his most fearsome enemy. For ten years he has watched the best men of his city, including many of his fifty sons, fighting to keep the invaders outside the walls. His men have succeeded, so far. But a few days ago their best hope, his most beloved son, died in single combat against the mightiest of the enemy soldiers. That enemy is a young man still, with the virtues and the failings of a young man: at once generous and hot-tempered, arrogant, impatient of advice, yet capable of deep affection. To him, one Achilles, the king goes alone, to beg on his knees for the body of his slain son Hector.

When Achilles sees him in the tent, such is his age and his suffering, and his courage that he appears to him, of all things, like a god. Achilles is stunned into silence. Then the king makes his appeal. He reminds Achilles of the father that he loves, whom he has left behind, far away in Greece, and whom he may never see again. The king comes bringing splendid gifts. He acknowledges Achilles to be the greatest of his city's enemies. The good king recalls the gods, and asks him to honor them, for suffering comes to all mortal men, especially to those who forget they are mortal:

> I have gone through what no other mortal on earth has gone through;
> I put my lips to the hands of the man who has killed my children.

And what does Achilles do? He is the man who felt dishonored by his fellow Greeks and their captain Agamemnon, and retired from the battle, sullen and cold. When the Greeks were put to rout by Hector, and were all but resigning to return to their ships and leave again for their homeland, Agamemnon sent to Achilles three men whose presence would most honor him: Odysseus, the army's shrewdest advisor; Ajax, second only to Achilles in strength; and Phoenix, Achilles' old servant, the man who nursed him when he was a toddler. They could not move him. Not even when his best friend, Patroclus, begged him to rejoin the battle would he budge—but he did grant Patroclus his armor to terrify the enemy. Patroclus did more than terrify them. He fought and slew Trojans left and right, until he came face to face with Hector, greatest of the Trojans. Hector killed him and took Achilles' armor. When on the next day Hector met Achilles alone on the plain outside the city, he tried to bargain for mercy for whoever would be vanquished—simply, the return of the loser's body to his friends. But the heroic Achilles will not be moved. Not even when Hector lies bleeding out his life before him, pierced with a spear through the neck, will Achilles give in. Says the iron-hearted man:

> No more entreating of me, you dog, by knees or parents.
> I wish only that my spirit and fury would drive me
> to hack your meat away and eat it raw for the things that
> you have done to me. So there is no one who can hold the dogs off
> from your head, not if they bring here and set before me ten times
> and twenty times the ransom, and promise more in addition,
> not if Priam son of Dardanus should offer to weigh out
> your bulk in gold.

An ordinary man would have yielded to Hector before the battle; but then, an ordinary man would have been roused by only ordinary affections. An ordinary man would yield to Hector now, accepting the ransom, and delighting in anticipation; but then, an ordinary man craves ordinary things.

It is this Achilles, no ordinary man, to whom old Priam appeals. And the hero does something we do not expect—but then, that is the way of heroes. He is mindful of his mortality. He honors Priam. He and the old man weep the tears of the great:

He took the old man's hand and pushed him
gently away, and the two remembered, as Priam sat huddled
at the feet of Achilles and wept close for manslaughtering Hector
and Achilles wept now for his own father, now again
for Patroclus. The sound of their mourning moved in the house.

I am not claiming that Achilles is a good man. But he is a great man. Other men's passions can be measured against the good things that men daily pursue. Those of Achilles cannot, or not so easily. The hero stretches our imagination. He introduces us, for better or for worse, to possibilities we had never considered. He extends the limits of what is human.

If he does so in the service of something good and noble, we love him so much the better for it.

This time the battlefield is a beach on the Kentish shores. Invaders—we know them as Vikings—have sailed there to exact tribute, what we would call protection money, from the English farmers near the coast. Their business is simple enough. If the people pay their tribute, the Vikings will leave them alone for a while, and will sail on to the next village, and harass it instead. In other words, buying them off only defers the trouble and passes it along right now to the countrymen nearby. An old and ready warrior named Byrhtnoth, the head of a small militia of mostly inexperienced men of the land, awaits the marauders. The Vikings are separated from Byrhtnoth by a narrow spit of sand, a high-tide causeway. They cannot force their way across. Instead they challenge him to let them cross, so that battle can be waged as a fair fight in the open. Byrhtnoth's honor, thus, is at stake; nor is it clear to him that if he refuses he will not soon have to fight them on the mainland anyway. He yields the ground. The battle rages, and Byrhtnoth, the best man on the English side, goes down to his death, taking several of the enemy with him as he goes.

Is it time then for the rest to turn and run? Some do, but others remain to the terrible end, rooted in place by their love for Byrhtnoth, their loyalty, and their emulation of his heroism. One Byrhtwold rises to the occasion, uttering words that only a man whose heart beats warmly in the sight of heroism can understand:

Our minds shall be the firmer, our hearts all the keener,
our courage the more as our strength dwindles!
Here lies our lord all hewn down,
good man, on the ground. Forever may he mourn
who thinks to turn now from this battle-play.
I am full glad at heart! I shall not go from here,
but by the side of my captain,
whom I loved so well, I intend to lie.
(*The Battle of Maldon*, translation mine)

What kind of practical sense does that make? None, perhaps; but then what practical sense does it make to fall in love, or to play with a small child, or to sing, or to do anything at all that makes life more than a calculation of profit and loss?

To an inattentive onlooker, there appears to be something wrong with the old priest. His body is hobbled and bent. His fingers—or what appear to have been his fingers—seem hardly to extend, like small stubs, from his hands. Indeed he himself believed he could not celebrate the sacred Mass, because he could not with due dignity lift up the host of bread during the consecration. But the authorities in Rome had ruled otherwise, granting him a dispensation. He should have lived out his days in his native land, but he has returned to America, and the Hurons whom he loved in vain, and among whom he has spent many years giving the best he believed he had to offer—the good news of a God who loves all men without distinction, and who sacrificed his Son upon a cross to show that love—are now hacking at him here and there with their tomahawks as he is made to run the gauntlet to his death.

His name is Father Jean de Brebeuf, and he arrived in the land north of the Great Lakes years ago, bringing the gospel, with indomitable courage, and simple love. Now it does not matter whether a child who hears this story is Christian. The first danger is that of the natural virtue, embodied in a heroic man. If we thought we knew what courage was, we hear of this holy priest, and we doubt again; our minds wander as if to a far galaxy, where beings dwell who seem like us but whose thoughts are like oceans to our puddles, stars to our fireflies. He came there, and he settled among the Hurons, teaching them and baptizing them; but when the enemies of the tribe he had baptized came on the warpath, he was captured and tortured.

They burnt his fingers down to the nub; yet he never cursed them, he never denied his God. Astonished by his stoutheartedness, they did not kill him. Instead, a Dutch Calvinist—it is remarkable how heroic virtue unites men across their national or sectarian divisions—learned of his whereabouts and saved him, procuring him passage on a boat back to Europe. And there his one longing was to return, to live and die a missionary for his faith.

We want to raise children who will think the man a fool for returning. Flippancy, says C. S. Lewis in *The Screwtape Letters*, is the evil parody of mirth, caustic to the soul. But the very Indians who put Father Jean to death knew better. They whose way of life exalted courage above all knew they had never witnessed courage like his. In a sense they were far more innocent than a despiser of this story would be. They knew what they were seeing. Their imaginations seized upon this new thing in their world. Some of them ate the priest's heart afterwards, so that they too could have a share in the man's courage.

"Our arrows will fall so thick they will block the sun!" cries the arrogant Persian to his Spartan opponents on the other side of the pass. The Spartans are vastly outnumbered, but they do not flinch. "All the better," said one of them. " Then we shall fight in the shade."

"Do you have anything final to say?" asks the enemy officer, as the handsome young man, captured as a spy, is led to the noose. "Yes," he says. "I regret that I have but one life to give for my country."

The leader of the expedition, his fingers all but useless, opens his log-book for a final entry. Winds are howling outside the little tent; the temperature is forty degrees below zero; they have no more provisions; the other men in the tent are barely alive. He, Captain Scott, had made his share of mistakes. He had underestimated the cold of this inhuman land. He had ignored good advice and had relied upon ponies for much of his trek to the South Pole; but the ponies could not bear the bitter cold, and had to be shot. He had not therefore brought enough dogs, not for pulling the sleds, and not for eating, once they could pull no longer. But he was also a chivalrous man, brave, generous, and kindly. His men were loyal to him. One of them, knowing that gangrene had set in his foot, that he could never make it back to the base, and that his fellows would never leave him, left their camp alone one morning to die, giving up his life for their sake. Consider the last entry that Robert Falcon Scott, who lost his race to be the first man to reach the South Pole, then lost his life but a few miles from their home station in Antarctica, wrote. I am quoting it from a story in a set of old Childcraft books (1965), which any sensible parent would want to keep far from the eyes of an impressionable young person:

> "We shall stick it out to the end, but we are getting weaker, of course, and the end cannot be far . . . for my own sake, I do not regret this journey, which has shown that Englishmen can endure hardships, help one another, and meet death with as great a fortitude as ever in the past. . . . It seems a pity, but I do not think I can write more."

We cannot indulge a sentimental admiration of the hero if we are to keep our children banal and safe. A hero, even a fictional creation, is like a pack of dynamite, ready to blow any mountain of heaped-up conformity and dullness sky high. Even a madman, if he is brave and if he follows a noble calling, can inflame the imaginations of all around him. So the good Don Quixote, who thinks he is a knight errant doing battle against giants (really windmills), saving damsels in distress (really a statue of the Virgin Mary carried in procession), and paying court to a beautiful princess named Dulcinea (really a fat peasant woman from the next village who raises pigs), has the power to entice everyone around him to join in his game. His squire and sidekick Sancho Panza has ridden along with him for many a long mile, with so far little but bruises and bad food and broken bones for his pains. Yet when someone suggests to him that his master is mad, and that he should leave him, Sancho replies:

> His soul is as clean as a pitcher. He can do no harm to anyone, only good to everybody. There's no malice in him. A child might make him believe it's night at noonday. And for that simplicity I love him as dearly as my heart-strings, and can't take to the idea of leaving him for all his wild tricks.

Boys in particular are natural hero-worshipers. Men hardly give up the habit. You are on the shores of a broad lake rich with fish, but ruffled with sudden storms. It's a dangerous place to make a living if you're a fisherman, and rough work, too, not for the gentle of speech and soft of hand. One morning, after a miserable night catching nothing, you are putting in to shore when your younger brother comes racing up to you. "We have

seen him!" he shouts. He jabbers something about a long-awaited redeemer
of your people, who have spent many centuries now being sacked and
destroyed by Assyrians, carted into exile by Babylonians, granted home
rule as a tributary to the Persians, bullied by Greeks, and protected by the
even bigger bullies in Rome. You don't believe a word of it. All you can see
is your empty net.

Then the man himself appears on the shore. He is one of those men
whose manhood it never occurs to anyone to question. Men are drawn to
him, as to one who knows things that they cannot fathom. "Peter," he says,
addressing you by name, in a quiet but commanding tone. "Take your boat
out again, over there, and cast your net." You swear to yourself. Who is
this landsman telling me my trade? But something in you responds to the
man. You do as you are told. When you and a couple of men haul the net
back into the boat, it is so full of fish that the net nearly breaks. You come
ashore and bow your head before him. Your world has been shattered to its
foundations. Now anything is possible—and you hang back, in timidity.
"Depart from me, Lord," says Peter. "I am an evil man." "Come, follow me,"
says Jesus, "and I will make you fishers of men." Which he did, and they
changed the world.

What shall we do to ensure that the fire of heroism never kindles in
the hearts of our children? I suggest the following easy steps. First, since
the likeliest place for a hero to show forth his courage is a battlefield, cast
aspersions on the military ideal. This you can do by belittling the intelligence of the soldier, by preaching an easy and self-serving pacifism, and
by reducing the military to a career option open for everyone, regardless
of physical prowess or even sex. Second, since the hero will often do what
is foolish in the eyes of the world—sailing to Molokai to minister to lep-
ers whom all the world had shunned, or enduring the contempt of former
associates while preaching against their trade in slaves, or taking a small
contingent of half-starved men across the icy Delaware on a night-attack
against professional soldiers at Trenton—instill in your children an easy
contempt for the more difficult and fantastic virtues. Encourage the snigger rather than the cheer; the knowing smirk, rather than the flush of ado-
ration. Lead them in laughing at what you do not understand. Finally, since
the hero stretches our minds and hearts by being so strikingly *different* from
the rest of us, even superior in some way to the rest of us, teach your children to hate and suspect excellence. This you can do in two ways.

You can attack excellence itself; a risky enterprise, since if you are going to bring the heroic genius of Michelangelo down to the level of, say, special effects in video games, you actually have to show your children the work of Michelangelo. One never knows what might happen then. The opposite strategy seems surer. You call anything and everything excellent. You democratize heroism. Everybody is a hero, and simply for doing (and often not well at that) the ordinary tasks of living as a half-decent person. Does your mother fix your breakfast? She is a hero. Does your father visit you every weekend without fail? A hero. Does your teacher mark your papers faithfully when you make a mistake? Unexampled heroism, that. If everyone is a hero, then no one is a hero; and genuine heroes will go unnoticed in all the mindless self-congratulation.

Let's now look at these methods more closely, one by one.

Let Us Make Men without Chests

"Courage," said Thomas Aquinas, that most earthy and commonsensical of metaphysicians, "is the virtue that has to do with danger and death."

We want, however, to shield our children from an encounter with those, not least because death or the risk of death can suddenly lift us out of the petty concerns of the day. We might consider the time before we were, and the time after which we shall be seen no more on this earth, and then we stand as on the shores of a vast and uncharted sea, listening to the waves lap at our feet, and knowing that sooner or later we must take that voyage upon it. So the old Germanic warriors would build a boat in honor of their fallen king, load it with treasure, place his body in state aboard it, and float it off into the mists. "No man knew," says the poet of *Beowulf,* "where that cargo went."

But the very occupation of the soldier requires him to live with death, his own death, at his side, bunking down with him, in the back seat of the jeep with him, flying with him and his comrades over enemy territory. That is a plain fact, no romanticization. The life of the soldier is prone to many a vice—and many a long hour of digging holes, scrubbing decks, peeling potatoes, signing requisition forms, and marching from nowhere to nowhere. Yet even so, it is a profession worthy of honor, because in entering it the man implicitly agrees to consider that his life is not his own.

When war broke out in Europe, the devil Wormwood wrote to his uncle Screwtape to revel in his glee. "The immediate fear and suffering of the humans is a legitimate and pleasing refreshment," Screwtape admits. But "how disastrous for us," he says, "is the continual remembrance of death which war enforces." For if war is the occasion for great cruelty and hatred, at best a necessary evil, yet it calls forth acts of courage and generosity and charity, and these often at the cost of limb or life.

What we want to do, then, is to see only the misery that war brings, and never ask such obvious questions as, "What would Europe look like, had Britain surrendered to Hitler and Mussolini at once?" Or, "What would Asia look like, if the Americans had come to terms with Japan after the bombing of Pearl Harbor?" Since we no longer trouble to teach history except as fashionable glances at wise people who did the politically correct thing and wicked people who did not, we need not bother to delve farther back into time, asking what it was like for the greatly outnumbered Poles to face down the Turkish onslaught at Vienna in the seventeenth century, or for the outnumbered sailors of the Holy League to kneel on the decks of their fleet as they waited to engage their Muslim enemies off the coast at Lepanto.

We need not think of any of those things, because we "know," without any particular experience, that war is evil, and that we ourselves are morally superior beings for having discovered the fact. By all means, keep your children in that mode. The virtues that really open the heart and the moral imagination are those that you must exercise with real effort, here and now—standing up in front of this bully, perhaps, taking a blow for what is right, and dealing one or two in return. Even friendship can be forged out of enmity when opponents of genuine courage meet one another. But that will not do. Instead, we should instill in our children the sense that they are virtuous simply because they have adopted the opinion that other people—particularly, the ones who agree to go off to war—are *not* virtuous. They fight; we are wiser than they are, and favor peace. It is a virtue for which we need not sweat one drop, or scratch one finger. We practice it in a warm cocoon of safety, and are praised for it.

This dismissal of what is quintessentially courageous is, fortunately, a staple of the modern textbook. Not the textbooks of old, mind you. In those it was assumed that men and women of any political party would look with gratitude upon the heroism of the soldier. So George Botsford's old high school history of ancient Greece tells of the death of the Theban patriot and general Epaminondas, struck in the eye at the Battle of Mantinea (362 BC):

> Epaminondas repeated the tactics of Leuctra with perfect success. His flying column, now in the form of a wedge, cut through the opposing ranks and shattered the enemy's host. But the great commander in the front fell mortally wounded with a javelin. Carried to the rear, he heard the victorious shouts of the Thebans, but when told that his fellow-generals were both dead, he advised his countrymen to make peace. The surgeon then drew out the javelin point and Epaminondas died.

There are plenty of such moments in the history of the world. Take, for instance, the Battle of Marathon, in 490 BC, between the Athenians and Persian invaders. Of old, every schoolboy would learn that the Persians had counted on sheer numbers to overwhelm the Greeks. They would also learn that the Athenians were fighting for their own land and their way of life, whereas the Persians, many of them mercenaries, all of them subject to the commands of a despot, were fighting for the despot's imperial ambitions. It was, then, a moral battle, as much as it was military; so the Greeks of the time saw it. And when victory came to them, they sent a boy courier named Pheidippides to Athens, to shore up the courage of the wavering city, by proclaiming, "Nike," victory! That boy raced the twenty-six miles from Marathon to Athens, and expired upon delivering the news. Here is how the incident is conveyed in a recent textbook:

> The Athenian infantry then hurried the twenty-six miles from Marathon to Athens to guard the city against the Persian navy. (Today's marathon races commemorate the legend of a runner speeding ahead to announce the victory, and then dropping dead.)*

But what if young boys still are fascinated with violent action? One thing we can do is to short-circuit the fascination by providing it with an easy and frivolous outlet. I don't mean creative outdoor play—of the sort

---

* Lynn Hunt, et al., *The Making of the West: Peoples and Cultures, to 1740*, 2nd ed. (Boston: Bedford/St. Martin's, 2005).

that might pit one boy's speed against another's strength, or one boy's strategy against another's tenacity. I don't mean that he should learn to handle a gun, and go target shooting with his father, and eventually hunt for food in the woods. Such activities require real practical knowledge, and knowledge, as opposed to some gauzy and free-floating "creativity," is always dangerous. Besides, it will put him outdoors, in the quiet forests, or on the open plains; it will invite many hours of silence, propitious for thought; it is difficult, and will instill in him both humility and a desire to work hard that he might master the art. No, the best thing to do both to satisfy a craving for violent action and to shut down the imagination is to glut it with a lewd and bloody video game, or with the noisy and imbecilic brawling of a television "rassling" match.

Meanwhile, we should load up our lessons with heroes too pallid to idolize. We should make it abundantly clear that we choose them not for their physical courage, nor for their moral virtue, nor for their artistic or intellectual excellence, nor for some gallant sacrifice for their countrymen, but for their politics. We choose not people who make peace, but people who talk about it a lot, preferably from a position of comfort. We choose not people who gave the last measure of devotion to their country, but people who despised their country in ways we now approve, because they are our ways.

A couple of examples should suffice. Aleksandr Solzhenitsyn, a communist sympathizer as a young man, and an officer in the army, returned to Russia and began to see the difference between what the communists had done to his people and what the heart and soul of the people really were. He began to write about it, and promptly found himself with a one-way ticket to a labor camp in Siberia. From there he wrote a small book that would gain him renown throughout the world: *One Day in the Life of Ivan Denisovich.* The one day was a day as a Siberian prisoner, with its inhuman deprivations and petty wickedness: bribing guards so as to get a ladle full of soup scooped from the bottom, where a chunk of potato or fat might be gotten; wiping oneself in the morning with a three-inch square of cardboard; and so on. Solzhenitsyn went on to write greater works, and eventually was set free, emigrating to the United States, where he became a prophet railing against the soulless materialism of both the West and the East.

Now there you have a man who has experienced many things, some of them impossible to consider without contemplating the mystery of human evil. He cannot be reduced to a political platitude. So you do not introduce your students to Aleksandr Solzhenitsyn. He has too much of the hero about him; he bursts the bonds of the everyday world.

Instead take your students to Seneca Falls, New York, where a group of well-to-do socialites are meeting to draft a resolution calling for women's suffrage. Now apart from the issue of the vote, none of these people are particularly interesting or accomplished or virtuous. Susan B. Anthony, one of the attendees, liked to wear men's trousers and get herself arrested at polling places; she was a singularly unpleasant person, who believed that women who depended upon their husbands or their brothers were simpletons. Elizabeth Cady Stanton, far milder of temper and contentedly married, wrote a good deal about the issue, but that is about all we can say about her. There are no great stories here, no bold deeds risking life or limb or even property. Let such people be "heroes." It will not matter from what political party you derive them, either. Pick anyone you like—John Birch, Robert La Follette, Samuel Gompers, Carry Nation—just so long as your *reason* for the choice is political. If, for instance, you pick Florence Nightingale, there's no need to describe her heroic ministrations on the miserable fields of the Crimean War; instead, make her into a modern feminist. Or if you pick William Wilberforce, there's no need to describe his saintly Christian faith and his arduous perseverance in trying to end the English slave trade. Focus instead on the political angle. The object is to induce the student to say, "I am heroic already, because I agree with William Wilberforce," rather than, "If only someday I could do something a tenth as noble as what William Wilberforce did."

Souls about Nothing

As I've suggested, when it comes to using humor to damn the soul, it is as Screwtape says to his nephew Wormwood, "Flippancy is the best of all." Not many people can cut a really good new joke, but anybody can be trained to speak as if the good things of this world were ridiculous. "If prolonged," he says, "the habit of Flippancy builds up around a man the finest armour-plating against the Enemy that I know, and it is quite free from the dangers inherent in the other sources of laughter. It is a thousand miles away from joy; it deadens, instead of sharpening, the intellect, and it excites no affection between those who practice it."

Therefore flippancy is to be indulged. It can accomplish remarkable feats with very little effort—just as it takes only a wrecking ball, or a kid with some gasoline and a match, to destroy in one night a town hall or a school or a church that dozens of craftsmen and laborers took a whole year to build. Flippancy—the habit of sneering at what is great or noble—is that sneak with the match.

Take the example of George Washington. He was, for generations of Americans, the Father of Our Country. He was a gentleman farmer, not a professionally trained soldier. He made more than his share of mistakes. He exposed himself to danger constantly—riding always at the front of his men. He was shot at but never killed. He owned slaves. His conversation was nothing special; he was rather on the quiet side. His rules for soldierly behavior were perfectly medieval: lashings with the whip for indecent talk, for instance. He kept his ill-clad and starving men together through the terrible winter at Valley Forge not just by inspiring them with hopes of victory. He had deserters shot. Well then, we should keep to those easy targets, and take them out of context.

Don't let students read, for example, what Washington wrote to the Marquis de Lafayette, just as he was getting ready to retire for good from public life, not knowing that one day he would be called upon to serve as president: "I am not only retired from all public employments, but I am retiring within myself, and shall be able to view the solitary walk and tread the paths of private life with heartfelt satisfaction. Envious of none, I am determined to be pleased with all, and this, my dear friend, being the order of my march, I will move gently down the stream of life until I sleep with my fathers." They might not be ready to snicker at the eloquence—notable in a man who never attended high school, and far beyond the capacity of most teachers and professors today. They might wonder at the man's strange reversal of priorities. They might not yet roll their eyes in disbelief at the statesman who has no love for running about to scramble up votes, but who instead wants to work his farm, where he was, as it turns out, an inveterate tryer-out of new inventions, a would-be pioneer.

There's not much to laugh at, there. Better to quote the teenage Washington's *Rules for Civility* on how to dress or bear oneself in public:

In walking up and Down in a House, only with One in Company if he be Greater than yourself, at the first give him the Right hand and

Stop not till he does and be not the first that turns, and when you do turn let it be with your face towards him, if he be a Man of Great Quality, walk not with him Cheek by Jowl but Somewhat behind him; but yet in such a Manner that he may easily Speak to you.

Do not trouble to discover here the combination of self-assurance and humility, the attractive deference to an elder, and the perhaps more attractive desire to speak with him. Enough of these directives, delivered with a knowing curl of the lip, will do: *we* wear our trousers below the hips, you see, and are therefore wise and advanced.

Or, since we are on the subject of presidents, take Abraham Lincoln. Do not let the students begin to ponder the theology, the wise, evenhanded politics, and the yet firm commitment to the dignity of all mankind, evident in the Second Inaugural Address:

If we shall suppose that American slavery is one of those offenses which, in the providence of God, must needs come, but which, having continued through his appointed time, he now wills to remove, and that he gives to both North and South this terrible war, as the woe due to those by whom the offense came, shall we discern any departure from those divine attributes which the believers in a living God always ascribe to him? Fondly do we hope—fervently do we pray—that this mighty scourge of war may speedily pass away. Yet, if God wills that it continue until all the wealth piled by the bondsman's two hundred and fifty years of unrequited toil shall be sunk, and until every drop of blood drawn with the lash shall be paid by another drawn with the sword, as was said three thousand years ago, so still it must be said, "The judgments of the Lord are true and righteous altogether."

Southern partisans still rankle over Lincoln's centralization of power and his assertion that the states are strictly subordinate to the federal government and have no real sovereignty of their own. Their position is one worthy of consideration; but do not consider it. We do not want students to support or oppose Lincoln's policies based upon some well-thought philosophy of government. We want them to snicker.

So, for instance, we assume that Lincoln was right to go to war against the South, because the southerners who prosecuted the war were all nasty slave owners. It isn't true, but it absolves us of the need to take the southern position seriously. Then we say that Lincoln himself thought that blacks were an inferior race. We neglect to mention that just about everybody thought so, too, including the abolitionists; it was the foolish "scientific" consensus of that day. Then we say that Lincoln mismanaged the war, and that his generals were bloodthirsty brutes. We don't actually discuss these or the Confederate generals and their tactics at any length, because then we'd stumble upon some mysterious personalities: the devout Stonewall Jackson, the hard-bitten agnostic Sherman, the hard-drinking Grant, the diminutive Catholic Sheridan, the gentlemanly Lee, the scholar Chamberlain. We want to encourage the curiosity-deadening smirk, after all. We say that Lincoln suspended basic political rights during the war—that he had men held under arrest without specifying the charge. We do this not to examine the questions of martial law, but merely to belittle. If possible, we toss in a modern rumor that Lincoln was a homosexual. There's no evidence for it, but the tactic works in a couple of ways at once. It diverts attention from the man's heroism, and it reduces him to a counter in a modern political game. It also—though it is politically incorrect for the teacher or textbook writer to admit it—makes him appear a bit contemptible. Similar tactics may be used, with similarly scant evidence, against Leonardo da Vinci, Michelangelo, and Shakespeare.

So far I've mentioned only specific people. The really effective killer of the moral imagination, though, will want to raise children who snicker at *anyone* who possesses a remarkable virtue. He must be trained to see all such people as fools or knaves. The perfect vice for instilling that attitude is small-souled envy. For pride, though a greater sin than envy, is dangerous too: a child who is proud of what he believes to be his own excellence may end up admiring it in his opponent, and as soon as that happens, we are well on our way to losing him altogether. Envy presents no such opportunity for the imaginative leap. The proud man wants to excel; the envious man fears lest someone else excel. So envy teaches us to see virtues inside-out, to turn them into despicable caricatures, and, at best, to laugh at them:

> And all he had of the magnanimous,
> all the sublime, the gloriously bright,

Gernando reprehended as mere vice,
artfully shading truth in an ill light.*

This inversion is easy enough. Humility—as, for example, in the country boy Alvin York, most decorated American in the First World War? Call it servility. He was a hayseed who didn't know any better. Or, if we find the virtue in a woman—say, in the great Joan of Arc, who led the French soldiers to battle against the English but did not wear a sword—we call it humiliation. She was all right in her way, but insufficiently liberated.

Chastity is absurdly easy to laugh at. First of all, no one is chaste. Second, it is stupid to be chaste to begin with. What's all the bother about, anyway? Elizabeth Bennett believes, in Jane Austen's *Pride and Prejudice*, that her family will be disgraced when it becomes known that her silly sister Lydia has run off, unmarried, with a soldier. Weren't they quaint and unenlightened in Jane Austen's day? Better that Elizabeth Bennett should follow her sister's lead, ignoring that prig Mr. Darcy, and make the cart-springs squeak with Colonel Denny or someone—anyone will do.

Self-control? Only for Puritans, like the horrible people of Salem, back when they burned witches. The Indians (of course, one mustn't *really* teach students about the Indians, unless they can be reduced to political markers) knew better, because they were in touch with nature. Temperance? Only hypocrites preach temperance. Besides, it doesn't work. Prohibition, you know. Pass the beer.

Honesty? Listen, everybody cheats. If you don't cheat a little, you will fall on the wrong side of the curve. So since everybody expects a little cheating, to cheat isn't really to cheat but to tell the truth. All politicians (or rather all politically incorrect politicians) are liars.

Fortunately, the attentive parent will be aided in this enterprise by what is called "popular culture." It isn't really culture, but mass entertainment; but that's another matter. Watch a half hour of television, and count how many times what is supposed to be humorous is based upon a flattening or a reduction. Is someone not humbled but humiliated—and just for our enjoyment of the humiliation? Is the jest merely a snide wisecrack, and not really funny unless you adopt the snideness of the jester? Is the predominant mode the flippant, the cheap, the snickering? If so, know that you

---

* Torquato Tasso, *Jerusalem Delivered*, 1591.

will have little to worry about. After years of watching the comic face of nihilism, your children will come to respect nothing, love nothing, believe in nothing, and long for nothing.

I'm a Hero, You're a Hero

When Johann Sebastian Bach was twelve years old, his family gave him enough money to go on a long trip to the city of Leipzig. He had learned that the great organist Buxtehude was there, and he wanted to meet him and become his student. So the young Bach traveled, by himself, by carriage and by foot, in tribute to the excellence of the master.

When the Scotsman James Boswell came to London, he sought an introduction to the most famous essayist, conversationalist, and scholar of his day, Dr. Samuel Johnson. For years he would call on Johnson when he was in town, and would jot down notes of dinner talk, philosophical debate, and humorous anecdotes, all in honor of the friend he admired so deeply. Johnson inspired that sort of devotion: Boswell tells that when Johnson was a boy, the other schoolboys would carry him about on their shoulders like a potentate. Boswell ended up writing probably the greatest biography ever, the *Life of Johnson.*

When Donatello was a young sculptor, he caught the fascination for works of ancient Greek and Roman art that had inspired Masaccio, the painter, and humanist poet-scholars like Petrarch and Boccaccio. He therefore traveled south to Rome and its environs, literally unearthing the old sculptures, studying them with mingled humility and emulation. He then sculpted the first bronze equestrian statue, and the first nude statue in the round, in over a thousand years.

What must have gone through the young Johann's mind as he trudged those hundreds of miles, through the rain and the mud, putting in at roadside lodgings, missing his family, and wondering whether his journey would end in vain? Without a constant yearning of the imagination, he could not have done it. No one would make such a journey merely for a tactical advantage in the pursuit of a worldly career. Bach was in love with music, and for him, Buxtehude was a giant, a man who knew much, from whom the young lad would learn.

Did such hero-worship make Bach a slave to the past? Far from it; it was the ground of all he accomplished as perhaps the greatest composer who ever lived. For Johann Sebastian Bach never ceased learning from other people whom he considered to be great: Vivaldi, Hassler, Crueger, Palestrina. He took the delicately interwoven melodies of Palestrina's polyphony and transformed them in chorales of unsurpassed imaginative power: as in the famous Passion Chorale, or the twelve-chord *Christ Lag in Todesbanden*. Had the soul of Bach not been exalted by the greatness he esteemed in others, he would have been but the organist of the cathedral of Leipzig, known for a stray odd melody here and there, and forgotten to all but the specialists. He might have been forgotten in any case, and *was* forgotten for a time, except that the young Wolfgang Mozart "discovered" him and fell in love with his excellence, making him known to the world.

Donatello would have been nothing without Masaccio, Masaccio nothing without the painter Giotto. Saint Augustine, an intellectual giant of the highest rank, said of himself and his contemporaries that they were dwarfs, but dwarfs perched upon the shoulders of giants: he had the pagan Plato principally in mind, as the greatest of those giants. Dante was twice the poet that the great Virgil was, but without Virgil—or rather without his admiration for the pagan Roman poet—he would have been but one of the more interesting of the dozens of love poets of medieval Italy and Provence. So Lucretius, the greatest philosopher-poet of the West, writes in *On the Nature of Things* of his master Epicurus:

> Out of such darkness you who were first to raise
> So brilliant a light to show us the best of life,
>   I follow you, glory of Greece, and in the deep
>   Print of your traces I now fix my steps,
> Not eager to strive with you, but longing in love
> To imitate your work.

So the English poet Spenser, in the *Faerie Queene*, pays tribute to his predecessor Chaucer, that "most sacred happy spirit," calling upon his spirit that he may "follow here the footing of thy feet."

Name but a work of prodigious genius, remaking the artistic or intellectual discipline, or even changing history, for better or for worse. You will see in it an admiration of greatness past. Machiavelli once wrote that during the day he would venture from his villa down into the back streets of Florence, to drink and gamble with ruffians; but when he returned home he would change his clothes, put on a robe of state, and read the authors he loved: the old Roman historians Livy, Sallust, and Tacitus. It is not enough to say that Machiavelli merely learned from them, or that he studied them. They were his *authorities*, his teachers; he bowed with reverence before them. He wrote, under their influence—whatever else one may think of it—the first truly modern work of political thought, *The Prince*.

Or take the most original of English poets, Gerard Manley Hopkins— a man who died decades before his work became known and admired. His strange and image-crammed poetry and his grammar-wrenching language would exert a tremendous influence upon English poets in the twentieth century, but Hopkins himself never suspected that that would happen. He had always admired the songs of the ancient Greeks and Romans, and had taken to heart the rhythms of his predecessors in English, particularly Shakespeare. But he fell under the spell of the medieval metaphysical philosopher John Duns Scotus, and from him learned to dwell with poetic contemplation upon what the poet called the "inscape" of things: what, by the glorious creative power and wisdom of God, a bluebell really is, or a lichen-covered rock on the bare heath, or the faint spectrum of mist around a full moon after the rain has cleared. That love *made him original.* Had he been merely his own, he would have been like everybody else.

And that suggests a fine method for stifling the imagination. We live in an age of putative "equality." It is our easy stand-in for the difficult virtue of justice. If things aren't equal, well, they ought to be. But just a glance at human variety will suffice to show that people aren't alike, nor would it be interesting if they were. People differ markedly in talent, virtue, fortune, diligence, cleverness, temperament, health, physical strength, and wisdom. Christopher Marlowe could write a blank verse passage so memorable in its rolling thunder that no Renaissance English playwright after him could quite avoid his influence. "Is it not passing brave to be a king," says his swaggering Tamburlaine, a glint of ferocious ambition in his eye, "And ride in triumph through Persepolis?" But Marlowe could fashion only carica- tures; he never saw deep into the heart of man, as his younger contempo- rary Shakespeare did. Monet could paint a watercolor sunset like no man else; but for sheer drama and bravura I prefer the watercolor paintings of the sea by Winslow Homer or J. M. W. Turner, any day.

The point is that excellence is there to be found and admired and learned from: but it is an offense to our self-esteem. Why should we not say that all things are equal? That frees us of the need to learn from what is great. Scott Joplin, the inventor of ragtime, learned from Mozart—the waterfall-spills of thirty-second notes are all over his compositions. He is not as great as Mozart is—who can make that claim? But we can draw a kind of equivalence to suit our own purposes. We can say, "Mozart was famous in Vienna in his day, and Scott Joplin was famous in America in *his* day. Scott Joplin learned from Mozart. So there's really no difference here; you can't say one was greater than the other. It's the same now with today's popular music. Styles change, that's all." Joplin himself would never have said or thought such a thing; had he done so, he probably would not have become half the composer and pianist he was.

You see how it goes? "Back in the old days," says someone who doesn't really know what he is talking about, "very few people could read, and few people went to see a play. Shakespeare was popular then. Nowadays we're in better shape. More people can read, and we all see dramas. They just happen to be on television. I think," and here you can fill in the blank; it hardly matters what you fill it with, "that _____ is as great as anything Shakespeare ever wrote." The strategy is not to engage young people in a *real* conversation about greatness, because, again, that would rouse the mind, and might eventually engage them in just the creative emulation and hero-worship we want to avoid. It is instead to use this argument as an excuse for not bothering to consider Shakespeare at all. It is to insist upon an equality from one age to the next, as an excuse for insisting upon a pretty much even distribution of merit within our own age.

The lesson applies to moral heroism as much as to works of art or of the intellect. In fact, applying it to moral heroism is quite easy. For it is obvious, even in our flattening schools, that some people are smarter than others. What is not obvious is that some people are *better people* than others. Merely to state such a thing is to make a judgment, and that, we must teach our children, is offensive. We must teach them to consider themselves better than others because they consider nobody better than anyone else. It may not entirely cure them of hero-worship. But it will ensure that if they do worship any hero, that hero will be themselves. Or perhaps the word "hero" is ill-chosen here. *Idol* may be more like it.

So if we wish to cramp the moral imaginations of our children, we must tarnish the genuine heroes of our past, and at the same time place mirrors for self-adulation everywhere. Everyone is creative, everyone is "original." Every one of the millions of lemmings is to believe himself a "leader of tomorrow," leading tomorrow in perfectly predictable fashion right over the edge of the cliff and into the sea. Everyone must go to college, not to learn something about Homer and Thomas Aquinas, but to *be a college graduate*, to be somebody. Deprived of the wellsprings of the imagination, they will seek gratification in mechanical sexual encounters, or in watching others try to make imbecilic idols of themselves on television. They will have nothing to be proud of, yet will scoff at humility. They will fancy themselves important, and will be slaves to the contemptuous marketers of the day. They will string after their names the letters of degrees from institutions of higher learning, and will not be able to read Milton— or be willing to read Milton. They will all be aspiring, breathlessly, for prestige, a promotion, a nicer house, the office of lieutenant governor—but will have no hero to love, no hero's memory to serve. They will parade their originality, all the same, and drab. If but a moment's love for someone truly great could crack their carapace of self-absorption, then they might be able to breathe freely again and be fully human. If they could say, "Not all the speeches I have ever delivered can weigh in the balance against a single sentence by Daniel Webster," or by Joseph Hayne, if you are from the south—then their hearts and imaginations might expand, and they might write a sentence or two that would make the old senators proud. But the carapace is thick. Education—and the mass entertainment—have seen to that.

Method 7

Reduce All Talk of Love to Narcissism and Sex

or

Insert Tab A into Slot B

The middle-aged warrior in Homer's *Odyssey*, his little raft smashed to flotsam on the stormy seas, has had to strip and swim for his life. When he reached land it was but a terrible outcrop of rocks, battered by the waves. He grasped hold of one, clinging, fighting to find a way into the island, when the backwash of a gigantic comber flung him off it, leaving shreds of his skin still on the rock, just as pebbles and sand stay stuck in an octopus's suckers if you yank it from its hold. Finally he finds a river mouth and is able to swim to it and drag himself ashore, purple with bruises, bedraggled with seaweed, blear-eyed and half dead. He stumbles across to a thicket, crawls underneath the branches, piles dead leaves over his body to hide from wild beasts, and falls into a dead sleep.

Meanwhile, a lovely young princess, inspired by a dream, has woken up to the sunny morning with a nice plan in mind. She asks her father, the king, if she can take a team of horses and a chariot out to the beach, where she and her girlfriends will do the laundry. "My older brothers will be looking to marry soon," she says, "and they like to look fine at the dances. And it's my job to see to the robes." The father smiles—he knows it's a grand excuse for a picnic—and agrees. So the princess and her friends take the basket of laundry down to the pebbly shore. They pound it with hands and feet in little natural basins scooped out of the rock, then spread each piece of clothing out in the sun to whiten and dry. After that they go for a bathe—there aren't any boys around, and bathing suits hadn't been invented yet. When they come out they make their skin glisten with olive oil, put their clothes back on, have breakfast, and start to play with a ball. It isn't a competitive game they play; it's more like jump rope. You pass the ball from one to another, while everybody claps her hands and chants a rhythmic chant.

But one of the princess's tosses sails wide and bounces over toward the thicket where the warrior lies. He wakes up and hears their shouts from far away. "What now?" he moans to himself. "What sorts of wild animals are these? As if I hadn't had enough trouble already!" But the shouts also sound as if they might be girls. So he scrambles to his feet, snapping off a bough to hide his nakedness, and breaks through the bushes, like a mountain lion. The girls run away, screaming—a natural enough reaction. But the princess, upon whom the goddess of wisdom has bestowed courage for this moment, stands her ground.

It is a moment tense with human suffering and the attraction of man and woman to one another. The warrior approaches carefully, even shyly, keeping a respectful distance. Then he speaks:

> O Queen, I do implore: Are you divine
> or mortal? If you are a goddess—one
> of those who have vast heaven as their home—
> then I should liken you most closely to
> the daughter of great Zeus: you surely are
> an Artemis in form and face and stature.
> But if you are a mortal, an earth-dweller,
> then both your father and your noble mother
> are three times blessed, and three times blessed, your brothers:
> their hearts are surely always glad to see
> so fair a blossom entering the dance.
> But one whose heart is blessed above the rest
> is he who, wooing you with comely gifts,
> will lead you to his house.

He tells the story of his wanderings, begs her to assist him in finding help so that he can sail home again, and concludes by reading her mind—reading her dearest wishes:

And may the gods grant you what your heart wants most,
a husband and a home, and may there be
accord between you both: there is no gift
more solid and more precious than such trust:
a man and woman who conduct their house
with minds in deep accord, to enemies
bring grief, but to their friends bring gladness, and—
above all—gain a good name for themselves.

Indeed she will find that help for him—and will wish, once Odysseus has bathed and dressed and become himself again, that the gods could grant her such a husband as he. She has already rejected many suitors, but they were only boys. What she desires, as she expresses in words that are noble and chaste and reticent, is that heroic man, even after she knows that he must return home:

I greet you, guest, as you take leave, so that—
when you've gone back to your homeland—you may
remember me and keep in mind how I,
more than all others, worked to save your life.

His reply is manly and gentle, exactly right:

Nausicaa, daughter of the generous
Alcinous, may Hera's husband, Zeus
the thunderer, now guide me to my house
and let me see the day of my return.
There I shall pray forever and each day
to you as to a goddess. Dearest girl,
to you I owe my life.

Lovely, isn't it? And don't we all recognize the strength and the keen sight of the man, and the grace and generosity of the woman?

It is not the sort of thing you will read nowadays. That would require the presence of those two fabulous beasts, called a "man" and a "woman," and the mystery they bring to one another. When that mystery is dispelled—or rather when it is papered over and ignored—we suffer the terrible loss of the beauty of manhood and the beauty of womanhood. But that is not the greatest loss we suffer. The greatest is that we can no longer appreciate why men and women were ever fascinated with one another in the first place. We lose the poetry and music of love.

If the *Odyssey* will not persuade you, listen to this verse from a wistful old ballad:

> Her brow is like the snow-drift,
> Her neck is like the swan,
> Her face it is the fairest,
> That e'er the sun shone on.
> That e'er the sun shone on—
> And dark blue is her e'e,
> And for bonnie Annie Laurie
> I'd lay me doon and dee.

The poem is said to have been composed by one William Douglas, who fell in love with the young Annie Laurie, but who never enjoyed the fulfillment of that love. He was a Scots partisan of the ousted Stuart claimants to the throne of England, and so Annie's father prevented the marriage. It's simple enough poetry—it does not require a master to compare the beauty of a fair woman to the whiteness of drifting snow, or to the slender elegance of the swan. Nor does it require a master to imagine, and utter, the sentiment of a man in love, that for his bonnie sweetheart he would lay himself down in one bed or another, the bed of married love, or the bed of a grave.

What strikes me most about the poem is that in its very simplicity it lifts the mind out of petty, selfish, daily concerns. Suddenly we are with the singer and his outlandish accent, striding over the braes of Scotland, and wondering what it must be like to be glad even for a love that is lost—to love with such abandon that we would lay down our lives for the woman we love, as simply as we would kneel at an altar. The power of love touches the ordinary, and suddenly we see that it is not ordinary after all: that the man before us, even the shepherd with his ragged cloak, is an Odysseus, and the woman, even the shy girl with braces, a Nausicaa.

Something of that wonder, and the gratitude that wonder inspires, we can hear in the sad verses that Stephen Foster composed, for the woman he loved, a woman he felt himself unworthy of (Foster had his troubles with money and the bottle):

> I long for Jeanie with the daydawn smile,
> Radiant in gladness, warm with winning guile;
> I hear her melodies, like joys gone by,
> Sighing round my heart o'er the fond hopes that die:
> Sighing like the night wind and sobbing like the rain,
> Wailing for the lost one that comes not again:
> I long for Jeanie, and my heart bows low,
> Never more to find her where the bright waters flow.

His wife Jane left him as his life dwindled away into penury. But he looks about him and finds her everywhere, in the sunlight, in the night wind; her gladness, and her sorrow, mingled now with his loneliness and longing. It is not great poetry. It is good poetry; what exalts us is not the poetry, nor even the haunting melody to which it is sung, but the call of love that leads us, in imagination, into a world of desire, and beauty, and disappointment. It is a world that is as old as man; and can be put to death only by the abolition of man.

Fortunately, the abolition of man is just what our mass entertainers and mass educators are about. Consider this passage from a modern "love" song:

> What a girl wants, what a girl needs
> Whatever makes me happy and sets you free
> And I'm thanking you for knowing exactly
>
> What a girl wants, what a girl needs
> Whatever keeps me in your arms
> And I'm thanking you for being there for me

It's not as bad as most. There are at least a boy and a girl in it. There are no obscenities (one almost wishes there were). It is self-infatuated drivel. You can't really tell what the phrase "sets you free" is supposed to mean, nor what the fellow would have to do to qualify as "being there," other than perhaps letting her do as she pleased. That's because, we see, "love" has to do with "whatever makes me happy," not with whatever makes me see beyond myself. It is an emotional itch, that is all.

Compare with this famous moment in Shakespeare's *Tempest*, wherein the young Ferdinand and Miranda vie to outdo one another in wonder and obedience:

> *Miranda.* Hence, bashful cunning,
> And prompt me, plain and holy innocence!
> I am your wife, if you will marry me;
> If not, I'll die your maid. To be your fellow
> You may deny me, but I'll be your servant
> Whether you will or no.
> *Ferdinand.* My mistress, dearest;
> And I thus humble ever.
> *Miranda.* My husband, then?
> *Ferdinand.* Ay, with a heart as willing
> As bondage e'er of freedom.

Miranda here is not thinking of what she "needs," but of how noble her beloved Ferdinand is. Even were he to refuse her as a wife, she would serve him; and he, in response, kneels to her, and offers her his freedom with as hearty a desire as that of a slave seeking release from bondage.

Now the trouble here is not that Shakespeare is the greatest writer who ever lived, and the woman who wrote the song above is barely lingual. That is a problem, no doubt, but it is not the worst. You can have terrible poetry, and still, somehow, a trace of the love that inspired the poetry will survive. The problem is that Stephen Foster could understand the love that inspired Shakespeare's scene. Any ploughman of old could understand it. We cannot. Or rather we want to ensure that young people will look upon a Ferdinand and Miranda, or even Stephen and Jane, or William and Annie, as creatures of a fundamentally different species. As indeed they will be.

How to ensure it? Reduce sex to hygiene, or to mechanics. Reduce eros to the itch of lust or vanity. Reduce the love of man and woman to something private, arbitrary, and socially indifferent. While you are doing these things, soak television and magazines with pictures of people in a state of undress, so that the only mysteries remaining will be in the cruel, the bizarre, and the disgusting.

Scratch Me Here

The poet Edmund Spenser in "A Hymne of Love" has a nice description of what sexual desire is like in a soul that is base:

> His dunghill thoughts, which do themselves enure
> To dirty dross, no higher dare aspire,
> Nor can his feeble earthly eyes endure
> The flaming light of that celestial fire,
> Which kindleth love in generous desire,
> And makes him mount above his native might
> Of heavy earth, up to the heavens' height.

The lust-burdened man does not "aspire," says Spenser. The problem with him is not that he ignores heavenly things, but that he reduces even the earthly things to the dunghill. He does not see, in other words, that the earthly beauty about him is shot through with rays of wondrous light. He cannot imagine anything other than the itch of animal desire.

Spenser will often show such "love" in action, as when, in *The Faerie Queene*, the worthless Braggadocchio encounters a beautiful and chaste huntress named Belphoebe. Now, Braggadocchio is *not* exactly hot-blooded. Indeed, Spenser is always careful to expose the itch of lust as finally cold, unproductive, and impotent. It might bear a handsome exterior, he says, but it brings on the disease "that rots the marrow, and consumes the brain." And so when we first meet Braggadocchio, he is doing nothing at all. He is sunning himself on a hill, not because he enjoys the outdoors, but because he hasn't the heart to exert himself to accomplish anything great or noble.

Such is the man, hardly a man, who meets Belphoebe. He asks her why she spends all of her time in the woods, rather than at court, where she can see and be seen—for the lazy knight, that's all that one does at court. She replies with a kind of hymn to honorable work:

> Abroad in arms, at home in studious kind,
> Who seeks with painful toil, shall honor soonest find.

But she never finishes her praising. Braggadocchio attempts to leap upon her—failing, of course. It is all he can understand.

The great poets and philosophers of our tradition understood that eros is *for* something beyond the satisfaction of a physical desire. None of the philosophy of Plato makes the least bit of sense unless we understand that we are given eros so that we may hunger for the good, the true, and the beautiful. So, in his dialogue *Phaedrus*, Plato's master Socrates likens the human soul to a charioteer with a pair of horses, one ill-natured, and one noble. The ill-natured horse, representing the appetite, has to be kept in check by the other horse, representing what the Greeks called *thumos* or spiritedness. It is that faculty of the soul that drives us on to seek greatness. Both horses are attracted by beauty—in Plato's dialogue, it is the beauty of a handsome and intelligent lad. The ill-natured horse seeks mere copulation, and thus would end the quest for greatness before it really begins. It is the spirited horse that obeys the commands of the driver, the intellect, not because it desires to possess that beauty any less, but because it desires it all the more, and in the noblest form. In the greatest souls, Plato suggests in the *Symposium*, eros results not in mere bedding down, or even in marriage, but in fast friendships bound by a mutual rivalry in noble deeds, or, more exalted still, by shared conversation about and contemplation of the good itself.

The young Dante is greeted by a lady named Beatrice one day as he is walking down the streets of Florence. So stunned is he by her beauty that, as he puts it, he surrenders his life to his lord, Love. That does not mean he seeks to enjoy her beauty in bed. In fact, Beatrice will marry another man, and will die young. Nor does Dante ever suggest that he so much as kissed Beatrice. But his youthful love, beginning in infatuation and culminating in a vision of his lady as his blessed guide through Paradise, spurs his imagination to heights that Western poetry has never exceeded. Because of this desire for a beauty that could not be reduced to its material accidents—a pretty eye, a fair cheek—or to its animal attraction, Dante forged a vision in which eros is merged with the longing of the intellect to know the highest truth, that is, to contemplate the beauty of the Creator, face to face. Had eros been demoted to a bodily itch—had Beatrice been the common trull that we encourage our young girls to be—there could have been no *Divine Comedy*.

Our experience of beauty is that it is something gratuitous, gloriously abounding over the bare needs of existence. It does not have to be there, yet it is, shining, summoning our wonder. And of all the things in the physical world, none, says John Milton, is more beautiful than the "human face divine," with its look of intelligence revealing the capacity to understand and take into itself all things. When the beauty of the human person, the face through which the mind gleams, and the body meant to stand upright and greet all the world, is an object of genuine wonder, then even lust does not lose all of the glory of true love. That wonder shines through a soldier's gruff talk in *Antony and Cleopatra*, when Shakespeare's Enobarbus describes the beauty of Cleopatra to a couple of other old campaigners:

> For her own person,
> It beggared all description: she did lie
> In her pavilion, cloth-of-gold of tissue,
> O'erpicturing that Venus where we see
> The fancy outwork nature: on each side her
> Stood pretty dimpled boys, like smiling Cupids,
> To glow the delicate cheeks which they did cool,
> And what they undid, did.

But when that same beauty is united with a pure and innocent soul, it can take the breath away, for innocence is more than mere absence of wickedness, just as purity is more than mere abstinence. In Dostoyevsky's *Crime and Punishment*, we find gentle and womanly innocence in Sonia, a girl who is compelled by the debaucheries of her worthless father to sell her beauty on the streets, just to keep a little food in the house for her family. When the young murderer Raskolnikov—whose materialism had led him to reject the law of good and evil as merely conventional—meets Sonia, her beauty and self-sacrificing innocence pierce through his brassy intellectual armor. Had she possessed the slightest taint of self-serving careerism about her, or had she not been a woman both strong and in need of a defender, he would have gone his way, unconverted. *Because* she is an obedient and humble girl, she can command him. She can even direct him to his true self, and to God:

> He suddenly remembered Sonia's words: 'Go to the cross-roads, bow down to the people, kiss the earth, for you have sinned against it, and proclaim in a loud voice to the whole world: I am a murderer!' He

trembled all over as he remembered it. And so utterly crushed was he
by his feeling of hopelessness and desolation and by the great anxiety
of all those days, but especially of the last few hours, that he simply
plunged head over heels into this new and overwhelming sensation.
It seemed to come upon him as though it were some nervous fit: it
glimmered like a spark in his soul, and then, suddenly, spread like
a conflagration through him. Everything within him grew soft all at
once, and tears gushed from his eyes. He fell to the ground just where
he stood.

He knelt down in the middle of the square, bowed down to the earth, and
kissed the filthy earth with joy and rapture. Then he got up and bowed
down once more.

'Plastered,' a lad near him remarked.

We can forgive that lad's snickering observation. After all, what would
we think if a man dropped to the ground in front of us to kiss it? Yet that
snicker is to be heard wherever our educators go, marching forth in the van-
guard of "progress," instructing our students in the technique of how-to-
rut-without-offspring, and shrugging away all questions of love. The result
is a constriction of the imagination. And that is exactly what we want.

Here I am embarrassed with a wealth of riches! So many banalizing
books for young people on sex, and so little space to devote here to them.
I shall content myself with four. The first is a work that for many reasons
should not be included at all: *Building Your Own Conscience (Batteries Not
Included)* (1992), by William J. O'Malley, SJ. Father O'Malley makes the
terrible mistake of including classical *stories* in his discussion of morality—for instance, the story of the adulterous Tristan and Iseult, and how
their faithlessness brought them to disaster; or of the interview from *A
Man for All Seasons*, when the self-seeking councillor Cromwell elicits false
testimony from Richard Rich, whom Father O'Malley aptly describes,
unsympathetically, as "a young man desperately trying to improve his lot
in the world"; or Scheherazade, saving her life by telling fascinating stories
to the Sultan. All these, with some probing questions appended, would
serve to stretch the moral imagination, and prepare it to ask *human* questions about sex.

Still, there are items in the book that are worthy of emulation (and we recommend them to the imagination destroyers lagging behind in schools run by the churches). Father O'Malley laces his prose with the snarky and the colloquial, bringing the mystery of love down to earth, or to regions below, with a bump. Of extramarital sex, he writes, "You knew this was coming, right?" Of the power of romantic love, he says that people in love dwell in a kind of womb: "Both are wonderful— in fact, essential—places to visit. But, all in all, you really wouldn't want to live there." He wavers between a sense that there is something to our experience with beauty that brings us out of ourselves, and a more reliable sense that "like all things subject to the laws of thermodynamics, the intoxicating love potion wears off." He lards his discussion with psychological jargon: a "male," he says, not a boy or a man, "'dumps off' his inner feminine (anima) on the female, and she 'dumps off' her inner masculine (animus) on the male. You hear it all the time." Not surprisingly, he sees no particular beauty in being a man or in being a woman; there is nothing *peculiarly* masculine or feminine for the boy or the girl to grow into:

> *Masculine* means, roughly, all those character qualities we wrongly associate solely with males, not *manliness* and *virility* that deal with sexuality, but attitudes and preferences: logic, analysis (taking apart), tough-mindedness, decisiveness, competition. *Feminine* means, roughly, all those character qualities we wrongly associate solely with females, not *womanliness* and *mothering* (sexuality), but attitudes and preferences: intuition, synthesis (putting together), openness, patience, cooperation.

Expose your children to enough of this, and they will be unable to see the beauty in, say, the manly Ferdinand courting the womanly Miranda. For "manliness" and "womanliness" here are reduced to the capacity to engage in sexual intercourse, and then, for the woman, to bear and nurse a child. That is all. Notice also that our associations of certain qualities with good men and good women are presented as merely conventional; it could and should be otherwise. Finally, notice the false dichotomies: as if tough-mindedness were not a part of patience, or as if competition were not a most splendid form of cooperation.

But Father O'Malley is not a reliable destroyer. After all, he retains more than the residue of a desire that his readers will be granted the ultimate in human flourishing: to see the face of God. For better works, we turn to the secular. Here, for instance, is a passage from the first page of Lynda and Area Madaras's *My Body, My Self: For Girls* (2007):

> We hope that you'll have fun with this book, that you'll learn a thing
> or two, and that you'll come back to it from time to time.... We hope,
> too, that you'll hang on to the book, and that if you one day have a
> daughter or another special woman in your life, you'll give her this
> special puberty book written by and about you!

That about captures the tone and the intellectual tenor of the book. The passage from girlhood to womanhood, from being a child to being capable of bearing a child, is reduced to twaddle and giggles. So we are presented with sections on all the requisite body parts, on what they look like in the mirror, how they grow, how they smell, how big they should be, and so forth, all so "special," yet strangely all so clinically reducible to measurements and functions, without the least connection to the *being* of a woman, much less her capacity to love a man, and to love children.

Banality has one disadvantage, for our purposes. It is too sometimes too dull to be flippant. For the marriage of the banal and the snigger, one might go to Mavis Jukes's *The Guy Book: An Owner's Manual* (2002), a title which plays upon the boy's fascination with machines, even as the author is at pains to insist that boys in fact are nothing special in that regard, or in any other. There is no special manhood to which the boy might aspire. Says Jukes, as delivering the news: "The roles of men and women have been continuously [*sic*] changing over the past few decades; it's okay to feel confused." Of course, feeling confused is one thing, but actually believing that there might be something called "manhood," into which a man could lead the boy, is quite another. So Ms. Jukes is all for what she calls mama's boys. Behold how a shrug and a laugh suffice to harden the heart against a real tragedy, and send thousands of years of male experience into oblivion: "So many boys don't have a dad in their lives! Whether you do or don't, keep hanging out with your mom; it's good for you." Toss that tight spiral, Ms. Jukes!

For being a boy, as Ms. Jukes sees it, is all about having a penis; the whole first chapter is devoted to that and that alone, and most of the rest of the book is devoted to what the boy does with it. Delicate matters of human desire and attraction are shrugged away with a laugh. Does the boy gaze at other boys in the locker room? It means nothing at all, says Ms. Jukes; which in one sense is right, since all boys do that, but in another is as wrong as can be—but then, she would not know anything about what boys really feel, never having been one herself.

And what happens when a boy and a girl fall in love? Not much, except that eventually they get around to wondering when they will have sexual intercourse. For the whole subject of sex has to do with controlling the hardware and keeping it clean. Natural virtues, the momentous giving of oneself wholly to another, the duty you owe to a child you might conceive, the duty you owe to your parents, the duty you owe to the people among whom you live, not to mention the duty you owe to the law of God—none of these enter into the pasteboard imagination of Ms. Jukes. All she says about it is what might come from a self-satisfied teenager who could occasionally write grammatical sentences and pretend to some degree of adulthood:

> Once grown and fully mature, you'll be aware of and ready and able to accept [*sic*] the risks and responsibilities involved in having sex with a partner.
> You'll be able to recognize when the situation is right.

But for sheer destructiveness, the prize goes to Michael J. Basso, *The Underground Guide to Teenage Sexuality* (2003). It is hard to know where to begin with a book so variously banal, flippant, vicious, and deadening to the moral imagination. Needless to say, this book, like the previous two, contains absolutely nothing on the beauty of manhood or womanhood. But this author is intelligent enough to make quite clear that words such as "beauty" are meaningless, as are "normal" and "abnormal," and, by implication, almost everything that people have believed to be sexually licit or illicit. "Normal," he says, begging the question, "means many people do a certain activity. Normal does not mean something is good or right. Abnormal means that only a few people do a certain activity. Abnormal does not mean something is bad or wrong."

That virtue of purity, which Ferdinand saw shining in Miranda, is first reduced to a physical state, and then, by a nice parrying move, rendered obsolete. Are you a virgin if you are a man who has not had sexual

intercourse? Or if you are a woman whose hymen has been torn acciden-
tally? Basso pretends not to know, because in fact he does not care. "Vir-
ginity is a term that seems to cause quite a bit of confusions [*sic*] and problems. Choose whichever definition you feel makes the most sense."

Of course, anyone who holds up to teenagers a responsibility to use
their bodies rightly—or who holds forth a vision of chaste love, before and
then within marriage—must be vilified. Answering the question, "Whom
should I believe when it comes to sex?" Basso will not be honest enough to
say, "Believe me," but rather casts aspersions on those to whom the young
person should turn, namely their elders. "Unfortunately," he says, wiping
the reptilian tear from the eye, "many adults are more interested in their
own values, religious beliefs, agendas (plans to accomplish their personal
goals [*sic*; Basso apparently believes that people who cannot understand
that simple word can fathom the depths of human sexuality]), and power
than in providing facts supported by research, equity, people's rights, and
the health and lives of others, especially young people." That there are
millions of young men in American prisons who grew up without fathers
in the home seems not to qualify, in Mr. Basso's mind, as a fact supported
by research, or as a concern for equity or human rights or health or anything else.

Where is he at his finest? When discussing the hydraulics of the male
member, with a sniggering "Thar she blows"? When recommending that
young people seek help from the hard-leftist Alan Guttmacher Institute?
When slandering those who, usually as volunteers, work at crisis preg-
nancy centers, to help poor women bear their children to term and care
for them afterwards? No; his powers are at full display when dissociating
sex from love. For he is not, finally, interested in the mysteries of love; they
only distract him from his true project, which is the promotion of hygienic
mechanical sexual activity among young people. So, in response to the
question, "Is it possible to be in love with two people at the same time?"
he does not trouble himself to ask, "What is love?" Or to try to explain the
difference between genuine love and sexual desire. Or to turn the question back at the questioner, to ask whether he would not be deeply hurt to
learn that his father had taken up with a woman other than his wife. No,
the severance of sex and love is abrupt and final. Says he, with a hearty
laugh, "There's that word again—love! If we're talking about companion-
ship love or a marriage type of love [*sic*], then we face a question that has

perplexed philosophers for centuries. There is no concrete answer that can be given here."

Brave New Family?

Why should we care whether our young people retain a sense of modesty, such as they might feel in the presence of something mysterious or holy? It is that insofar as they do so, they remain partially unassimilated by the world of the masses: mass education, mass entertainment, mass politics. In particular, people with a strong sense of being embodied creatures, rather than being bundles of appetite provided with the machinery of a body to work upon, will prove difficult to persuade in the coming century of the biotechnocrats.

Someone who retains the ideals of manhood and womanhood will not see the great advances to be made, for instance, in providing men with lactating breasts, or with wombs, to suit some individual whim. People who cannot think of the naked human body without thinking of its being fulfilled sexually in marriage, will look askance at the possibility of cobbling together a zygote made up of genetic material from three or four people. People who see children as the natural expression of the marital embrace will knit their brows with suspicion, when others come along to say, "Let us, with our intelligence that is far vaster than yours, help you select what kind of child you want, from the following menu of possibilities." They will blanch at the prospect of transforming the human race into biological products at the end of an assembly line, or on the counter of a reproductive boutique, reduced to jiggered parts, or to the latest wear in the salons of the rich.

It used to be taken for granted that in speaking to young people, one was speaking to a maturing human being, not to a brute with debased tastes, ill-governed appetites, no practical skills, no sense of high purpose or great art, and no yearning for the quest to find goodness and truth and beauty. Here, for instance, is advice given to young men by a priest long ago, on whether it is a good thing to "sow wild oats":

He has begun wrong, and a shaky foundation always threatens the building that is upon it. True, he may hold the building up, but it will be with ugly props or binding braces. At his best he will lack always the purest touch of beauty in his soul, always miss the serenity of spirit that dwells with the pure of heart.*

Or, from the Protestant side, the preacher Charles Parkhurst reminds his young men readers that marriage is the natural state for man, and that therefore they should prepare themselves for it morally and intellectually. What Parkhurst insists upon is the greatest respect due to manliness and to womanliness, "making manliness to mean the most possible, and womanliness to mean the most possible, not dragging the distinctive qualities of either over the ground of the other."†

What we want to produce, instead, are people incapable of glimpsing, with awe, the unfathomable mystery of people; of man and woman, whose bodies, when they unite, produce that one-flesh union which allows us to link one generation to the next. Machines must be lubricated; so let our children be, with the slick sweat of unthinking, mechanical sexual activity, something thirty or forty degrees below the old-fashioned warmth of lust, and a million degrees below the heat of "the Love that moves the sun and the other stars."

---

* Joseph P. Conroy, SJ, *Talks to Boys* (St. Louis: The Queen's Work Press, 1918).
† Charles H. Parkhurst, *Talks to Young Men* (New York: The Century Co., 1897).

Method 8

Level Distinctions between Man and Woman

or

Spay and Geld

Thou following cri'd'st aloud, Return, fair Eve,
Whom fli'st thou? Whom thou fli'st, of him thou art,
His flesh, his bone; to give thee being I lent
Out of my side to thee, nearest my heart
Substantial Life, to have thee by my side
Henceforth an individual solace dear;
Part of my soul I seek thee, and thee claim
My other half: with that thy gentle hand
Seiz'd mine, I yielded, and from that time see
How beauty is excell'd by manly grace,
And wisdom which alone is truly fair.
   —Milton, *Paradise Lost*

The child grew red with pleasure, for she knew well that her father
was held to be the comeliest man far around; he looked like a knight,
standing there among his men.
   —Sigrid Undset, *The Bridal Wreath*

More than a mile across the wilderness
They sat together halfway up a cliff
In a small niche let into it, the girl

Brightly, as if a star played on the place,
Paul darkly, like her shadow. All the light
Was from the girl herself.
　　　　　—Robert Frost, "Paul's Wife"

Masculinity and femininity are the more superficial aspects of being
a man or a woman and it is quite possible to put on the trappings of
masculinity without being truly male, or the trappings of femininity
without being truly female.
　　　　　—Mary S. Calderone, "An Approach," in
　　　　　Sex Educations: Issues and Directives

When I was young there was, I confess, something intriguing
about the television set. Not for what was generally showing on it, but for the thing itself, picking up airborne signals
from far away and translating them into a code of electronic dots that
would make up a picture. Or half a picture: often something like a fuzzy
compromise between coherence and chaos. In my mind, half the fun was
in seeing how you could turn the set in a particular direction, with the
antennae poised just so, to see if you could pick up stations from places
I'd never been, mysterious patches on the road map named Elmira and
Binghamton.

　　　It was the strangeness of it all that attracted me. The same thing happened when I'd try to find radio stations late at night from Pittsburgh, Cin-
cinnati, and even Saint Louis, fifteen hundred miles away from my house,
to listen to my favorite team, the Cardinals. Usually I'd hear only a sentence or two—"curveball in the dirt, full count to Alou—and the runners
will be going"—garbled up with bad music from a competing station from
Charlotte, over a thousand miles away in a completely different direction,
and with the haunting static of the universe. But I'd sit in the dark, hunched
to the floor, the radio pressed to my ear, trying to extend its little power by
making an antenna of my body.

　　　The imagination of man, unless it is stifled early, is restless. We grow
used to the things we see about us, taking for granted the beauty of the
stream without a name that only runs after the spring rains; overlooking
the ordinary houses straggling up the hill nearby; missing the pleasant lilt
in a voice we hear every day. We long for what we have not yet seen. We

track a brook to its source, because maybe there's a spring there, and who knows what's down in that cave, or in the crates up in the attic?

Man must have the faraway, the separate, the unknown—and, strange to say, he must keep it nearby. That, as I've said, explains the fascination of the holy. The ancient Romans kept small figurines or death-masks of their ancestors, in a special chest near the fireplace. These were taken out on holidays—they were not the objects of familiar handling. My father did not like to write letters, but when he did, he saved them; and my mother saved the letters he wrote to her when they were engaged, and he was stationed at an army base in Colorado. These letters they kept in a certain drawer in their bedroom. It isn't that they were filled with embarrassing expressions of passion. They weren't. It is simply that they were precious to them, and therefore things to be looked at seldom, and not by just anybody.

We have sent men to the moon, and even to Alaska. Yet we human beings wherever we go will always have one frontier right before us, one source of wonder, precisely for the fascinating strangeness of the land. Women will have men, and men will have women.

I need hardly say that it will do no good if we snicker at wedded love and demote sexual intercourse to matters of plumbing, if then we are still so foolish as to leave boys and girls to fall in what used to be called "love," looking at one another with longing and incomprehension. Eros has been known to blossom forth in great art and music and poetry, not to mention its dangerous proximity to longings for the divine—as Plato could teach us, or Saint John of the Cross. We want sex, as a kind of recreational drug, like the *soma* of Huxley's *Brave New World*. But we don't want sex, as the distinction between male and female. We are still, at least until the technocrats have perfected artificial conception and gestation, going to produce the next generation in the old-fashioned and mysterious way, the mingling of bodies giving rise to, as Scripture quaintly puts it, a new "living soul." But we want that to happen as the result of the life-career decisions of the modestly contented couple. We don't want a woman to look at a man with any kind of wonder and reverence, and say to herself, "He is the one whose child I want to bear." We don't want a man to look at a woman in the same way, saying, "She is the one I wish to bear my child."

We want a superficial—might we say epidermal?—familiarity, masking a deep and impenetrable ignorance of men for women and women for men. We want sexual satisfaction, like the routine filling of the belly with sandwiches and potato chips, but no joy. We want a regular parade of bodies profaning themselves for a buck or two, with all the romance of an itchy scab. How, since we are for the time being stuck with biological males and females, can we insulate ourselves against the dangers of wonder?

The answer is simple enough. Flatten the children.

Herd 'Em Up

This we can accomplish most effectively if we remember that often the same tool can serve two functions at once. If, for instance, the imagination is essential to genuine humanity, and if that imagination is kindled by the strangeness of one sex to the other, then anything we do to blunt a child's humanity will probably also blunt his sense of wonder for the opposite sex. And if human nature thrives on friendship on the one hand, and solitude on the other (as I'll show), then we can work against both friendship and solitude by gathering the children together in enormous herds, say, up to a thousand or more in a single building.

Just as individual personalities are washed flat by the tidal passions of a mob, so too individual distinctions, including distinctions of sex, grow less and less visible in a herd. The sheer magnitude of the herd prevents it. Yes, boys will notice that there are such things as girls, and girls will notice that there are such things as boys, but that will be lost in the general anonymity and relative indistinguishability of all the faces.

Beyond that, a herd or a mob is indiscriminate. There is no male cohort in the mob, no bleachers for old people, no children's wing. If, then, you want to raise herds that will perform exactly the function the state needs them to perform, using no initiative, you will be wise to pretend from the outset that there are no distinctions of sex, or none that matter for anything really important. That is why Socrates, in his *Republic*, decreed for his imaginary totalitarian state an educational regimen wherein young men and young women would exercise together, naked. The idea was not that they would then fall in love with one another—precisely the reverse: they would take one another for granted. They could sing patriotic songs if they wanted to, but not something as dangerously erotic as Yeats's "He Tells of Perfect Beauty":

O cloud-pale eyelids, dream-dimmed eyes,
The poets labouring all their days
To build a perfect beauty in rhyme
Are overthrown by a woman's gaze
And by the unlabouring brood of the skies.

Or as delightful and whimsically bawdy as Theodore Roethke's "Light Listened":

O what could be more nice
Than her ways with a man?
She kissed me more than twice
Once we were left alone.
Who'd look when he could feel?
She'd more sides than a seal.

Or expressing so innocent yet passionate a longing, as Keats's *The Eve of St. Agnes*:

They told her how, upon St. Agnes' Eve,
Young virgins might have visions of delight,
And soft adoring from their loves receive
Upon the honeyed middle of the night.

Eros, passion, and bawdiness are unacceptable. Boredom is all.

When I was young, the engineers of schools had not yet fully understood this principle. The Catholic schools I attended were particularly far behind the times. If we arrived at the "playground" early in the morning—the playground, I'll add, was no more than a sandlot next to the school, with no equipment at all in the way, and therefore a fine place for the invention of games—we were to walk quietly over to the church and take our places in the pews with the rest of our class, girls to the left of the main aisle, boys to the right. We were thus seated with (and we prayed beside) children with whom we would be most likely to strike up a good friendship; and we were seated opposite children who by their very separation from us piqued our interest. What's more, this division seemed to us natural and to be respected. We were the ones who wore trousers and jackets and ties. They were the ones who wore tartan skirts and weskits. They could no more imagine wearing coats and neckties than we could imagine wearing skirts and weskits. That, of course, made us interesting to one another.

When Mass was over—Mass, said by a priest, assisted by altar boys—we trooped back to the school, led by the nuns in their distinctive habits, in single file, boys on one side, girls on the other. That apparently was not unique to Catholic schools. Many an old public school building preserves a fossil of the old delight in distinction: a boys' entrance on one side, a girls' entrance on the other. Even state colleges, until fairly recently, maintained not only separate dormitories but separate deans for men and women—people still laboring under the fanciful illusion that there are such things as men and women, with different strengths and different weaknesses, or that sometimes a young man might not want to talk about a personal problem with a bossy or patronizing woman, no matter how kindly-intended she might be.

We did a lot of playing on that school sandlot, too. For the most part the girls played with the girls and the boys played with the boys, as was natural. Sometimes we played together—tag, or crack the whip. But girls did not join in playing King of the Hill, which was pretty rough, and would have been awkward for everyone concerned. It was the same way in the neighborhood. A couple of tomboys were all right for Wiffle ball and touch football, and we loved to have them along (especially when we boys got a little older), but never for tackle football, never for hardball, and never for tramping far into the woods (that would have been unseemly).

The upshot was that we looked over at one another and wondered—at least I did, and I assume I was hardly alone in this. That was so in our organized sports, too, what blessedly few there were at that time. Little League was open to boys; there was a softball league for girls who wanted to play, but it wasn't very popular. Now I was small for my age back then, and no doubt there were plenty of girls in town who could have performed at least as well on the ball field as I did. But nobody thought that would be right—not the boys, not the girls. It was fun for us to wear our uniforms together, as boys, especially if we weren't all that good at the game; it gave us a sense of being what we were, namely, boys. It was fun, too, for the girls to gather together in their girl-klatsches, eating Popsicles and cheering for their brother's team, or for the team with the boy on it whom they liked—the girls were mainstays at those games.

When the nuns who ran our school were ordered by the state to provide regular physical education (our hour on the sandlot being insufficient for the purpose), they conceived the remarkable idea of hiring a dance instructor. This, it is true, brought the boys and girls together, but not indiscriminately; the distinctions were preserved and even sharpened. When boys and girls dance a polka or a waltz, the boy has a job to do and the girl has a job to do. That also felt natural.

When I went on to high school, some of those distinctions were already being blurred away. Yet we did not have to suffer the indignity of coed gym classes, as were becoming common in the public asylums. That again made all the difference in the world to some of us. We could be free to be ourselves, letting ourselves go in dodgeball or football or wrestling. Since we shared the big basketball court with the girls, we could steal a glance across the way at them once in a while, and they could steal a glance at us. That too was fine.

All for One, and One for All

Meanwhile, keeping the boys more or less with the boys and the girls more or less with the girls —following what has been common sense in every culture and every age—had the effect of fostering interests within those groups.

At the turn of the century in my hometown, boys would get together in the wintertime to sled down a steep hill a quarter of a mile long, picking up tremendous speed, launching themselves into the air at a ramp formed by the bed of a railroad, and finally sliding to a halt almost a half a mile away, past the church and the Catholic school and the public high school. In my own time they would take motorbikes to the woods to try to zigzag up the enormous mounds of coal waste, two hundred feet or more from base to summit. Those were sporting activities, but boys used to get together to pursue intellectual and technological interests, too: they were ham radio operators, coin collectors, auto aficionados. My cousins put together dozens of model cars, gluing together the tiny parts, painting them, pasting them with decals. When they were not much older, they got themselves underneath the chassis of real cars, and learned about carburetors, distributors, timing chains, and crankshafts partly from overhearing the grown-ups and watching them closely, but also partly from one another.

I wasn't interested in machines, but I was interested in maps, and grids of numbers, and these things too were fostered by our being left alone to enjoy boyhood as boys. The neighborhood boys, for instance, were expected to go into the woods a little way—never as much as a mile, when we were young, but still far enough to be out of sight of grown-ups and, of course, girls. There we discovered things—and in part discovered ourselves, what we dared to do, and what we didn't. There were rock formations we climbed, and we painted our initials on them in the immemorial habit of boys everywhere from the cave paintings at Lascaux to the scrawled gang graffiti on the concrete sides of a highway overpass. My cousins collected sand from the sloping side of what was otherwise a sheer cliff, to make cement, as they said. We marked trails and named them; we set small pit-traps in one of them and then lured one of the duller neighborhood boys to run down the path to see him trip. And we drew maps of our territory.

Hobbies also spread from boy to boy. I collected coins because one of my older cousins did. He collected them because another older cousin did, who collected them because his father did. My younger brother collected them because I did. Sometimes we got together to look at our collections, and we traded. That too was full of high-stakes dickering:

"I'll give you these two Indian pennies for that Mercury Dime."
"Naw, I already have those dates. What about that 1932 quarter?"
"I am not giving you that for anything. I have two V-nickels with no date. I'll give you one of them for the steel penny with a D."
"OK, it's a deal."

Although we still enjoyed the residue of a genuine boy's life, it was nothing so powerful a source of ingenuity and imagination as such lives used to be. Partly the television was to blame, that excellent tool for isolation and indoor gaping. But partly we were already losing the sense that boys and girls were to be kept separate for their own healthy development, intellectual and emotional.

I speak from the point of view of someone who was a boy; I assume that many of the things I say would apply to girls, in a different way and for different activities. A judicious separation of the sexes made it possible for boys and girls to try their hands at this or that, without the distraction of the opposite sex—in particular, without fear of being embarrassed by, or in front of, the opposite sex. Take singing, for example.

It is hard for us to imagine it because it is so far from our current experience, but for many centuries in the cathedrals of Europe, boys not only sang, they were sought after for their voices, and choral music was written with their vocal quality specifically in mind. Until their muscles thicken and the cords of the larynx deepen into tenor and baritone, boys sing soprano, but still they don't sound like women. Their voices are clearer, less mature, youthful—not shrill or reedy, but rather like the pure or colorless sound of a recorder. They didn't generally sing alone. They sang the soprano parts in choral arrangements for tenors and basses, too. That it was a normal state of affairs we can gather not only from the written music and from written testimony but also from the paintings and sculptures of choir lofts: boys, singing together, *not* in some annoying children's choir, but in the real choir, to perform masterpieces of the most complex musical and theological beauty, such as Palestrina's *Credo* in the *Missa Papae Marcelli*, or Allegri's haunting *Miserere*.

About twenty years ago or so, Catholics in America got the idea that it was unfair for boys alone to assist the priest at the altar. I won't argue about the theology behind their position. I only note that what happened next could have been predicted by anybody who knows anything about boys and girls. The girls volunteered—it was, after all, not anything new for them to wear gowns—and the boys faded out of the picture. It wasn't that they didn't like the girls; it was simply that they had been deprived of something essential to the experience of being an acolyte. Without perhaps being conscious of it, they wanted to be a part of a gang of their own kind, boys, assisting a man at man's work. If one of them would do it, then two or three might; if two or three might, then ten or twenty might. The same thing goes for singing, or for any number of things. Whatever boys do together is by that very fact all right; it may be painting or dancing or singing or learning Russian or building go-carts. The separation from girls makes it possible; and the being-with-your-kind makes it enjoyable, and gives your imagination room to expand.

Anybody who really pays attention to these creatures can see that even when they are doing the same thing, they aren't doing the same thing. Take boys and girls to the lake, and the girls will go for a walk around the lake, or will swim and talk, while the boys will play chicken fights in the water. Give them a room full of hammers, boards, nails, and saws, and the girls will make something nice to go on a wall, and the boys will build a battering ram to knock the wall down. This is all pretty normal. But we don't want it. We want to stifle their spirits. So we compel them all to do the same thing, and that usually means we will choose something so banal as to interest nobody in particular. It will be the artistic equivalent of a doctored ball-yard game that boys and girls will play equally well, because it will be equally dull to both.

In short, sometimes it's not a question of embarrassment. It's rather the possibility of friendship, unencumbered by feelings of attraction or shyness; the possibility of working on the same wavelength, as it were, with someone who understands you because he's a boy as you are, or a girl as you are. Committee work stifles the imagination, because people have to work down to the common denominator of what would be minimally acceptable to everyone. But friendship exalts the imagination. Indeed it is one of the things that the ancients said friendship was *for*. Plato suggests in *Symposium* that one of the highest forms of friendship is one whose love issues forth in beautiful and virtuous deeds, for thus "the partnership between [the friends] will be far closer and the bond of affection far stronger than between ordinary parents, because the children that they share surpass human children by being immortal as well as more beautiful."

Everywhere in history and literature we see the creativity of friendship—I know I am speaking about the band of brothers here, leaving to others more knowledgeable than I to speak about sisterhoods. When the Babylonian hero-king Gilgamesh finally meets his match, Enkidu, and struggles mightily to best him in a wrestling match so titanic and so dangerous that the walls of the city shake, he and Enkidu become fast friends. "My little brother," Gilgamesh calls him, and proposes to him an adventure to benefit the whole kingdom: the conquest of the ogre of the cedar forest, Humbaba. We see in the myth the dynamism of such a brotherhood: it not only helps to civilize Gilgamesh, who had, before Enkidu challenged him to the fight, been in the habit of calling all the young men off to war and taking newlywed brides to himself. It also results in bold deeds undertaken for the sake of civilization itself: in this case, to slay the ogre is to bring back to the mud-brick city the decorative cedar, beautiful and fragrant, from hundreds of miles away in the mysterious and treacherous mountains of the north.

Michelangelo was in some senses a naturally solitary man, perhaps what we would now call autistic. But he could never have painted the Sistine ceiling or sculpted the *David* had he not been given the chance to develop his talents in the company of other young men, and had he not chanced to find close friends, inspirers, along the way. It is probably not accidental that in the most creative city in the most artistically bustling era in the history of mankind, a young lad with a knack for drawing would be apprenticed to a painter's studio at a very early age. There he would learn the humbler skills of the trade: how to erect scaffolding, how to mix paint, how to amend errors, how to draw relatively simple figures, and so forth. He'd be given gradually more and more responsibility—allowed to paint in a dog in the corner of a fresco, for instance—until he could set forth on his own. We refer to the paintings as the work of Ghirlandaio (the man to whom Michelangelo was apprenticed) or Raphael or Correggio, but in most cases the man we are naming is but the chief of a band of men working together at the project in hierarchical order, enabling the master to achieve the masterpiece.

But friendship seldom implies uniformity of mind. When Michelangelo was a young man, for instance, he was invited to attend the meetings of learned men in the gardens of Lorenzo de' Medici, the de facto ruler of Florence. In one room he would have heard at once a hedonistic poet like Angelo Poliziano, and the Platonic moralist (and young genius himself) Pico della Mirandola, and the dour and shy textual humanist Cristoforo Landino, and the expansive and somewhat self-aggrandizing Platonist, the acknowledged head of the Academy, Marsilio Ficino. The friend, in such circumstances, may be the worthy opponent, the iron that sharpens iron. Such for instance were the guildsmen of the Middle Ages: groups of craftsmen who bonded together not only for fellowship and camaraderie but also for mutual help in time of need, for insurance for their widows and orphans, for celebrating their special saint's day, for keeping prices high enough for everyone to do well, and for keeping the quality of work high enough that they might not be outdone by guilds from neighboring cities. If you want an example of what guilds could do, walk into any medieval cathedral or palace in Europe. It is not exactly true that illiterate *people* built Chartres Cathedral, perhaps the noblest building to grace the earth. It is that *brotherhoods* built it.

And what went on inside it, and inside the schools nearby? A medieval school was also a brotherhood: a guild of scholars who ensured the high quality of their work, so that one could become a master at the University of Paris and be accorded the right to teach at Oxford or Padua or Prague. Friendship, even rivalrous friendship, was of the essence of that newly created thing called the university (the name means, roughly, "union"). Thomas Aquinas, one of a band of brothers called Dominicans, discoursed on Aristotelian philosophy and its application to Christian theology at the University of Paris, at the same time that Bonaventure, one of a band of brothers called Franciscans, cast a cold eye upon the pagan rationalist Aristotle and developed a mystical philosophy meant to assist the soul in its journey into the mind of God. Now if a young man entered such a place, he didn't simply take a course, sit in his seat, nod off, drink too much in the evening and abuse the townsfolk, spend too much money, write home for more, and so forth. He entered friendships. He and his fellows slept in the same dormitories, ate together, heard Mass together, attended lectures together. It was a corporate enterprise—sometimes an enterprise involving the whole town. For when one of the scholars was ready to be examined by the masters to see if he would receive his license to teach, the examination was oral, and public, and set up in the form of an intellectual wrestling match, the student pitted against his questioners.

If it is objected that herding the sexes together will not entirely obliterate the opportunities for friendship, I agree. It won't, by itself. It will, though, severely hinder those friendships, both in their number and their kind. It will reduce friendship to a surface agreement in temperament—the "friend" is just somebody I can have a laugh or two with and maybe play a game with, but not much more. It will also provide all kinds of opportunity ensuring that such friendships as do develop never go far. For whenever boys and girls are together, the thing most prominent in their minds will not be the distinction between essence and existence, or what Dante meant when he placed the idolatrous king Solomon in the circle of the wise, or how to construct a telegraph. It will be who is eyeing whom, who is attending whose party, and so forth—it will be those things that males and females do *together*, rather than those things they can more easily do apart.

But I should not focus solely on the uses which friendship serves. The principle danger of friendship is the friendship itself. Men who once served in the army sometimes seek their buddies, people with whom they may have nothing else in common, after forty and fifty years' separation; a bond is forged between them that time can wear away but not break. My wife, who attended school just when the indiscriminate herding of girls and boys was getting into full swing—in, for instance, coed gym classes, the bane of her school days—used to get together with another girl, her best friend, to play the guitar. They learned together the songs of James Taylor and the Mamas and the Papas and Joni Mitchell. Back then, schools were not quite the small police states they have thankfully come to be, so occasionally she and her friend would steal away to a closet to play music. That creative friendship was severed, for many years, when each of them moved far from home and went to college. They have, however, recently found one another again. And that friendship stands as a small affront to the total control of all things by mass entertainment and mass media and mass education and mass politics. For wherever such friendships persist, there persists the possibility of imaginative leaps that threaten the comfort of the banal

For you look at the friend and you remember the past, and treasure it. You love the friend, and suddenly you understand that this life of ours cannot fully be described by the motion of particulate matter in empty space. You see instantly that politics fades into unimportance, with all its noisy glamour and empty promises. You feel that others before you have known what it is to have the true friend, the one before whom you can, as Cicero put it, think out loud. You feel that, and it is like an earnest of eternity, of being grounded in a love and beauty and goodness that is at the heart of all ages, and that transcends them all. Pals we may have, in the flatlands of contemporary life. Political allies, sure. Coworkers, aplenty. But not friends.

Male and Female He Created Them

The space traveler in C. S. Lewis's *Perelandra*, sent to a newborn world to help its first inhabitants ward off a temptation to evil, sees before him the spirits of that world and of another, older world. The spirits, possessing no bodies such as we can conceive of them, are nevertheless somehow masculine and feminine, and indeed they make our own biological maleness and femaleness seem shadowy and paltry by comparison:

> Malacandra seemed to him to have the look of one standing armed, at
> the ramparts of his own archaic world, in ceaseless vigilance, his eyes

peer roaming the earth-ward horizon whence his danger came long ago. "A sailor's look," Ransom once said to me; "you know . . . eyes that are impregnated with distance." But the eyes of Perelandra opened, as it were, inward, as if they were the curtained gateway to a world of waves and murmurings and wandering airs, of life that rocked in winds and splashed in mossy stones and descended as the dew and arose sunward in thin-spun delicacy of mist.

There's a village in rural China with a quaint custom. Every year, all the boys of the village line up on one side of a hill, dressed in red ceremonial garb, while all the girls line up on the other side, in flowing robes. The boys then commence to chant and sing about their bravery, and about how much they love the favorites of their hearts, a twinkle in their eye, because they know that most of it is delightful exaggeration. The girls for their part sing back, doubting the boys, egging them on to prove themselves, laughing at them and admiring them. In Austria, in the old days, a boy who was in love with his sweetheart showed his love and his manhood by braving the Alpine cliffs in search of edelweiss, which he would pick to give to his beloved. Even in secular, unsentimental, and politically correct Sweden, on Saint Lucy's Day the eldest daughter in the house, garbed in the most feminine of long, white robes and wearing a candlelit crown on her head, will wake her parents in the morning with a breakfast of tea and the traditional saffron buns.

I will not bother to argue here that there are such things as manliness and womanliness. The customs of all cultures testify to them, as do all the artists and musicians and poets. That is not the point. The trouble with believing in these things is that they are beautiful and bracing; they give a young person a recognizable ideal for which to strive, and to grow into, and—this is most important—it is an ideal not of their own devising. When the Jewish boy had learned to read the words of the Holy Torah and uttered them in the synagogue before his family and his community, he did not then say, "This day I have become a grown-up." Growing up is what we do naturally. A weed grows. He did not say, "This day I have become an adult." All that means is that he is physically mature and perhaps morally responsible. He said, "This day I have become a man." And if you do not understand the danger of giving boys the notion that they must become men, then you know nothing about either boys or men, and probably you know little about girls and women, too.

Sometimes the initiation of a boy to manhood is deemed as central to the health of all the people. In the Kwoma tribe in New Guinea, the initiates are taken to a hut far from the village, where they are given instruction in gong beating and intricate flute playing by the older men. This is to prepare them for the religious ceremony centered upon the cult of the yam crop, when the boy, led by an older sponsor, will have a roasted yam thrust into his hand as he dances alone within a circle of men. The boys are told that the spirits that rule over the earth do not actually visit the huts for the ceremony, but that they are still responsible for the success of the yam crop. After the dance, the boys are invited to sit with the men—because then they are men—to "smoke cigarettes, chew betel, and gossip"*

When girls in America outgrew their rag dolls, they began to collect things that might be useful or beautiful for their lives as women—as wives and mothers. They would save napkins, tablecloths, silverware, or whatever they treasured most, and keep them in a cedar chest, their "hope chest." Note the significance of the act. A young girl would be encouraged not simply to daydream but to act in a determined way to bring about some joy for herself and for those whom she would love, far in the future. They might as well have called it an "imagination chest," as it exercised their capacities, practical and moral, to see what it meant to be a good woman, and to prepare themselves to live up to that calling.

The Canadian writer Louis Hémon tells the story of a family of farmers in the countryside around Lac Saint-Jean, where the soil is rich but the fields are hard to plow, where the summers are warm but short, and the winters cold and long. Without the virtues of manhood and womanhood no family could survive there. Even to clear a small field to get it ready for plowing would require a half a dozen men with pickaxes, then a team of oxen hitched to the tree-stumps with iron chains, then coals and fire to burn out the thousands of remaining roots. It is bitter work, toughening the muscle and the soul. Were it not for a vision of possibilities far outstripping the meager yield of the present, no one would do it. But were it not also that men accepted the challenge as men, the place would be abandoned to the wild animals. One of the boys in the family, thirteen years old, is big

---

* John M. W. Whiting, *Becoming a Kwoma: Teaching and Learning in a New Guinea Tribe* (New Haven, CT: Yale University Press, 1941).

enough to take his place among the men, and work beside them, sunup to sundown. That grants him the privilege to smoke a pipe with them, and to give counsel, which the men hear with respect, no less than if he were thirty. For the women the work is equally difficult, but of a different sort, and it too calls forth an act of imagination almost heroic: to be a real woman in a place like this, responsible for feeding and clothing your family, and for keeping a house fit to dwell in, is a task calling forth every resource of ingenuity and diligence.

The heroine of the novel, Maria Chapdelaine, falls in love with a handsome young man who leaves one fall to go trapping in the far north country, promising to return. He does not survive. Brokenhearted, she seems ready to leave her forbidding homeland forever, following another young man in love with her, who wants to take her to Boston, where she will see the bright city lights, and shop in rich stores, and meet all kinds of people from all over the world. It seems an easy choice to make. But Maria is a woman in love—and one should never underestimate a genuine woman, in love. She decides in the end that she will remain in Quebec, among her people, on her land. The girl would have gone to Boston. The woman dwells where she belongs.

I trust the reader will see that we cannot kill the imagination if we allow children to look forward to anything as noble as manhood and womanhood. Yes, the children will grow up, and they know that they will do things when they are grown up that they cannot do as children. That might threaten to breathe life into the imagination, did we not have the antidotes against it.

First, one must never speak of "manhood" and "womanhood." Those words remind us of the mysteries of our bodies and our souls. They cause us to wonder why there should even be such fascinating creatures as men and women. We cannot use the words without calling up pictures to mind. We think of stories. We think of someone like Pier Giorgio Frassati, a young medical student in Turin, an avid skier and a popular athlete, who ministered to the homeless and destitute in his city, sharing their suffering, and eventually dying of the plague that ravaged them. We think of the gentleness and humility and womanly endurance of a Mother Teresa—aptly named "Mother," who begged the world not to make away with their unloved children, because she would love them if they would bring them to her. I cannot think of manhood without thinking of *a man*, and there comes to my mind my father, a severe judge of human character, who yet never stooped to say an unkind word about anyone; I see him sitting in his chair, relatively young, fully conscious on the day he knew he was going to die, telling me and my brother to shovel the snow out of the driveway lest anybody's car get stuck. I cannot think of womanhood without thinking of *a woman*, and there comes to mind my grandmother, who when her right arm was withered and nearly useless rolled out the dough with her left, who loved her sixteen grandchildren, changing all of their diapers, singing to them, feeding them, and brightening whenever they came to visit.

We cannot talk of such; so instead we replace "man" and "woman" with "adult." Now, the word "adult" rouses no imagination. It is a biological term, a technical term referring to physical maturation. First we have a larva, then a pupa, then an adult. At most the term connotes a kind of low-level responsibility, mainly in the service of one's selfish purposes, like showing up for work on time and keeping an orderly briefcase. No child ever says to himself, "I want to be an *adult*," just as nobody says, "If only I had to pay the monthly bills," or "The day when I fill out my first tax form will be the happiest of my life." So we must talk, in suitably banal and disheartening terms, of adulthood—and of course, whether boys and girls like it or not, their bodies will grow to adulthood eventually. Whether they become men and women is a different matter, but we can keep them unaware of that.

The other thing that talk of "adulthood" does is to flatten any residual ideal of manhood and womanhood down to a mediocre evenness. Christopher Marlowe once wrote of the beauty of Helen of Troy in *Dr. Faustus*:

Is this the face that launched a thousand ships,
And burnt the topless towers of Ilium?
Sweet Helen, make me immortal with a kiss!

That's what might come to mind if you conceive of the beauty of woman; the "beauty of an adult" sounds like a joke. In *Jane Eyre*, Charlotte Brontë's young, titular heroine meets the brooding and mysterious Mr. Rochester—who, like Helen of Troy, is no moral paragon, but who is every bit the man as she is the woman. Jane considers the capaciousness of his forehead and the strength of his countenance, marks of years of concentrated thought, self-control, and inflexible will. It may not be the best thing in the world to be a Helen or a Rochester, but it is at least *something*. And we should prefer to avoid it altogether.

And we can do that, if we instill in our students the easy habit of sneering at beauty and virtue. I say it is an easy habit, because a little veneer of intelligence will usually suffice to persuade one that all the people in the world who lived before one's time—say, all the people who lived before two in the afternoon on July 2, 1965—were fools or knaves. They all believed the world was flat; they kept slaves; they burned witches; they smoked cigarettes; whatever easy stupidity or immorality can be pinned on them, we pin it. They cannot answer the charges themselves, and students ignorant of history can't answer them either. So we talk glibly about *traditional* manhood and *traditional* womanhood, with a knowing wink—meaning brutality and idiocy. That such men and women, possessed of virtues we ignore, tamed a continent, is not to be considered.

Meanwhile what is miscalled popular culture, and what is actually mass entertainment, will help us out considerably. Have children understand that manliness and womanliness are contemptible. The true man is a cartoon figure, a crazy mixture of steroid-exploded muscle mass, grunts, and a bad shave. Otherwise men are fat, sloppy, and stupid. They paint their bellies for football games and drink beer. They are incompetents in the workplace. Their conversation revolves around fast food and fast women. For their part, the women are skinny to the point of emaciation. They wear clothes that would make the whores of old blush. They are fussy, snippy, and feline. They enjoy humiliating men, who always come back for more anyway. They have studied martial arts, and can be choreographed into delivering a backhand slap from a thin-wristed arm that will defy all the laws of physics and send a 250-pound man reeling. They have foul mouths, but they don't come by the foulness honestly; a sort of sneaky, sniggering arch foulness.

Let these be the creatures held up for our children's emulation. They cannot excite the imagination, no more than cardboard can excite the appetite. They may possess a lot of money, a sharp wardrobe, and a glamorous job, but those things are the false goods that glut the soul rather than whet its longing for what is beyond our immediate range of sight. They not only possess no virtue; they corrode what virtues are left in the young. They leave children with the cynicism of a twice-divorced harridan or cad. Men are not worth looking for, women are not worth looking for. Feed young people enough of that, and you will not only ensure that they lose the ideals of manhood and womanhood. You will go far toward making souls incapable of imagining any real virtue at all. They will be wiser than all that traditional rot—and, for our purposes, more manageable.

Method 9

Distract the Child with the Shallow and Unreal

or

The Kingdom of Noise

"Let him who has ears to hear, hear."
—Mark 4:23

And the winds whistling in the hollow of reeds
Taught them to play the rustic hemlock pipe.
Then little by little they learned the sweet complaints
That the pipe pours forth at the fingering-pulse of the players,
Heard in the trackless forests, the shepherds' dells,
Places of sunlit solitude and peace.
—Lucretius, *On the Nature of Things*

On a night of darkness,
In love's anxiety of longing kindled,
O blessed chance!
I left by none beheld,
My house in sleep and silence stilled.
—John of the Cross, "The Dark Night"

Tradition has it that Homer, the man who wrote the defining epics of the West, the *Iliad* and the *Odyssey*, was blind. Perhaps the tradition arose from one of the figures in the *Odyssey*, the old poet Demodocus. He is led by hand to his honored seat at the banquet table, bread and meat placed before him, and his lyre hung from a peg nearby. He was loved dearly by the Muse, says Homer, who gave him both good and ill: "she blinded him in the eyes but gave him a sweet song." There is just the hint there that the misfortune was a blessing: because he was blind, it became all the easier for him to hear.

Homer was not the only blind poet or blind musician in history. Ray Charles and Stevie Wonder, both exceptionally talented musicians and composers of popular music, were blind. John Milton lost his vision writing political pamphlets in his middle age, having deferred his heart's wish, to write the great Christian epic of the fall of man. Many millions of people have read *Paradise Lost*, but Milton was not one of them. When he "wrote" the poem he was stone blind, dictating it to his daughters, who would read it back to him. He "saw" his work as a totality in his mind, but he could never have seen it had he not heard it first. That's a strange thing to say: how could he hear what he had not yet composed? But Milton describes the exercise of his poetic imagination not as declaiming, but as hearing. So he prepares for the climax of his poem, the temptation and fall, by appealing to his Heavenly Muse,

> . . . who deigns
> Her nightly visitation unimplor'd,
> And dictates to me slumb'ring, or inspires
> Easy my unpremeditated Verse.

This hearing is not just the sharpening of one sense at the expense of another. It is, as the poets struggle to tell us, a kind of receptivity to something that comes to us from without. This is why we can do a fine job curdling the imagination by stressing "creativity," for the creative child is encouraged to think of himself as a little god, with all his bright ideas coming from within. The older tradition has the poet as hearer before he is a crafter of verses. The Muse comes to him.

It is an attitude that leaves us open to all possibilities. I have in mind a young man, about sixteen years old, not at all busy making a career for himself, or being creative, or speaking endlessly about his qualifications for admission to this or that university. In some ways, he was a kind of lazy fellow; a lover of music to the end, who played the violin for the sheer joy of it. He was daydreaming on one of the hillsides in Tuscany, its slopes dusky with olive trees and dotted with the dark conical cypresses, bathed in the Mediterranean sunlight coming down from a clear blue sky. And in that silent place he wondered about light—about what it would be like to ride a ray of sunlight. We might say he lay there listening to the light's whispering. His name was Albert Einstein.

Or I am reminded of the famous account of the prophet Elijah in the wilderness. He was told by the Lord to stand before a cave, for the Lord would pass by. And Elijah witnessed all the pyrotechnics nature has to offer. First came the whirlwind, a dust storm not uncommon in the arid east. But the Lord was not in the whirlwind. Then came an earthquake, but the Lord was not in the earthquake. Then came fire from above, but the Lord was not in the fire. Finally Elijah heard a faint whispering sound, or, as the King James translators brilliantly render it, a "still small voice." And immediately he entered the cave and hid his face in worship.

When I was a small boy, in the days before children had been trammeled up for safety's sake, I'd take my sled out at night after supper to join my cousins on one of the hills nearby. The snow lay heavy on the earth and the bushes and the trees, muffling all sound but,

> . . . the sweep /
> Of easy wind and downy flake

and the cries of the boys, and the soft *ssshh* of sled runners on snow, and the panting and occasional bark of the happy dog who could not bear to be apart from us. One of the hills was blessedly treacherous, a drop of about forty feet over a two-hundred foot span, concluding in a sidewalk at right angles to the road. You'd have to lean your body on the sled or stick your right foot out like an oar to swing the sled right and keep going—or you'd bail out at the last moment and let the sled fly on to its impact. So there was plenty of laughter and an occasional smash of sled against stone. But no cars, and nothing electronic; and when you pulled the sled after you back up the hill, you might be alone with that openness to the night that speaks more eloquently than thought.

One night of bitter cold, the snow a deep and dry powder, I remember sledding down from the wooded hill above my grandfather's house, hardly able to see the path to steer in the dark, and hearing, as if by small and faraway bells, the sound of a hymn:

> A mighty fortress is our God,
> A bulwark never failing.

Such moments remain with you; they are the wellsprings of a human life, rich in thought, though not perhaps in worldly consequence. I met a man recently with a humble enough job. He is one of the caretakers of a provincial park in Nova Scotia, an island no longer inhabited, out in a bay beyond which lies nothing but the ocean between it and Europe. He told me that when he was only a boy, he and his brother would take their father's motor-powered boat out twenty miles to a point they knew of, and set anchor there and fish. They'd have provisions for a week. They fished, or napped, or stripped and swam, or talked for hours, or thought; and when he described it, I knew that he had never since known a time as happy as that. For he enjoyed solitude, and yet was not alone.

What is the point of these ruminations? Recall that the imagination is a natural faculty in man. Some people make the mistake of fostering it, but it is often so powerful on its own that it will assert itself if we simply allow people to live what used to pass for an ordinary life. If you are breathing hard from the airborne soot of a city, all it may take for your lungs to clear again is to spend a week in the country. And all it might take for the imagination to breathe again is some time in solitude and silence. Then solitude and silence must be abolished. You can deny the existence of God, and of any meaning in the universe. You may take out the democratic steamroller and flatten all heroes in sight, or, perhaps more wisely, raise every ordinary selfish fool to the status of a hero. You may laugh at manhood and womanhood, and deprive boys and girls of ways to express longings natural to their sex. You may douse the flames of love of country, and convict your forefathers of wickedness, for not doing everything as you do. You may see all the world through the lens of politics. You may schedule a child into submission. You may keep him from witnessing honest and ingenious labor. You may muffle him up indoors. It will be in vain, if you allow him moments of silence and solitude.

As always Screwtape is instructive. Here he reproaches his nephew Wormwood for two colossal mistakes, both involving that receptivity to reality that marks true imagination: "On your own showing you first of all allowed the patient to read a book he really enjoyed, because he enjoyed it and not to make clever remarks about it to his new friends. In the second place, you allowed him to walk to the old mill and have tea there—a walk through country he really likes, and taken alone." So much for the blundering. What should the patient have been taken up with instead? Says Screwtape, "Vanity, bustle, irony, and expensive tedium." In other words, instead of music and the whisperings of the natural world, noise. Instead of solitude, the bustle of modern life, made all the more soul-deadening by its loneliness. Instead of solid realities like earth and wind and star, and dare I say intimations of the Maker of earth and wind and star, vanity: hours crammed solid with things of no real significance. We must turn up the noise.

Murders and Toothpaste

People have long complained about the wasteland of television. Children, it was said, were spending too much time in front of the box, gaping at inanities, sometimes as much as two hours a day. The shows, moreover, were punctuated by moronic sales pitches for toys and toothpaste and luxury cars, appealing to lust, vanity, greed, envy, pride, and various other sins deadly and disheartening. Children were losing the ability to concentrate on anything for any length of time: television was replacing the more strenuous and active exertion of the imagination required to read a good book.

All of that was true, but it did not go nearly far enough. Every hour spent in front of the television was an hour *not spent doing something else:* playing ball, building a snow-fort, talking to friends, collecting coins, watching the men tear down a condemned building, hopping a train to Scranton, hiking in the woods, reading *David Copperfield*, taking apart the engine of a dead lawn mower, or damming up a creek just to see what would happen. Moreover, television didn't merely spend the time, it spoiled the time it didn't spend. For everybody has to have some time doing something pointless, like playing cards. But television engaged the imagination in a false and easy way, as playing cards does not. That meant that when a real effort of the imagination was required, the child could not make it. Books would be dull because they were not like television. If your ear is trained up on bad music, you'll still be able to play cards, but you just will find it hard to listen to Beethoven.

Yet as beneficial as television was, it was still quite imperfect, and presented dangers of its own. Many of the old shows were an attempt to translate to television what the writers and directors conceived as shows for a playhouse. Most of these were filmed in the imagination-stirring medium of black and white. They offered dangerous possibilities for moral thought. A show called *Playhouse 90*, for instance, featured an episode called "The Comedian," wherein a wicked man torments his comedy writers and destroys his brother's marriage. The acting (Mickey Rooney, Edmund O'Brien, Kim Hunter, Mel Torme) is first rate; we are led to plumb the depths of human evil, and we see—the ending is quiet and unhappy—what happens when a good man indulges his weakness. That sort of moral exploration was common enough, particularly on what I consider the two best-written shows in the history of television, *The Twilight Zone* and *Gunsmoke.*

These shows, I dare say, would not be popular now. They would feel too slow. The black and white film of *The Twilight Zone* and of the early seasons of *Gunsmoke* allows for almost no glitz, no visual noise. Special effects, those cheap mind-shutting thrills, were nonexistent in the latter and rare in the former. The dialogue too was stripped of the glitzy: no political posturing (except when Rod Serling wrote in defense of human liberty), no easy and unfunny snideness, no cleverness for its own sake. We were encouraged to focus on the human face, lit up against the surrounding dark. What good or evil or tangled knot of motives burns in this mind, here, now, in this situation? Why can the down-and-out boxer not believe the little boy who admires him, against all reason? Why does the executive long for a country place called Willoughby? Why does the old woman who fears death so much let the young stranger through the door?

Television has developed considerably since then. Shows about ordinary life no longer exist. There is no delight in the innocence of children, no reverence for age. Shots are quick, disjointed. Conversation takes place at several removes from reality, reflecting not what human beings say and do, but what long-established television pasteboard figures say and do: the clever quipster, the oafish husband, the snappy wife, the snotty teenager, the sluttish secretary, the tough lady cop, all of them eliciting only an immediate recognition of the category and the appropriate salivary response. Add then the background music, bombastic scores, even sequences wherein image after image is shown, as in a so-called music video, dispensing with the need for dialogue and careful plot. The result is not so much that people will not watch, let's say, *A Tale of Two Cities* or *The Third Man.* Plenty of film enthusiasts do (though they would do better in both cases to read the books). It is that the great majority of people now can neither read those books nor watch the movies. They have been fed on noise, and have no taste for melody.

What is noise, then, and why is it so useful? Children certainly make a lot of noise, or at least they used to, in the days when they engaged in what was called "playing," hollering that the batter couldn't hit the side of a barn, or that the pitcher's arm was a noodle, or chanting jump-rope chants in rhythm. Noise as I use the term here has nothing necessarily to do with decibels, though they can help. It is instead a kind of mental and spiritual interference, like the blitz of tiny explosions in radio static. It is best when it is not purely meaningless, because then it compels the mind to attend to it, at least for a moment. And that will often be enough to derail real thought.

Consider what an old fashioned schoolroom used to look like. How retrograde our ancestors were! They assumed that all you needed to do to kill the imagination was to line students up in rows, boys on one side and girls on the other, drilling lessons into them, and keeping order. But while they were keeping that order, they abandoned the great weapon of noise. And see what happened. The students, though they had to keep still during their classes, had a lot of time to play at recess. Since the classes were small, they knew one another, too—indeed they might have many years to get to know one another. Since order was the rule of the day, the teacher instilled in them a certain reverence and a regard for hierarchy. One old schoolroom I know, now used as a place for community gatherings, had a small platform in front for the teacher's desk, behind which stood an American flag and a portrait of George Washington. Up on the ceiling was mounted a model of a planetarium. To one side stood a piano, for playing hymns and singing. The room otherwise is handsome but spare—old wainscot painted light blue, and plaster walls. There wasn't enough noise in that room. So even if you had a teacher of narrow mind and smoldering dislike of children (which teachers, it is pleasant to reflect, are still with us and still doing yeoman work), you also had quiet, and in that quiet a child's mind might open, and his ears might hear a thought. In all my life I have not met a single person who ever attended such a school and did not look back upon it with a nostalgia that itself is food for the imagination.

Now enter a modern school building. First consider the scale. Five people can have a conversation. A thousand people can only make noise. And they do, they must. Children are herded down halls of their "center"—for schools are now "centers," though what is the circumference, no one is allowed to tell. The look of the school is drab and gaudy at once. That is, there is nothing exalting or beautiful or even quaintly picturesque about it; it does not resemble a town hall or a church or a farmhouse, but a factory or an office building or a warehouse. As it should: but warehouses are insufficiently distracting, and factories, if you know anything about machines, can be fascinating. So the walls must be festooned with noise. Behold the great cardboard poster blaring out in loud colors and loud slogans the appropriate sentiments about recycling or global warming. Behold another poster boasting school spirit, or community involvement, or leadership, or some such. Enter a classroom and behold—what can you not behold? A chaos of self-advertisement meets the eye, blue, green, red, pink, yellow, white. Open a schoolbook. Not a page passes without a bright color picture, or an inset, or a smiling cartoon figure teaching you that a noun names a person, place, or thing.

Sit at your desk and wait for the bell to ring. No, not yet; announcements first from the speaker. And what is that on your desk? A computer monitor. What is playing in the halls? Television sets. Where is there a single spot either of beauty or of visual and auditory quiet? Nowhere at all. But who wants quiet? Go to the fast food restaurant: televisions there too, providing noise. Look at the ticker at the bottom of the screen: you cannot help yourself, you must look. The Giants lead the Eagles, 16–13. Do you care that the Giants lead the Eagles? No, but you notice it, and a thousand things like it, minute by minute, day after day. Suddenly the volume on the television rises. Is it a report on a mass murder in Oklahoma? No, that was last week. This time it is a commercial for something called male enhancement. You don't really want to hear the warnings the drug company must issue, but you hear them anyway. Noise, all noise.

I was at a library one summer day; a library is a place where people used to house books, so that other people could borrow them and read them. Not so now. A library is a place filled with noise. Outside the full-length windows the sun was shining on the sea, and the weather was perfect for swimming or fishing. Seagulls were circling about and crying their unearthly cry. Ospreys—those "bonecrackers," as their name in Latin means—had built an eyrie atop one of the telephone poles. A whole world lay in wait beyond the windows, a world of sound and silence, of both solitude and that genuine friendship that needs no words to express itself. And inside the library, I am pleased to say, were perfectly healthy children. They were not tanned by the sun. Their bellies were already a little soft, a little pudgy—an earnest of years of inactivity and boredom to come. They sat in front of the machines of noise: computer screens, playing pointless video games. Or they did what is called "chatting," but not face to face. We are not talking here about someone looking you in the eye, talking about football, or whether God exists, or what it must be like in the winter in Newfoundland. The sentences they hammered out on the keyboards were sublingual, like the grunting of brutes.

People whose eyes cannot rest on something as beautiful as a stretch of sea and sky can hardly be expected to dwell upon an imaginary sea or an imaginary sky. Just as their eyes have been trained to jitter with the skips and blips of visual distraction, and their ears to jitter along with incoherent wailings, so their minds will not rest on something as challenging as, let's say, *Pride and Prejudice*. Who cares whether Elizabeth Bennett ever learns that Mr. Darcy is in love with her, and that she has misjudged his character? What difference does it make, and what is a "moral conversion," anyway? Why don't they just "do it" and leave us be? So teachers indulge the jitters. Some students, they say, are incapable of such a feat of the imagination as is required to read Jane Austen. These students are given comic books to pore over, with lots of noisy pictures and exclamation points.

This kind of schooling is exactly what our children need, if they are to hold their places in the kingdom of noise. Take political thought, for example. Take it; we don't want it. We can have no political thought. That requires a mental discipline out of keeping with a faceless proletariat we should like to control. Dictators of old, with their mistaken authoritarian impulses, tried to wipe out political thought by force. But that produced martyrs, real heroes—and heroes rouse the imagination, as the plain-spoken and fearless electrician Lech Walesa united the Poles against their Soviet overlords. What we want instead is not political thought but a glut of political noise, a great, never-ending garbage dumping of sloganeering, inanity, polling, up-to-the-minute coverage of non-events, polling about polling, coverage about coverage, slogans about slogans, without pause, without anyone stopping to ask a single question about what is Good or

True or Beautiful. We want people not merely to forget what a Washington or a Jefferson said. We want to make them wholly incapable of ever hearing and understanding what they said. We want to stupefy them with information without form. We want readers deeply illiterate *because they have learned to read*. We want people who have forgotten what they have forgotten, because they cannot forget what has just passed by on the bottom of the screen.

The still small voice? Drown it with noise.

Who Is My Neighbor?

I could answer that question well enough when I was a boy. I cannot begin to answer it now.

In stifling the imagination, we must take care to understand that people, too, can be "noise" to one another. The point requires some elucidation. Let us say that you are so foolish as to allow your children the free run of their neighborhood. The trouble with that is the same as the trouble with allowing them to wander the woods, where they might come upon a wild riot of things being their own particular selves. I remember a swamp perched on a ridge, like a great birdbath—to this day I cannot tell how so much water could collect and stand idle several hundred feet above the surrounding valley. Birch trees grew in that swamp, but when they got to be of a certain size they would rot from within, and you would see the blackened stumps of them sticking out of the water, like the bones of an alien race.

No, there's no telling what you might find in an ordinary walk on a heap of glacial rubble, and no telling what you might find if you got to know your neighbors. I am not speaking here of criminals—of people who abuse children, and who in a saner day would be rendered incapable of committing a crime again, by imprisonment or rough surgery. I'm simply speaking of the human race, the people who happen to live nearby. Getting to know these, when you are young, can be like rummaging through the attic of the local American Legion. The old man with the limp, whose elbows have nubs of muscle on them still, was a miner. He can tell you how they hauled the coal up in small carts on wheels, and how people who couldn't get a job—boys and crippled men—would "pick" fallen pieces of coal and put them in their own wheelbarrows, to sell them at a discount in town. The old lady across the street, who runs her grandchildren out of her yard, used to take in boarders, and that made her the richest woman around. The short guy over there says that he used to be a minor league pitcher and threw hard till he hit a batter in the head and could never pitch inside again. He says he knew Robin Roberts and Bobby Shantz. The skinny old man who grows tomatoes and petunias came from Italy fifty years ago, and you still can't understand what he's saying.

The people that a child meets this way—in the ordinary run of human life—are not noise. If he goes to a barber shop by himself, for instance, even if he doesn't open his mouth, he will be introduced to a world of men he hardly understands, with their talk about money, cars, sports, politics, the mayor, and the cops. I heard that talk when I was a boy, all the time, at the local shop, with a picture of Pope Paul VI on the wall behind the barber chair, and a list of prices for various haircuts and a shave on the other wall, and the name of the manufacturer of the chair in relief on the pedal, an Emil somebody from Chicago. I was a little timid going to the barber's, as was just and right. Or you go to watch the local football team on a cold fall night with your uncle and cousins, sitting in the bleachers, drinking hot chocolate from a thermos, and overhearing the men talk about the merits of the running back, and where he's going to school next year—and again, the people are like mysterious portals opening out into strange worlds.

Even your own relations can be like that. On the wall of my grandmother's house stood a framed studio photograph, in that light wash of color that captures the essence of someone's personality better than photographic accuracy ever can. It was of her eldest daughter, who died of leukemia at age ten, on the very day my father was born. She loved that daughter dearly, and always thought she was the most intelligent of her children. She liked to show me scraps of her daughter's notebook paper, on which she had written out some homework for school. This little girl was my aunt, yet she was only a girl, only as young as I was. When my grandmother talked about her, in her broken English, the very fact that she had almost nothing she could say made the girl seem all the more present in the room beside us.

Now that is not noise. In fact, there is in such an encounter between a child and someone else, someone who has dwelled in a world other than his own and maybe far bigger than his own, something akin to silence, and listening, and peace. Therefore we want to ensure that such encounters never happen, or that the child will be such as it will never occur to him that such an encounter could happen. We want him to regard other people as noise. So we make sure that other people *are* noise.

When I go to the sprawling Shop and Slop for groceries, and roll my cartful of food the mile and a half to the counter, I may trade a pleasant word with the person at the checkout, but that's all. She performs a function for me; I perform a function for the store. The encounter is brief and efficient. That is the way it has to be, given the proletarian life to which we aspire.

Mankind did not grow up on such functional relationships. The Miller in Chaucer's *Canterbury Tales* was a hilarious drunken sot who would overcharge you for flour by crooking his thumb on the scales when weighing it out. If you lived in his village, you knew he was a bad man—nothing sentimental about that. But you knew he was a man, too. He was Robin, the cheating miller. In Sigrid Undset's epic *Kristin Lavransdatter*, Kristin marries and becomes the mistress of a large estate, which she manages well not because she is morally pure (she is not), but because she knows every manservant and maidservant in her employ. She knows who loafs, who drinks, who works the extra hour, who can be trusted with money, and who cannot. Even Harriet Beecher Stowe, who despised slavery as deeply as anyone ever has, and who strove to illustrate how it corrupts the spirits of the slave owners, does not show that the relationship between master and slave was indifferent and merely functional. Uncle Tom's owner Mr. Shelby, hard up for cash, betrays his loyal servant, and he knows he is betraying him when he sells him away. But at least Shelby *could* betray Tom. You cannot betray a cam or a cog.

So let us see how we can ensure that the child will grow up taking it as normal that other people will simply be the operators of impersonal *functions*. The first thing to do is to remove him from people he loves, and who love him in turn. I cannot stress too much the wisdom of replacing the relationship of mother and child with that of worker and client. The mother is a world of mystery. She loves; she does all kinds of interesting things throughout the house; she sings; she reads; she loses her temper; she may be as peaceful as a summer evening or a whirlwind of fury. But she is always the mother, and her love for her child, even when it is shot through all the flaws of her character, will be a *human* love. It may be far from perfect. But it will be something real.

Now take the child from that mother, and place him somewhere else. Not in another home, among different people who love him—and who will be sources of mystery to him, too. Not with his Aunt Violet or with his grandmother, nor even with the kind old lady next door. Place him with—here is the crucial word—a *professional*. Place him in the context of a money-making—here is another crucial word—*industry*. Take him to those functional places with tellingly abstract and impersonal names, like the Early Learning Center, or the Tiny Tots Academy. Place him among professional caregivers, rather like people who will walk and feed your dog at the kennel, only much nicer. They will feed the child, will parcel out the child's day with appropriate Learning Activities, will enforce the scheduled Naptime, and will send him home clean, well-fed, generally contented, runny-nosed, patted, played with, and unloved. Thus will his natural hunger for love be filled instead with the pleasantly functional. He will have no complaints about the Choo-Choo Child Connection. It may, in fact, be the only time in his day that he will run into other children. And he will be all the readier for school. Not only because he will be able to say his ABC's. He will be ready to see himself and everyone else in the school as a cipher in an institution built to serve a certain function.

Charles Dickens long ago exposed the cruelty of many a private school. In his novel *Nicholas Nickleby*, Mr. Wackford Squeers, the headmaster of Dotheboys Hall, is nothing but an illiterate brute, pocketing their tuition, skimping on their rations and their clothing, and teaching them absolutely nothing. Here is Nicholas's first impression of the boys:

> There were little faces which should have been handsome, darkened with the scowl of sullen dogged suffering; there was childhood, with the light of its eye quenched, its beauty gone, and its helplessness alone remaining; there were vicious-faced boys brooding, with leaden eyes, like malefactors in a jail; and there were young creatures on whom the sins of their parents had descended, weeping even for the mercenary nurses they had known, and lonesome even in their loneliness.

We cannot now do likewise. Our problem is twofold. We want to squelch the imagination, but not necessarily warp it until it becomes criminal; for criminality would upset the smooth running of the mass machine. Also, the relationship between Squeers and the boys engenders deep hatred, and hatred too can rouse the imagination. It roused Dickens's own, to rise up in indignation against injustices.

So instead we want what is pleasant and smooth. It should not be a perversion of the human, so much as an evasion of it. We want a system that cannot be convicted of any identifiable crime: nothing so direct and understandable as a flogging, for instance. We want a deadening routine without order, acts of affability without love, rebukes without anger, and schedules, timetables, five-year-plans, objectives, and output assessments. This is what we get in schools. It is indeed what schools are for: to habituate people to a world of routine, affable impersonality, schedules, timetables, five-year plans, objectives, and output assessments.

We cannot do this without building large schools—institutions in fact, where no one will know everyone else, and therefore where a certain superficiality of acquaintance and anonymity will rule the day. The child is to be hustled from this group to that group, mainly among other children whom he will never get to know, developing a passing familiarity with a few teachers, and generally muddling through his clocked hours without anybody ever noticing that he has memorized the records of the 1927 Yankees, or can sing songs from the Civil War. He will have a name—we have not yet found a way conveniently to dispense with those—but he will be treated as if he were a counter in a vast board game, and will learn to treat other people similarly.

Should he still wish to make a friend, rather than a shallow acquaintance, we will deprive him of the opportunity. No recess; no unsupervised play. He will choke down his food in a few minutes and be recharged—like Charlie Chaplin in *Modern Times*, belted down into the Billows Feeding Machine.

After-school activities will but continue the routine. First, there will be such things as "after-school activities." There will not be free time to play, or read, or think. Let the child be hustled from one functionary to another, among a welter of children whose parents are availing themselves of the same service. Here is the karate teacher you do not have time to get to know, and all the students in the karate class whom you do not get to know. Here is the piano teacher you do not know, and here are a few of her other pupils in the waiting room, some of them squirming like they are about to see the dentist.

When Kermit Roosevelt attended the boys' boarding school at Groton, he wrote home often—about the barracks life, but also about the books he had been reading. He discovered the works of a young poet named Edwin Arlington Robinson and thought highly of them. When he learned that Robinson was in New York looking for employment, he wrote to his father, the president, who also was an avid reader of poetry, to ask whether he could find him a job, so as to give encouragement to the struggling artist. Teddy Roosevelt agreed. I mention the story because Kermit's very loneliness at Groton brought forth in him human responses: he turned to literature he loved; he wrote to his father; eventually he made real friends. We want our children to be lonely in the sense that they know no one before whom they would freely reveal their souls. We don't want them to know that they are lonely, however, because that disquiet might revive the imagination and send them in quest for true human relationship.

The constant herding and hustling of our children accomplishes just that. We use the word "friend" to describe someone we hardly know, because the real depths of friendship are inaccessible to us. When children who are brought up among dozens of quasi-anonymous people who are their "friends" and who know nothing about them, and about whom they know nothing either, then that will go a long way toward destroying in them the possibility for romantic passion. They will have libido—bodily chemicals see to that—but they will obtain mechanical release for the libido by contractual arrangement. "Friends with benefits," it is called, if among people who know slightly more than one another's names, and "hooking up," if not.

In His Will Is Our Peace

Here I could rehash the usual arguments about how television has shortened our children's attention span to that of an insect—a notable injustice against the bee, but in other regards true enough. Or I could turn to the philosopher Philippe Beneton and note how modernity is a form of confinement: a way of life wherein we are free to "express" ourselves, so long as the differences between one person and the next are not considered of any account. Everyone is different, and the differences make no difference; everyone walks in the gaudy wear of his own whims, and therefore everyone is a prisoner of the fads of the passing moment.

But the wellsprings of the imagination lie deeper than that. There is a graver danger to our children than that they might someday pick up good books and read them, and see how thin and paltry the modern soundtrack is by comparison with Homer or Augustine. Graver, too, than the chance that they might begin to judge the good and the bad, the noble and the silly, the true and the false, and therefore learn to appreciate what makes the one different from the other. True, they might then begin, for the first time, to look at bad people as human beings, genuine sinners with stories of folly or vice or weakness behind them, and not as placeholders in what passes for social analysis or political debate. The danger, rather, is that in a moment of silence the strangeness and wonder of this world, and perhaps of the self-concealing and revealing Maker of this world, might overtake them. And if that happens, even if they should insist that they belong to no religious sect at all, they will be lost to us. They will live in the world, but as if it had an extra dimension or two invisible to most.

Blaise Pascal lanced the heart of modern man when he said that our greatest misery was that we could not sit quiet in our rooms. "Teach us to sit still," wrote the poet T. S. Eliot, praying in "Ash Wednesday" for release from the distractions that keep our minds bound fast. If our children learn to be comfortable in silence—and worst of all, in silence when they are among other people they love, feeling their presence nearby without need-ing to say a word to them—then a door will be opened that it might take many years of careful schooling, overexposure to the jitters of electronic media, and inundation under the inanities of breathless news that are not news, to shut. For in that deep quiet of the heart we hear things. We hear that the world as we know it is passing away. We are passing away. Yet the world is beautiful, and good is no illusion. Evil is the illusion; it is weak, a shadow, a parody of good, a specter. We seem to crowd many years into a single instant, or we recall an instant years later, as if it were present now in all its power and life.

When I was a boy, my father took me, my little brother, and our dog up to the top of a nearby mountain to pick blueberries. Up there they grew on scrubby bushes, close to the ground. That meant you had to crouch low to pick. It wasn't easy. My father loved picking blueberries, and I grew to love it too, but over the course of two hours we might hardly say a word. "Here's a good bush for you," he might say, and I might reply, "I have a good one here—I'm picking five or six at a time." The dog would trot from one of us to the next, panting, loving being there, sometimes nibbling a few berries from the bush. For some reason, talking gets in the way of picking. Mainly it got in the way of the joy and peace of not needing to say anything.

There were sounds, though: an occasional car from the back road in the distance; the strange low beep of an army radar station at the summit; the dog doing her doggish duties; birds whose twittering and chattering I didn't recognize then; the muffled scuff of our shoes on the dry paths and the rocks; the tumble of a handful of berries into a plastic pail. I still pick blueberries, and other wild food too; and I sense my father's presence nearby, after these forty years. It is the silence that brings him back—or in the silence I hear that he is not gone.

That silence has a strange way of inverting everything we think is important. I should not be picking blueberries; there's no money in it, after all. I am missing a sporting event on television that I don't really care about. I am not mouthing slogans at a rally. Yet when the silence overtakes me, I can almost believe that a life of imagination is close at hand, and is so rich as to put all the glamor and the noise of "real life" to shame.

Is it not so? Thomas Merton, a man firmly in the grip of the world, weary and cynical though he was still very young, wandered one day into a church in Manhattan, and was overcome by the stillness of the place. Not that he was alone. He entered by himself, true enough, but heard, as he lingered there, the priest's sermon on Holy Communion, using terms many centuries old, heard and understood by the common people scattered in the pews: workingmen, housewives, ordinary people, yet as mysterious as fabulous beasts. Merton gave up his life of vanity, and eventually became a Trappist monk, a member of the order following the strictest rules of silence. Those who follow the Trappist rule say that their minds open in the silence, and their hearts do too. The rarity of the speech they are allowed makes their words all the more powerful to one another. They know both solitude and deep friendships, expressed by a gesture, a nod, a smile, or a simple abiding presence.

Most people, of course, will not be Trappist monks. But something of that stillness abides in a home—not the flophouses we typically inhabit, but a home. Laura Ingalls Wilder looked back upon her childhood spent in the most forbidding places: a deep forest in Minnesota, or the plains of the Dakota territory (prone to great heat, violent storms, and long and treacherous winters). But there was little noise in that life. And so she heard things: the roar of a snow-melt swollen creek at Christmastime in Kansas, or the plaintive wailing of Pa's fiddle, as he played his favorite old songs of an evening, while Ma was sitting at her needlework, and the children were falling asleep in their beds. Such a place, a home, fit for human beings, and all their endless yearnings, is a place of stillness even when the neighbors come in stamping their boots and hollering their greetings. Its days follow the rhythms of the season and of the hard and noble work to be done. Its nights grow hushed in the sounds of the great world beyond, and the greater world within, the human world, with its quiet breathing, and silent and astonishing thought.

Jesus went into the desert to pray. The Pharisees accused him not of being a loner, but of hanging around too many people, especially the wrong sorts—harlots and drunkards and raffish fishermen. Yet Jesus went into the desert to pray, and stayed there for forty days and forty nights, one day for each year it is said the Israelites spent in the Sinai on their journey of liberation from Egypt to the Promised Land. There in the desert, apart from cities and kingdoms, their leader Moses had heard the name of God, who called Himself I AM, or Being, or Love: since His saying "I AM" to the Israelites was also to say "I AM *with you*." It was a revelation that shook the world. Likewise when Jesus returned from his prayer, his rich solitude, it was not to be some aloof guru, approachable only by the few. He traveled the length and breadth of Galilee and Judea, preaching to people one by one, or by thousands and thousands. He came preaching in parables, imaginative stories crafted to reveal to man both where his heart really lay, and where it should lie instead. He preached, and the noise was stilled, and people began to hear, just a little, and to know the love to which he came to give witness. "Know," he says in his farewell to his disciples, "I AM with you, to the end of time."

And at a stroke, they who follow that wisdom—whether they acknowledge it or not, and whoever they suppose the wisdom may come from—are set free, if but now and then, to stand erect beneath the star-powdered vault of heaven. They are free to wonder, and free to love. They will be, if but now and then, shiningly human, the terrible creatures against whom no empire can stand. If, then, our current empire of the mass man is to survive, we must resist the temptations of the One whom Elijah heard in the still small voice. For unlike the serpent in the garden, He really would make us be as gods, and set us free. We prefer our bonds instead.

Method 10

Deny the Transcendent

or

Fix above the Heads of Men the Lowest Ceiling of All

One of my earliest memories is that of a book. I was not quite four years old when I started to read—nobody could ever tell me how it happened. We had only a few books in the house. My mother and father, children of Italian miners, had more urgent things to worry about, like putting food on the table and saving money for a down payment on a house. But there was one book I can never forget.

I still have it with me—I asked if I could keep it after my father died. You have seen similar books, no doubt, but for me it was the only one of its kind. It is bound in red leather, with a red tassel attached, to help you keep your place. Its pages too are edged in red dye. There are small thumb-shaped indentations periodically set in the open side, with gold decals pasted on them. They are to help you find the sections of the book you want to look up: "Gen Exo," "Lev Num Deu," "Jos Jdg Rth," read the first three.

These portions of the book had numbers all over them, fascinating numbers. The part called Isaias had sixty-six parts to it, and the part called Jeremias had fifty-two. Jonas had only four, and Abdias had but one. I had no idea why a Book of Abdias should be a single page, but it was not up to me to determine these things, and I was strangely stirred by the great differences. There were also small letters everywhere, in the text and at the margins, referring by abbreviation to other portions of the book. I understood nothing of all that.

There were pictures too, with bold faced titles and illuminative verses beneath. Here was Cain, hairy on the jowl, writhing in envy against smooth-faced Abel to the right, who stood with palms uplifted before a stone table with fire rising from it. Here was the boy David, wearing a light tunic, standing with one foot on the earth and one planted on the body of a great hulking fellow with a head as big as a washtub. The boy had raised a silver sword over his shoulder, held two-handed, like a hockey stick. Here was Job—whose funny name my mind's ear rhymed with "Bob"—sitting greenish and naked in a pit, with his friends, who were clothed and looking well-fed, staring at him in astonishment. I didn't understand that one, either.

The book had a fragrance to it, not like paper from a mill, but something like perfumed parchment. That too set it apart as holy. *The Poky Little Puppy*, after all, did *not* have fragrant red-dyed pages. On the inside of the front cover was a drawing of a man in a beard, and horn-like shafts coming from or penetrating into his forehead. The man was climbing down a mountain. He was carrying big tablets of stone, that began, "I am the Lord thy God, thou shalt not have strange gods before me." I did have an inkling, even then, of what that meant—a childlike intimation of the Being beyond beings, of the God who made all and rules all, who Himself was strange because He was God, while all the "strange gods" were not gods at all, as strange as they might be. On the inside of the back cover was a similar drawing of Jesus (I do not remember a time when I did not recognize a drawing of Jesus) standing on a hillside, preaching to people below. This time the caption began, "Blessed are the poor in spirit, for theirs is the Kingdom of Heaven." I am still working on that one.

I never saw my mother or father reading the book. Not that I would have noticed if they had. But there were special laminated pages set between the Old Testament and New Testament, illuminated with small drawings and red letters, for recording births, baptisms, confirmations, marriages, and death. My name is there, in my mother's handwriting. That alone gave me an idea as to the importance of the book. Here was something that had to do with what for me were, and still are, the deep mysteries of birth and death, not to mention the marriage between a particular woman and a particular man, without whom I would not have come to be.

That such love and reverence should be accorded a book, a family Bible, is not surprising. But perhaps it should be. Nobody would think of recording births, marriages, and deaths in laminated insets of Darwin's *Origin of Species*, or Freud's *Interpretation of Dreams*, or Marx's *Das Kapital*. Even an atheist would not do so, or would do so only as a poor and self-conscious jest. Then why the Bible? And what does all this have to do with the fostering of a child's imagination?

To say that it's simply a tradition only shifts the question back a little way. Why should such a tradition have developed in the first place? Maybe we would do well to open that book again, with the eyes of a child, as I did long ago. For in those days I had no idea that many of the greatest books are like a forest, and that the best way to get to know them is to wander right into the middle and get lost. So I started at the first page, and read these words: "In the beginning God created heaven and earth, and the earth was void and empty, and darkness was upon the face of the deep; and the spirit of God moved over the waters."

Saint Augustine would write a voluminous commentary on the first chapters of Genesis, unfolding the text sentence by sentence, almost word by word, but of course I knew nothing of that, then. I did not know what "waters" meant. I imagined darkness like a sea, and God brooding upon the sea. I found it strange that the "earth" was there but wasn't there. God hadn't made the earth yet, so it was nothing, or worse than nothing, just empty. But the words that fixed their wonder in my mind were those first three: "In the beginning."

Here was a time before any I could remember. Here was something older than my dog or my house, or even my mother and father. Here was not "once upon a time" or "a long, long time ago" but "in the beginning," meaning that every other story came *not in the beginning* but some time later, like my dog, my house, my mother and father, and me. It stirred the mind with its dark and unfathomable depths. I could ask my father, "What was it like when you were a boy?" and "Tell me about how you used to hop on the train cars," and "How could you see anything when you were down in the mines?" but I could never ask him, "What was it like, *in the beginning?*" A question like that would be infinitely far from my little world, yet here I was being taught that what it was like in the beginning helps to explain what it is like here and now. That too was a mystery. I knew that I had been born—and now I felt the tap on the shoulder, as of a stranger whispering into my mind, "And you were not simply born."

Then came the words that flooded my mind, strange words that no storyteller I have ever heard of would conceive: "Then God said, 'Let there be light,' and there was light."

I didn't stop there. I read on. I read about Adam and Eve and the serpent. I read about Cain and Abel. My eyes were dazed by the great lists of begats, of unpronounceable names, living prodigiously long lives, and occasionally inventing metalwork or settling in the land of Edom, named after a cheese. I read about Abram and Sara, and how hard it was for her to get a child, though I had no idea why she couldn't get one from the same place where other people got them. I read about concubines, and had no idea what they were, though they all seemed to be women, like secretaries. I read about Lot and Mrs. Lot, and their visitors, and the tremendous rain of fire from heaven. I read through all of Genesis and Exodus—Moses in the wicker basket, the burning bush, the staff of Aaron, the gnats and locusts and boils (what were boils?), the frogs and the river of blood and the angel of death; then the Ten Commandments, the golden calf, the earth swallowing up Korah and Dathan and Abiram. Finally I stalled, not with the decorations for the Ark of the Covenant, but with the law of purity in Leviticus. "What does the word *is-sue* mean?" I asked my mother. "Let me see," she said, taking the book and considering. She paused. "I don't know," she said.

After that I stopped reading in order, but bounced around the book, mainly in the Old Testament, reading about Gideon and the night assault on the Midianites, Samson and the honeycomb in the carcass of the lion (the business with Delilah I found pretty dull and incomprehensible, but a lion carcass and a honeycomb, that was another story entirely), Tobias and the fish (we were Catholics), Balaam and the talking ass, Joshua and the trumpets at Jericho. I remember particularly how the prophet Elisha was mocked by a gang of rotten boys, "Go up, thou bald head, go up," and he cursed them, and they were eaten up by some bears from the woods. I was getting my first taste of kindergarten then, and that seemed about right to me.

But do not think that my imagination was stirred primarily by the excitement of these stories. I have no objection to children reading stories—but that is not exactly the point. If a man named Bill is about to do something stupid and is suddenly rebuked by his dog, that may make a pretty good story for a little child. But these were not simply fooleries for children. They were stories rooted in the heart of our being human.

Balaam was rebuked by the Lord, in the form of the miraculous speech from the beast, because in his willingness to disobey what he knew was the right, Balaam was behaving more stupidly than a beast, and was setting himself on the road to a dreadful death which the dumb animal could see and he could not. In other words, you couldn't read a line without being aware of those first lines, "In the beginning," because these stories were always finally about the works of that mysterious Father who made all.

The imagination opens out not principally to what it knows and finds familiar, but to what it does not know, what it finds strange, half hidden, robed with inaccessible light. The familiar too can be an object of wonder, but not by its familiarity: as when the hills I looked upon every morning of my youth suddenly seemed to reveal the thousands of years they were building, long before any man ever left his traces on their slopes. Even the dog at my heels, then, like the dog who wagged his tail when Tobias and he finally came home, reveals itself the more, and is the greater object of wonder, the more I turn to it in love and see that, after all, I do *not* know him; for a dog too proclaims the wisdom of God.

It is, in the first instance, the very *idea* of God that guarantees that we can never reduce anything in creation merely to the stuff of which it consists. And, as for God Himself, what greater object of wonder can there be than one who is not the greatest thing-in-the-world, but beyond the world, of whom all things great and small declare, "He made us, we did not make ourselves"?

Therefore I think it is a grave mistake, even if only for the sake of education, to suppose that schools can or should be neutral with regard to the being of God. One cannot be neutral with regard to dynamite powerful enough to blow the earth as high as heaven. There are only three choices, as I see it. We can do as the McGuffey readers did, taking for granted the nobility of faith. We might, for instance, introduce students to the brave words of the blind poet Milton as he prayed not to see the human face again, but to glimpse heavenly truths in his mind and heart:

So much the rather thou celestial Light
Shine inward, and the mind through all her powers
Irradiate: there plant eyes, all mist from thence
Purge and disperse, that I may see, and tell
Of things invisible to mortal sight.

We might have them hear once again music that used to resound in every school hall in the nation:

Our fathers' God, to thee,
Author of liberty,
To thee we sing!
Long may our land be bright
With freedom's holy light;
Protect us by thy might,
Great God, our King.

The danger in this option is obvious. It is not, as inattentive people will say, that such sentiments as these tend to divide people and make government impossible. It is that they tend first to make young men and women sufficiently independent to scorn the passing fashions, desiring to see what Milton saw. Then, when such people sing the words of the song that used simply to be called "America," they *unite* around that call for a freedom born in obedience and virtue. Such people govern themselves. They do not make government impossible. They make despotism impossible.

Failing that, we could show ourselves unremittingly hostile to the whole idea of God. But that runs the risk of a reaction, as we have seen among the hundreds of thousands of families who are trying to pull their children away from the benign influence of the schools by teaching them at home. And that's doubly harmful, in that a child who is taught at home will quite often have a *home* to be taught in, with all of its deep associations of love and duty and strife and grief and joy, which we do not forget as long as we live.

No, probably the best thing to do is to flatten the mystery. Here we could hardly do better than to follow the lead of those churches that seem determined to produce as many people as they can who will look back on belief with the same seriousness with which they remember a cartoon. These churches produce "children's Bibles" and "children's liturgies," so that what is left imperfect during the week, Sunday school will complete. A child who never hears of God in school may yet be aware, from church and from his family life and from his own reading, of the tremendous mystery of that Father who is utterly different from us, yet who knows our inmost thoughts. But the child for whom God has been reduced to a googly-eyed cartoon of a smiling old man will reject it as he grows older, just as he rejects dressing up as Batman and running around the house in his shorts.

When I was small, there were no cartoons in my church—not yet. Paintings and statues there were, quite a few, ranging in quality from ordinary to superb, as there were stained glass windows. It would be some years before I could "read" any of those works of art, but even at four or five years old I knew that it was Jesus on the cross behind the altar, and I recognized the names of the Old Testament figures painted in the niches between the windows: Moses with the tablets, David with the crown, Gideon with the trumpet, the young boy Samuel, and the white-bearded old prophets Isaiah and Jeremiah. Yet there was much more that I did not know, but that called out to me in a powerful way. Here was a stained glass window of two men in what my mind registered as "old foreign" clothes—Renaissance tights. One of them was talking to the other, and the caption read, "What doth it profit a man to gain the whole world?" Underneath it was a small medallion of one of the men, in a brown robe, lying at a seashore and holding a cross.

What should I have made of that? It was not meant for a child. There wasn't anything cute or cuddly about it. That's why it was dangerous for a child: it opened the child's world out into vistas of ultimate meaning. How can you "gain the whole world"? Why would that not be a good thing? Who was that lonely man abandoned on the seashore? Had he gained the whole world, and then lost it? Only much later (for at my church, thankfully, the flattening of the imagination had already been well underway, with its loss of stories and cultural memory) did I learn that the man at the seashore was the missionary Saint Francis Xavier, who by losing all that he had in the world had attempted to gain the whole world, even Japan, for Christ.

Many powerful symbols do I recall from those early years, symbols that spoke to me in a language that leaves the vernacular hobbling far behind. There was a rail up at the back of the church, in front of the great white marble altar. The rail's columns were inset with pictures made out of tiny pieces of colored stone—I did not know the word "mosaic." There were three loaves of bread on one, a bunch of grapes on another, then two fishes, an anchor, and a lamb clutching a white banner with a red cross on it. I figured that the bread had to do with the grapes, and the anchor had to do with the fish, but what they had to do with the lamb or with one another I had no clear notion. But when I saw, in my mother's missal, the words "Behold the Lamb of God, who taketh away the sins of the world,"

I knew that here was a clue to investigate. And when I saw the priest raise the host of bread as he said the corresponding words in the old language, *Ecce Agnus Dei, qui tollit peccata mundi*, I concluded that somehow the loaves of bread were involved. I was handed, at that time, no answers, but I was given a universe of questions.

The Latin, too, fascinated me, because I didn't know what it meant, but occasionally I could figure out something or other. I noticed right away that "Lord" could be spelled *Domine, Dominus, Domini, Domino,* or *Dominum,* and I thought that that was great, a real richness of words. I noticed that *Et cum spiritu tuo* meant "and with your spirit," and that meant that anything that looked like *tuo* must have something to do with "you." My mother's missal, too, divided the Mass into recognizable parts, like the *Fraction* (which was not one half) and the *Pax Domini,* and explained them very briefly, just enough to give me the impression that I knew a little bit about something miles beyond my comprehension. When nobody was in it, the church was the quietest place I ever knew, a place not for visiting but for dwelling.

Paintings on the Wall of a Cave

One day a small boy in the Lascaux region of southern France wandered off in search of a lost sheep. He came upon a cave and, as boys will, entered it, probably not so much hoping to find the sheep as hoping to see what was inside. The result was one of the most stunning archaeological and artistic finds in the history of the world.

Imagine a haunted-house maze of passages and tunnels, in absolute darkness, leading ever inward. Suddenly they open out into a room, vaulted high, like a natural cathedral. You cast the smoky light of your torch upon it, and it blazes with color, red ochres and yellow and green. It is a wall and ceiling festooned with animals and hunters. The bumps and crevasses of the limestone make flat painting impossible, but that is of no importance to our master artist. He will *use* the very strangeness of the wall to render the strange: the lithe turn of the flank of a buck in flight, the heave of a bull trying to get free. Whoever he was, he knew the joy of the hunt, the patient wait, the tracking, the breathless attack from men on many sides, the rich and powerful life of the animals he loved. His reds are deep and vital, the eyes he painted seem to gleam from the darkness of the rock.

Wherever we find man, said Chesterton, commenting upon these same paintings, we find art—and what is the first art we find? Nothing "primitive," nothing at all like the first faint scratchings of an ape. Rather, we find masterpieces, which, given the severe limitations of the technology and the "canvas," are worthy of a Michelangelo. We also find, inseparable from that art, acts of worship. It is almost certain that these paintings, so vast and so difficult, were part of a community's celebration of the successful hunt, and their prayers that the god of the hunt should grant them more. Into this sanctum, said the anthropologist Joseph Campbell, our ancestors led their boys, to initiate them into the rites of the hunt, to make them sons of their fathers once and for all. In other words, in the deepest heart of man, the motive for art and the motive for worship are bound together.

That is not accidental. In both art and worship, the heart seeks out something beyond itself—a beauty or a power that is not its own. That seeking involves a great deal of what can best be called "play." Why, if the painting of the deer is only a practical superstition meant to help catch another deer, is the deer the artist paints so deer-like—not photographically true to life, but lovingly true to what it must be like to be a deer? Why lavish so much care upon a caveman's version of bookkeeping, if that is all it is?

But that is not all it is. The play of the artist's hand is one with the praise of the artist's heart. He cramps his knuckles and strains his eyes in the poor light to reproduce in the cave a hint of the wonder of his life: that there should be a god who gives him and his people the deer, for their feasts, for their clothing, and for their enjoyment of their odd and familiar ways. The painting bears the style of his hand, yet he does not at all mean to express *himself* in it; rather it allows him to pass beyond himself, to the animals he knows in part, and to the mysterious forces that govern his life and the life of his people, forces that he hardly knows at all.

In other words, man's imagination, when it is not corrupt, yearns for the holy—to behold its beauty from a distance, to be possessed by it. All the greatest art of the past, pagan and Christian, testifies to this desire. It is what inspires the poet Pindar and his *Pythian Odes*, for whom human glory is but a reflection of the divine. How can you celebrate a lad's victory at the games, if you do not contemplate the beauty and vigor of the immortal gods, from whom such blessings flow? So Pindar, praising the strength of a boy named Aristomenes, who defeated his fellows at wrestling in the

Pythian games—games in honor of the god of music and medicine, of poetry and archery, Apollo—rises to praise the gods:

> Man's life is a day. What is he?
> What is he not? A shadow in a dream
> Is man: but when God sheds a brightness,
> Shining life is on earth
> And life is sweet as honey.

Such sentiments burst from the heart of the Psalmist, who sees the vast *distance* between man and God, and yet feels that God Himself has bridged that distance and touched us with his favor:

> I look up at your heavens, made by your fingers,
> at the moon and stars you set in place–
> ah, what is man that you should spare a thought for him,
> the son of man that you should care for him?
> Yet you have made him little less than the angels,
> you have crowned him with glory and splendor,
> made him lord over the work of your hands,
> set all things under his feet.

And with that same longing for the ineffable glory of God, Dante begins the crowning work of all his mighty poetry:

> The glory of the One who moves all things
> penetrates the universe with light,
> more radiant in one part and elsewhere less:
> I have been in that heaven He makes most bright,
> and seen things neither mind can hold nor tongue
> utter, when one descends from such great height;
> But as we near the One for whom we long,
> our intellects so plunge into the deep,
> memory cannot follow where we go.
> Nevertheless what small part I can keep
> of that holy kingdom treasured in my heart
> will now become the matter of my song.

It isn't just the deeply learned art that finds God the object of devotion and imaginative wonder. The common people also find their highest flights of fancy when they dwell upon that something more-than-man whereof all cultures everywhere have had some intuition. Look at this rose window from Chartres Cathedral, with its mad play of light and color, its network of visual patterns and theological symbolism. That is *folk art* at its most ambitious. The glaziers who put those windows together were well paid for craftsmen of their day, but they weren't graduates of some art academy, and we don't know their names, because in all likelihood they could not even read or write. They and their friends the masons and the carpenters and the sculptors were common people inspired by the truths of their faith to build those soaring spires, to extend the lacy walls of ribbed stone upwards, held in place by filaments of stone called flying buttresses, and to perforate the walls with colored glass, a kaleidoscope of prayer.

And there were other forms of art that the muscular faith of the Middle Ages revived, and not for a few wealthy donors either, but for everyone with eyes to see and ears to hear. In the early thirteenth century, to celebrate the resolution of a theological conflict regarding the real presence of Christ in the Eucharist, Pope Honorius III declared a new holy day: the feast of Corpus Christi. In our day, the federal government will declare a "holiday," and people use it to take a long weekend *away* from their neighbors. I suppose that not one young person in twenty can tell what Labor Day is all about, unless it is to mark the end of their all too short parole, and their return to the house of bondage. But in those old days the people of Europe, from England to Italy, from Portugal to Prague, celebrated the new holiday by engaging in a burst of local, folksy, imaginative art the likes of which we will no longer see. Taking their cue from the liturgy of the Mass—itself a complex theological drama in word and gesture, spoken and sung—they began to put on cycles of plays, treating the whole history of salvation, from the Fall of Adam (indeed, sometimes from Creation and the Fall of Lucifer) to the Last Judgment.

They revived an art—the drama—that had lain dormant *for over a thousand years*. Imagine that everyone in your small town spends a couple of months getting ready for the festival. It's no small deal. You won't be putting on one show, but twenty or thirty, on floats that you yourselves have hammered together, proceeding from church to church throughout the town, over the course of the three days beginning with the Thursday of Corpus Christi and ending on the eve of Trinity Sunday. If you want costumes (and you do; with spiky tails for devils and firecrackers to delight the children), the tailors and seamstresses have to stitch them, or patch the old ones from the year before. If you want props (and you do; for instance the spring-loaded gates of Hell, ready to explode open at one touch of the victorious Christ who has descended to set free Adam and Eve and all the other faithful Jews who have awaited his coming), your carpenters and blacksmiths have to forge them and hammer them together. Most of the people can't read, but that will be all right, since the priest and another clerk or two will write the scripts, often with fine dramatic sense and profound theological import, and these scripts too will be passed down from one year to the next.

The results were often astonishingly good. For instance, in "The Buffeting," from the cycle of plays at Wakefield, Christ is on stage along with the high priests Caiaphas and Annas, a couple of torturers, and a mysterious figure named Froward, and all while they take their turns trying to compel him to admit his guilt, mocking him (Caiaphas calls his mother a harlot), spitting upon him, beating him, and pressing the crown of thorns upon his brow, he says nothing. Caiaphas nearly explodes in impatience and the filthiest of blasphemies:

> Say, to speak art thou afeard?
> I will not be thus fleered,
> Alack! The devil's dirt is in thy beard,
> Vile false traitor.
> Whatso thy quirks betoken, yet still thou might say, mum;
> Great words hast thou spoken, then wast thou not dumb;
> Be it a whole word or broken, come, out with some,
> Lest my rage be awoken, or thy death the outcome
> Of all!

They talk on and on about the laws Jesus has broken, the sacred laws they must uphold, the laws they abide by in their trial, and all that talk of law and law and law begins to weigh upon the minds of the audience like a weary burden, because the people know that by the law they are all doomed. It is a miracle of grace they celebrate, an undeserved gift, and not the condemnation they deserve, if the law that all sin merits destruction should have its way. Amid all the abuse—and the abusers themselves begin to fall out and squabble—Jesus remains silent, until Annas, who pretends to feel a touch of mercy for him, begs him to answer the single question upon which the whole trial hinges: are you the Son of God? Jesus answers:

> So thou sayest even now,
> And right so I am.
> For after this shalt thou see when that I come down
> From heaven shining brightly in the clouds
> that form my gown.

They are his only words in the play. He is the central figure; all eyes are on him; but if we do not know who he is, then it matters not what he may say in his defense. His identification of himself is his great "crime," and is at the same time the lifeline thrown out to all who watch the play, who will say, "I believe in you." What might have been an ordinary meditation upon man's cruelty to man, the "lawful" assassination of an innocent man, becomes a statement written upon the vault of the heavens. *This* is what man's justice does to what is good and holy. *This* is man's gratitude to God—and God's love for ungrateful man. It may lack polish, but I'd affirm that you could distill all the genuine art from whole shelves of modern, jaded, diminished, gray-on-gray literature, and not discover a moment as exalting as this one, from a no-account village in the Middle Ages.

People do not paint, in rapture, the rise of the dollar on the world money market. There is no Bach to compose a fugue like a waterfall, joyously heralding the advent of some political hack, the joy of man's desiring. No one will travel over half the world to look at a mural dedicated to Collaborative Learning, or Development of Social Skills. The ancient Hebrews dared not sculpt the Lord God, because they had been warned that any representation of him would be an idol, a lie—such was the awe wherein they were to hold the craftsman who sowed the skies with stars thick as a field in grain. We now must take the commandment given to the Hebrews and twist it inside out. We will not sculpt anything that has to do with the Lord God, because we do not wish to feel the awe that makes all our efforts seem puny. We do not want to say, with Dante, that to describe what we have seen, our words are no better than a baby's "who wets his tongue still at his mother's breast." Such visions are too strong for our nerves. They probably would not do our economy any good, either.

The Abolition of Man

I like to imagine a blaring sign over a gigantic shopping mall, with these messages alternating every five seconds, forever and ever:

WELCOME TO THE MALL OF THE WORLD
ABANDON ALL HOPE YOU WHO ENTER HERE

And not only hope, but community life, personal independence, common sense, virtue, and money.

For the great threat of the imagination, roused to life like Lazarus from the grave by the faintly heard voice of God, is that it makes a man a man, not a consumer, nor a clotpoll to be counted off in some mass survey. The praise of God is inscribed upon the heart of man, says Saint Augustine, "man who bears about within himself his mortality, who bears about within himself testimony to his sin and testimony that you resist the proud." Yet even so man longs to praise and cannot truly be himself unless he praises God, for as Augustine says in *Confessions*, "you rouse him to take joy in praising you, for you have made us for yourself, and our heart is restless until it rests in you." If we have the love of God, the saints all testify, what do we need from anything else? And if we do not have that love, not all the creature comforts and tricksy gadgetry and rubbings and itchings of appetite can fill up the tiniest corner of the chasm that remains. Yet we will try to fill the chasm anyway. That is what shopping malls are for.

In the old days, when man still walked the earth, there were bright points of light in the night sky, which people who spoke English called "stars." Some were a pale red, like Antares the heart of the Scorpion, others blazing white, like Sirius the Dog Star; most were far and cold and dim, yet twinkling if you glanced at them a little out of the corner of your eye. Such were most of the stars that formed the Little Dipper, concluding in Polaris, the star that seems fixed in one place while all the others wheel about it.

Now the odd thing about man is that he cannot help himself, but when he goes outside on a clear night he must look at the sky. The dog does not do it. If birds do it, it is not because they wonder at the beauty above them; they are only using those lights as roadside reflectors or signposts on their aerial highway. They do not wonder at them. But man, if he has nothing above him to gaze upon in wonder, ceases to be man. He not only can behold the heavens; he must. Regardless of what you may think about the birth of the cosmos presented in the first chapter of Genesis, one thing is certain: it is a brilliant piece of psychological wisdom. The first thing our imaginations seek is the first thing God creates: the primal light. And God beheld that light, and saw that it was good. So too all of the wild variety of creatures that dwell in the heavens and on the earth, concluding in man. Yet man is made not primarily for work. Man is, in that account, oriented toward the day of rest, the Sabbath, and worship of the God who made him. We could put it this way: he is man, and like God, because he too beholds the light and sees that it is good. None of the other beasts do that, and none of the other beasts sum up their work in worship on the day of rest. Man is not only that creature that forges tools, that reasons, and that walks upright. Man is the creature that looks up. Man praises.

We can suppose, then, that to remove from the child the possibility of praise—to rob him of any intimation of the Being that lends existence itself to all things that exist—would be like confining his mind to a room with a low ceiling. "This is all there is," we say, "and don't ask us where it is going, or what it means, because it is going to destruction only, and it means nothing. Now build a cathedral in honor of that. Write an epic poem about universal heat-death. Compose a song of love for what cannot love. Just try. When your head gets too sore from all the bumping against the ceiling, you'll learn better, and be a good and useful citizen."

Can we imagine human life under that spiritual lid? If we can't, the great Dante has done it for us. He and his guide Virgil have descended into the eternal coffin called Hell. They have entered the gates of the city of Dis, and come upon a field of scattered tombs, with their lids set to the side and flames erupting from within them. Those are the tombs of the heretics, says Virgil. And which heresy among the dozens he could have chosen does Dante focus on? The fundamental heresy, which is to believe that there is nothing to believe, because all is matter, and matter, finally, has no meaning. Says Virgil:

These will be bolted on the day of doom
when from the Valley of Jehosophat
the souls bring back their bodies to the tomb.
On this side, in his cemetery, lies
that Epicurus with his followers who
put it that spirit dies when body dies.

They are the materialists. They are, more or less, the people who write textbooks for our children today.

What you use to fill up the chasm of your life when there are no heavens to behold, Dante knew long before the shopping mall rose up from below. You grasp for wealth or power or fame. That is what the two spirits whom he speaks to in this cemetery have done. One, the father of his friend and fellow poet Guido Cavalcante, lived vicariously in the fortunes of his son the genius. The Harvards of the world would not exist if it were not for parents like Guido. The other, the great-souled and fearless Farinata, lived for the political fortunes of his party and family. Much good it has done them. Guido will die soon after the events described in the scene, and Farinata's family have been exiled from Florence, with the man's very name tarred for treachery, though he was a patriot who once saved the city from destruction.

Now something peculiar happens in the middle of Dante's conversation with these men, and it puzzles him. Dante has learned, from the upper reaches of Hell, that the spirits of the damned are granted some vision of what will happen on earth. They can play the prophet now and again. Yet the elder Cavalcante did not know that his son was still alive on earth, and Farinata did not know that his family had still not managed to return to Florence. How, then, can they see the future, but miss the present?

It's a mockery of how man comes to know, and of the cramped vision of the world that the materialists possessed. We remember the past, we perceive the present, and our minds grope forward in anticipation toward the future. That is a hint of the immortality of the soul, say the Church fathers. All creatures experience things in a succession of moments, but only man can, in memory, perception, and foresight, stand outside that succession—a shadow of God's simultaneous vision of all things in one eternal present. But the materialists insist that matter alone exists; all our thoughts about matter are only fictions, without reality. So it is fitting that they are the ones to reveal to Dante the great inversion of Hell. They are granted a dim prevision of the future, not by their own power but by God's. It is the present they miss entirely. Farinata explains:

"As a man with bad vision," he replied,
"we dimly see things far away. So much
splendor the sovereign Power still shines on us.
When things draw near, or happen, emptiness
is all we see. If no one brings us news,
we can know nothing of your human state.
Hence you can understand that evermore
dead will be all our knowledge from the time
the future ends, and Judgment shuts the door."

On that last day, as we have learned from Virgil, the now open lids of these tombs will be sealed shut. And just as the souls in Hell will never again look upon the sky—never mind heaven, but even the stars that beckon to us above—so the materialist heretics will never again even look upon the beetling ceiling of Hell. They will see only the lid above their heads. But in fact that is all they have ever seen. When they walked the earth, they argued that it was nothing but a vast morgue. It was no sky for them, but the vault of a mausoleum.

Now the thing about a mausoleum is that no matter how big you build it, it's too cramped for man. It's too cramped for love. "The grave's a fine and private place," says the poet Andrew Marvell, "but none, I think, do there embrace." In the *Symposium*, Plato will argue that the highest form of love is made manifest when two souls spur one another either to perform deeds of deathless heroism, or to behold in wonder the never-changing beauty of the Good:

The man who has been guided thus far in the mysteries of love, and who has directed his thoughts towards examples of beauty in due and orderly succession, will suddenly have revealed to him as he approaches the end of his initiation a beauty whose nature is marvellous indeed, the final goal, Socrates, of all his previous efforts. This beauty is first of all eternal; it neither comes into being nor passes away; neither waxes nor wanes.

And once you have beheld that beauty, says the sage woman Diotima to Socrates, you will never again be distracted by the fading beauty of flesh alone, or by flashy trinkets and rich toys. Your love will be too big for that.

Consider then how much perilous art should be hidden away from the child whose imagination you wish to stifle, or if not hidden, at least rendered ineffectual. *Moby-Dick* is out: that terror-inspiring book, with its relentless search for a God who does not appear, will rise up from the deeps, whale-like, and smash any complacent belief or disbelief to matchsticks.

Shakespeare is out. You can't follow Macbeth spiraling down into the Hell of his own wicked choosing. You can't have, in *The Winter's Tale*, a woman appear to be raised from death, most especially not when the raising is the climax of a long penance on the part of the husband whose jealousy caused her to die in the first place.

Chaucer is out. Well, you can reduce him to some bawdy jokes, while poking fun in a flippant way at the earthiness of the Middle Ages. But don't ever suggest that the cathedral at Canterbury is a symbol for the Kingdom of God, or that the free dinner which the best storyteller will win is a comic metaphor for the wedding feast of the Lamb, to which all Christians are invited.

Cervantes is out, unless you reduce Don Quixote to a bumbling mad-man, and not a Christian humanist who understands mankind and heaven more profoundly than anyone he meets; and you'll have to reduce Sancho Panza to a wisecracking know-it-all, and not the rough-edged ordinary fellow whose Christian humility and love of his master raise him in our estimation far above the aristocrats who are *not* trying to save the world from evil magicians and giants, but who maybe ought to be.

Dickens is out. You can't read *A Christmas Carol* unless you reduce Scrooge to a petty little miser who used to hoard his coins and now gives to the United Way—rather than a man dead inside, raised to life by the grace of God. "Returned to life" is the theme of *A Tale of Two Cities*, but you'll have to say it refers only to the old doctor's release from the prison in France, and *not* to the prodigal Sydney Carton's noble deed in the end, to die in place of the husband of the woman he loves. "I am the resurrection and the life," says the narrator as Carton proceeds to the guillotine, quoting the words of Jesus just before he would raise Lazarus from the dead. You will have to avoid talking about that. Call it Victorian sentimentality instead.

Eliot's *The Waste Land*? Out. It's a waste land because we have lost the food, the Eucharist, that heals the maimed and replenishes a world gone dry and dead. Talk about world economic troubles between the wars, if you have to read the poem at all.

Solzhenitsyn is out. Yes, he suffered the brutal conditions of a concentration camp in Siberia, for daring to affirm that there may be other things to affirm than how water flows through a pipe, or how much a cubic meter of lead weighs. Say that he was right about how bad it was in the Soviet Union, but he just didn't understand the nice materialism of the West. Say that the Soviet Union was bad because the people were deprived of meaningless creature comforts, and that the West is good because the people are flooded with them.

Bach? Well, you can listen to some of the *Brandenburg Concerti*, but don't click on the *Saint Matthew Passion*, or anything that came from the deepest wellsprings of his musical inspiration—because those were also the wellsprings of his faith. Mozart is similarly dangerous.

Don't go to the Sistine Chapel. If you do, you must reduce that sprawling drama of God's glory and man's shame to the technical and trivial. Talk about the vibrant color of the flesh. Do not talk about the empty space between the finger of God and the finger of Adam, the most dramatic example of painting nothing in the history of art—it is the space bridged by the will of God, who "breathed into Adam the breath of life, and he became a living soul."

Don't visit Salisbury Cathedral. Don't even visit Salisbury plain, where the monoliths of Stonehenge testify to man's longing to understand what is beyond man. If you do, turn it into a faddish dabbling in nature-worship, or something else that you can buy a T-shirt for at an overpriced specialty shop.

"The beginning of philosophy is wonder," said Aristotle, and if that is so, then what is its end? Nothing other than the fulfillment of wonder: the contemplation of truth, the unchanging Good, the First Mover. Aristotle is reticent about it, as befits someone who does not wish to reduce his dearest love to a checkout slip in some educational cafeteria. But dogs do not wonder, nor do the birds contemplate. Man, when he is thriving, does both. And that is what we must ensure that our children should not do, lest their hearts move toward the unpredictable. They must not be stirred by what David Hart has called "the beauty of the infinite." Will it make them less than human? Yes, indeed. But the fully human, wild and prone to fighting and loving, destroying and building anew, is not what the modern world requires. We are past all that.

No, it is best to keep the word "*only*" ready in the arsenal at all times. The flame of the sky at sunset is "only" the part of the spectrum that penetrates the atmosphere at that angle—or better, because we don't want our children to play with dangerous facts, it is "only" something or other material that scientists know about, and no big deal. The idea of God is "only" a projection of the father, or a wish, or an old-fashioned explanation of things we know all about now (such as matter, energy, gravity, electrical charge, the origin of the universe, the meaning of good and evil, chance, order, intelligibility, the end of man), or at least somebody knows all about them in some Important Places. Beauty is "only" a neurological tic, or a personal opinion. Love is "only" the drive to reproduce the species, which in turn is "only" the replication of genes. And man, man then is "only" a scurf of biomass on a speck of dust in some cranny of the universe. At which point, as C. S. Lewis shows us in *The Abolition of Man*, we have conquered all our natural inclinations toward what is beyond us and our nature, and abolished—ourselves:

> At the moment, then, of Man's victory over Nature, we find the whole human race subjected to some individual men, and those individuals subjected to that in themselves which is purely 'natural'—to their irrational impulses. Nature, untrammelled by values, rules the Conditioners and, through them, all humanity. Man's conquest of Nature turns out, in the moment of its consummation, to be Nature's conquest of Man. Every victory we seemed to win has led us, step by step, to this conclusion. All Nature's apparent reverses have been but tactical withdrawals. We thought we were beating her back when she was luring us on. What looked to us like hands held up in surrender was really the opening of arms to enfold us for ever. If the fully planned and conditioned world . . . comes into existence, Nature will be troubled no more by the restive species that rose in revolt against her so many millions of years ago, will be vexed no longer by its chatter of truth and mercy and beauty and happiness.

There you have it, my dear reader. That is what the destroyers of the imagination will do, whether they are aware of it or not. If we are but wise enough to let them have their way, they will wipe that cursed thing called "man" from off the face of the earth, to replace him with something more convenient to social planners, more manageable. Then go thou and do likewise.

Selected Bibliography

Augustine. *The Confessions of Saint Augustine*, translated by John K. Ryan. New York: Doubleday, 1960.

Austen, Jane. *Pride and Prejudice*. Garden City, NY: Doubleday, 1945.

The Battle of Maldon and Other Old English Poems, translated by Kevin Crossley-Holland. New York: Macmillan, 1965.

Beneton, Philippe. *Equality by Default: An Essay on Modernity as Confinement*, translated by Ralph C. Hancock. Wilmington, DE: ISI Books, 2004.

Beowulf, translated by Howell D. Chickering. New York: Doubleday, 1977.

Berry, Wendell. *Jayber Crow*. Berkeley, CA: Counterpoint Press, 2000.

Boswell, James. *The Life of Johnson*. New York: Modern Library, 2000.

Botsford, George Willis. *A History of Greece*. New York: Macmillan, 1908.

The Boy Mechanic, Volume 1: 700 Things for Boys to Do. Popular Mechanics, 1913.

"The Buffeting," in *The Wakefield Mystery Plays*, edited by Martial Rose. New York: Anchor, 1963.

Burnham, Smith. *The Making of Our Country*. Philadelphia: John C. Winston and Co., 1921.

Calvino, Italo. *Marcovaldo*, translated by William Weaver. San Diego: Harcourt, Brace, Jovanovich, 1983.

Cervantes, Miguel de. *Don Quixote*, translated by J. M. Cohen. Harmondsworth: Penguin, 1970.

Chaucer, Geoffrey. *The Canterbury Tales*, in *The Complete Poetry and Prose of Geoffrey Chaucer*, edited by John H. Fisher. New York: Holt, Rinehart, and Winston, 1977.

Chesterton, G. K. *Saint Francis of Assisi*. New York: Doubleday, 1957.

———. *The Everlasting Man*. New York: Doubleday, 1955.

Dante. *Inferno*, translated by Anthony Esolen. New York: Random House, 2002.

———. *La Vita Nuova*, translated by Mark Musa. Bloomington, IN: Indiana University Press, 1973.

———. *Paradise*, translated by Anthony Esolen. New York: Random House, 2007.

———. *Purgatory*, translated by Anthony Esolen. New York: Random House, 2004.

Dickens, Charles. *A Child's History of England*. New York: Harper and Brothers, 1854.

———. *A Christmas Carol*. New York: Airmont Books, 1963.

———. *David Copperfield*. New York: Random House, 1950.

———. *Hard Times*. New York: New American Library, 1961.

———. *Nicholas Nickleby*. New York: New American Library, 1981.

———. *A Tale of Two Cities*. London: Penguin, 1971.

Dostoyevsky, Fyodor. *Crime and Punishment*, translated by David Magarshack. London: Penguin, 1952.

Eliot, T. S. "Ash Wednesday" and *The Waste Land*, in *The Complete Poems and Plays, 1909–1950*. New York: Harcourt, Brace, and World, 1971.

Epic of Gilgamesh, The, translated by Andrew George. New York: Penguin, 2003.

Fielding, Henry. *Joseph Andrews*, edited by A. R. Humphries. London: Dent, 1973.

Frost, Robert. "Paul's Wife," in *The Poetry of Robert Frost*, edited by Edward Connery Lathem. Boston: Henry Holt and Co., 1969.

George, Jean Craighead. *My Side of the Mountain*. New York: Puffin Books, 2004.

Golding, William. *Lord of the Flies*. New York: Capricorn Books, 1959.

Hakim, Joy. *A History of US*. Oxford: Oxford University Press, 1994.

Hawthorne, Nathaniel. *The Scarlet Letter.* New York: New American Library, 1959.

Hémon, Louis. *Maria Chapdelaine.* New York: Doubleday, 1954.

Herodotus. *The Histories,* translated by Aubrey DeSelincourt. London: Penguin, 2003.

Hesiod. *Theogony,* in *The Oxford Book of Greek Verse in Translation,* translated by C. M. Bowra. Oxford: Clarendon Press, 1938.

Homer. *Iliad,* translated by Richmond Lattimore. Chicago: University of Chicago Press, 1961.

———. *Odyssey,* translated by Allen Mandelbaum. New York: Bantam Books, 1990.

Hopkins, Gerard Manley, SJ. "Harrahing in Harvest," in *The Major Works,* edited by Catherine Phillips. Oxford: Oxford University Press, 2002.

Huxley, Aldous. *Brave New World.* New York: Harper and Row, 1969.

John of the Cross, Saint. "The Dark Night," in *The Collected Works of Saint John of the Cross.* Washington: ICS Publications, 1991.

Keats, John. *The Eve of St. Agnes,* in *Selected Poems and Letters,* edited by Douglas Bush. Boston: Houghton Mifflin, 1959.

Kugelmass, J. Alvin. *Roald Amundsen: A Saga of the Polar Seas.* Chicago: Kingston House, 1955.

Lewis, C. S. *The Abolition of Man.* New York: Macmillan, 1978.

———. *The Chronicles of Narnia.* New York: HarperCollins, 2001.

———. *Perelandra.* New York: Simon and Schuster, 1996.

———. *The Screwtape Letters.* New York: Macmillan, 1960.

———. *The Weight of Glory.* San Francisco: HarperCollins, 2001.

Livy. *The Early History of Rome,* translated by Aubrey DeSelincourt. New York: Penguin, 1971.

Llewellyn, Richard. *How Green Was My Valley.* New York: Macmillan, 1964.

Lucretius. *On the Nature of Things,* translated by Anthony Esolen. Baltimore: Johns Hopkins University Press, 1995.

Macdonald, George. *At the Back of the North Wind.* New York: Airmont, 1966.

Machiavelli, Nicolo. *The Prince,* edited by Lester G. Crocker. New York: Pocket Books, 1963.

Male, Emile. *The Gothic Image.* New York: Harper and Row, 1972.

Marlowe, Christopher. *Doctor Faustus* in *Complete Plays and Poems*, edited by E. D. Pendry and J. C. Maxwell. London: J. M. Dent and Sons, 1976.

Marvell, Andrew. "To His Coy Mistress," in *The Complete Poems*, edited by Elizabeth Story Donno and Jonathan Bate. London: Penguin, 2005.

Melville, Herman. *Moby-Dick*. New York: W. W. Norton, 1967.

Merton, Thomas. *The Seven Storey Mountain*. San Diego: Harcourt, Brace, Jovanovich, 1978.

Milton. John, *Paradise Lost*, edited by Merritt Y. Hughes. New York: Macmillan, 1988.

Morgan, Alfred Powell. *The Boy Electrician*. First published 1913. Bradley, IL: Lindsay Publications, 1995.

Mowat, Farley. *The Dog Who Wouldn't Be*. New York: Bantam, 1984.

O'Connor, Flannery. "A Good Man Is Hard to Find," in *The Complete Stories*. New York: Farrar, Straus, and Giroux, 1978.

O'Malley, William J., SJ. *Building Your Own Conscience*. Allen, TX: Tabor Publishing, 1992.

Orwell, George. *1984*. New York: New American Library, 1981.

Pindar. *The Odes of Pindar*, translated by C. M. Bowra. London: Penguin, 1969.

Plato. *Collected Dialogues*, edited by Edith Hamilton and Huntington Cairns. Princeton: Princeton University Press, 1961.

_____. *The Symposium*, translated by Walter Hamilton. Harmondsworth: Penguin, 1951.

Pyle, Howard. *The Merry Adventures of Robin Hood*. New York: New American Library, 1985.

Roethke, Theodore. "Light Listened" in *The Far Field*. New York: Doubleday, 1971.

Roosevelt, Theodore. *In A Bully Father*, edited Joan Paterson Kerr. New York: Random House, 1995.

Sabatini, Rafael. *Captain Blood*. London: Penguin, 2002.

Scott, Sir Walter. *Ivanhoe*. New York: New American Library, 1962.

_____. *Old Mortality*. Oxford: Oxford University Press, 2009.

_____. *Tales of a Grandfather: A History of Scotland*. Boston: Ticknor and Fields, 1861.

Shakespeare, William. *The Complete Signet Classic Shakespeare*, edited by Sylvan Barnet. New York: Harcourt, Brace, Jovanovich, 1972.

Shute, Henry A. *Real Boys*. Chicago: M. A. Donohue and Co., 1905.

Sidney, Philip. *Apology for Poetry*, edited by Forrest G. Robinson. New York: Macmillan, 1970

Solzhenitsyn, Aleksandr. *One Day in the Life of Ivan Denisovich*, translated by Ralph Parker. New York: Penguin, 1963.

The Song of Roland, translated by Dorothy Sayers. Baltimore: Penguin, 1961.

Sophocles. *The Theban Plays*, translated by E. F. Watling. London: Penguin, 1947.

Spenser, Edmund. *Epithalamion* in *Poetical Works*, edited by J. C. Smith and E. DeSelincourt. Oxford: Oxford University Press, 1912.

_____. *The Faerie Queene*, edited by Thomas P. Roche Jr. London: Penguin, 1978.

_____. "A Hymne of Love," in *Fowre Hymnes*, in *Poetical Works*, edited by J. C. Smith and E. DeSelincourt. Oxford: Oxford University Press, 1912.

Stout, William B. *The Boy's Book of Mechanical Models*. Ottawa: Algrove, 1999 (first published 1912).

Stowe, Harriet Beecher. *Uncle Tom's Cabin*. Harmondsworth: Penguin, 1981.

Tasso, Torquato. *Jerusalem Delivered*, translated by Anthony Esolen. Baltimore: Johns Hopkins University Press, 2000.

Tolkien, J. R. R. "Leaf, by Niggle," in *The Tolkien Reader*. New York: Ballantine, 1966.

_____. *The Lord of the Rings*. New York: Mariner Books, 2005.

_____. "Smith of Wootton Major," in *Smith of Wootton Major and Farmer Giles of Ham*. New York: Ballantine, 1975.

Twain, Mark. *The Adventures of Huckleberry Finn*, edited by Henry Nash Smith. Boston: Houghton Mifflin, 1958.

_____. *The Adventures of Tom Sawyer*. Oxford: Oxford University Press, 1998.

Undset, Sigrid. *The Bridal Wreath*, vol. 1 of *Kristin Lavransdatter*. New York: Knopf, 1951.

_____. *The Master of Hestviken*, translated by Arthur G. Chater. New York: Knopf, 1952.

Virgil. *Aeneid*, translated by Robert Fitzgerald. New York: Vintage Books, 1990.

Washington, George. *Rules for Civility and Decent Behavior.* Naperville, IL: Sourcebooks, Inc., 2008.

Wilder, Laura Ingalls. *Little House in the Big Woods.* New York: Harper Collins, 1953.

Wyss, Johann. *The Swiss Family Robinson.* New York: Penguin, 2004.

Yeats, William Butler. "In the Seven Woods," and "He Tells of Perfect Beauty," in *The Collected Poems of W. B. Yeats.* New York: Macmillan, 1977.

Index